THE SHADOWS IN MY RAIN

A Journey of Isolation, Self-Discovery and Growth

Omomaro Okekaro, PhD

Table of Contents

Foreword

The author's reflections on his past experiences serve as a powerful invitation to readers, urging them to delve into their journeys and uncover the hidden truths that have shaped them. While yesterday may have come and gone, it left its mark, molding the essence of who we are today. This book is a poignant reminder that the shadows of our past often hold the keys to unlocking our potential, pushing us toward growth and transformation.

In *The Shadows in My Rain*, the author takes us on an extraordinary journey through the intricate tapestry of his life, navigating treacherous terrains, confronting inner demons, and solving the intricate puzzles that life has thrown his way. Each challenge he faces becomes a stepping-stone, each victory a lesson, and each moment of reflection an opportunity to level up. Through his narrative, we understand that life's battles are not merely obstacles but invitations to grow stronger, wiser, and more resilient.

The book is not merely a recounting of the author's experiences but a guidebook for readers ready to embark on their epic adventure. It challenges you to embrace the shadows in your rain—the moments of doubt, fear, and uncertainty—and transform them into opportunities for self-discovery and empowerment. With insightful tips and practical wisdom, the author demonstrates how to unlock hidden skills, build resilience, and conquer the challenges that lie ahead.

Whether you're navigating your own dark landscapes or seeking clarity in the chaos of life, *The Shadow in My Rain* is an essential companion. The author has masterfully crafted a roadmap for embracing your past, confronting your present, and creating a brighter future. This is more than a book—it's an invitation to grow, evolve, and rise to the challenges that define your unique journey.

Are you ready to explore the shadows and emerge stronger? Step into the author's world and let his story inspire you to illuminate your path.

John P. Tucker, PhD.
Professor/Clinical Therapist
Neumann University &
Delaware County Community College

Introduction

Embark on a compelling journey of self-discovery with "Shadows in My Rain," a biographical exploration that delves into the intricacies of personal growth, identity, and the shadows that shape our lives. This poignant narrative unfolds against life's unpredictable storms, revealing the nuanced interplay between joy and sorrow, success and setbacks. As we navigate the storms of existence, we'll uncover the shadows accompanying our achievements, casting subtle veils on our paths to self-realization. Join the author on a reflective odyssey, where the essence of human experience is laid bare, offering solace and insight to all who have weathered the storms in their own lives.

The journey commences with a prologue. Within this opening chapter, readers are welcomed into the author's world, where rain-drenched shadows reflect the intricate nature of existence. Acting as a tantalizing preview, the prologue provides a glimpse into the emotional terrain destined to unfold throughout the narrative.

In the intricate tapestry of his existence, the author is a multifaceted individual encompassing roles as an author, counselor, spiritual guide, mentor, and life coach. His presence in the healthcare industry transcends mere profession; it radiates a luminous force of compassion and wisdom.

1

Genesis

My deep-rooted commitment to serving others marks my mission through healing and guidance. I weave threads of empathy and insight with each interaction, offering solace to those sailing across life's challenges. Through the written word or face-to-face encounters, my essence shines brightly, illuminating paths to healing and self-discovery. In my hands, the intricacies of human experience become threads in a montage of transformation, each knot tied with care and understanding. As I walk the corridors of healing, my presence is felt as a beacon of hope, guiding others toward the light of self-awareness and inner peace.

The genesis of my expedition into writing and counseling can be traced back to high school corridors, where the sparks of passion for both ignited within me, creating a flame that has burned brightly ever since. Life, for a significant portion, was a series of endured circumstances. However, this realization became the fulcrum, the turning point that transformed my narrative. I discovered a profound sense of purpose and direction as I researched literature and psychology deeper. Through the written word and the art of listening, I found avenues to channel my experiences into avenues of healing and understanding of others. Each challenge I faced became a stepping-stone, propelling me forward in my exploration of self-discovery and service to others. From the corridors of high school to the expansive landscapes of my career, my passion and dedication have remained unwavering, guiding me toward a path of fulfillment and meaningful connection.

Armed with the formidable trio of self-awareness, forgiveness, and an acute understanding of the power inherent in my attention, I have evolved into an explorer heading the intricate terrain of existence. No longer marked by endurance, my adventure is now characterized by the active creation of a reality that is not just lived but is fulfilling and harmonious.

With each step forward, I embrace the intricacy of life as an opportunity for growth and transformation. Through self-awareness, I gain insights into my strengths and limitations, allowing me to maneuver challenges gracefully and resiliently. Forgiveness becomes a beacon of light, freeing me from the burdens of the past and opening doors to new possibilities. With a keen understanding of the power inherent in my attention, I focus on creating a reality that reflects my deepest desires and aspirations.

My exploration is no longer passive but active and intentional, as I consciously shape my destiny with every thought and action. In this journey of self-discovery and empowerment, I find fulfillment and harmony, emerging as a beacon of inspiration for others seeking to embark on their transformation paths.

At the heart of my aspirations is a profound longing for freedom transcending the tangible and monetary realms. Yet, I have come to recognize that true freedom demands a price. The question echoing within me is not simple—it explores the depths of self-discovery and personal growth. What is the cost of freedom for me? It's a query that goes beyond the material, beckoning me to unearth the essence of my being.

In my quest for answers, I embark on a quest of introspection and exploration, probing into the depths of my soul to uncover the truths that lie dormant within. Each step I take towards understanding comes with its challenges and revelations as I confront my fears and embrace my vulnerabilities.

As I steer the twists and turns of my inner landscape, I began to unravel the complexities of freedom, realizing that it is not merely the absence of constraints but a state of mind and being. Forge my path, unencumbered by societal expectations or external pressures.

Through this pilgrimage of self-discovery, I find liberation in acceptance and self-love, recognizing that the cost of freedom is nothing less than the willingness to confront and overcome the limitations of my mind. As I seek truth and meaning in my life, I embrace the campaign ahead with open arms, knowing that freedom is not just a destination but a lifelong pursuit of growth and fulfillment.

Reflecting further, I realized that embracing love as my aura wasn't just a fleeting sentiment or a passing emotion—it was a profound shift in perspective, a deliberate choice to embody love in every aspect of my being. I imagined it as a radiant glow from within, touching everything I encountered.

I continued to ponder, understanding the significance of choosing love in my approach to life. When I let love be my aura, I approached life with an open heart and a compassionate spirit. It was about seeing the beauty and goodness in myself and others, even amid challenges and imperfections. Instead of reacting with fear or anger, I responded with empathy and understanding, recognizing that we're all human and deserving of love and kindness.

In the canvas of my life, each stroke is a deliberate act of creation, each chapter a testament to the resilience of the human spirit. I embarked on this campaign purposefully, guided by the light of wisdom and fueled by the flames of passion that first ignited in high school. This narrative is not just mine; it's a story of transformation, of finding and packaging a message that transcends the pages of my books and the echoes of my counseling sessions—a message that resonates with the universal quest for freedom, self-discovery and the harmonious dance of existence.

With unwavering determination, I determine the direction of traveling through the complexities of my adventure, recognizing that my experiences can inspire and uplift others on their paths of self-discovery. Through my writing and counseling, I endeavor to illuminate the way forward, offering guidance and support to those who seek to break free from the constraints of the past and embrace the fullness of their potential.

Words become transformation tools in my hands, weaving a collage of hope and possibility for all who dare to dream. As I continue to dig into the depths of my being, I remain committed to sharing my insights and wisdom with the world, knowing that true freedom lies not in isolation but in the interconnectedness of all living beings.

In the ongoing mosaic of my account, every twist and turn becomes a chapter, every challenge an opportunity for growth. Through the lens of my multifaceted roles, I have learned that the power to shape my reality lies in the circumstances and conscious choices I make along the way.

With each new chapter, I embrace the sophisticated life, recognizing that adversity can catalyze transformation. Through my various roles and experiences, I have gained insight into the profound impact of intentional decision-making. Understanding that external forces do not solely determine the course of my description, I cruise with a sense of urgency, actively shaping my reality through mindful choices and actions.

In this odyssey of self-discovery and empowerment, I find liberation in the realization that I hold the reins of my destiny. Each conscious decision aligns my life with my deepest values and aspirations. As I continue to weave my story, I remain steadfast in my commitment to living authentically and embracing the boundless possibilities that lie ahead.

Planning the route, I wear the hats of the author, counselor, spiritual guide, mentor, and life coach with a deep sense of responsibility. It's a calling to share the wisdom gleaned from my experiences, the insights unearthed through self-discovery, and the profound transformations that have shaped my understanding of freedom.

In each of my roles, I see an opportunity to serve others and facilitate their paths of growth and self-realization. With each word written and each session conducted, I strive to offer guidance and support to those who seek it. My traveling period becomes intertwined with the objectives of those I assist, creating a montage of shared experiences and mutual growth.

Through my work, I endeavor to impart knowledge and inspire and empower others to embrace their expedition of self-discovery. I understand the importance of leading by example and embodying the principles of authenticity, compassion, and resilience in all that I do. I also remain committed to helping others find meaning, purpose, and fulfillment. And with each interaction and moment of connection, I reaffirm my belief in the transformative power of human connection and the infinite possibilities within each individual's voyage.

Finding and packaging my message is a dynamic process—an ongoing exploration of articulating the complexities of personal growth, spiritual awakening, and the pursuit of a harmonious reality. It involves distilling the essence of my insights into words that resonate with others, offering guidance and illumination for those on similar paths.

In my safari of expression, I searched into the depths of my experiences and reflections, seeking to capture the essence of my trip in a way that speaks to the hearts and minds of my audience. With each word carefully chosen and each sentence crafted with intention, I strive to convey the richness and depth of my message.

Through my writings and teachings, I aim to inspire others to embark on their quests for growth and enlightenment. I understand the power of storytelling as a tool for transformation, and I harness it to weave narratives that resonate with the universal human experience.

As I continue refining my craft, I remain committed to exploring truth and meaning, sharing my insights with sincerity and authenticity. In doing so, I hope to ignite a spark of curiosity and possibility in those who encounter my work, guiding them toward a deeper understanding of themselves and the world around them.

In the realm of writing, each word becomes a brushstroke, painting a vivid picture of the landscapes of the mind and the vast horizons of the soul. As a counselor, I serve as a compass for others, guiding them through the intricacies of their expedition. The role of a spiritual guide is to illuminate the path toward self-discovery, assisting others in unlocking the potential within.

Mentoring and life coaching involve imparting knowledge and creating a transformative space for me to recognize my strengths and capabilities. It empowers me to embark on my pilgrimage with courage and resilience.

As a writer, I understand the profound impact of words in painting the accumulation of human experience. I craft each sentence with care, each paragraph imbued with meaning, and I strive to evoke emotions and provoke thought in my readers, inviting them to explore the depths of their minds and souls.

As a counselor, I draw upon my empathetic nature and keen insight to guide others through their challenges and triumphs. With patience and understanding, I help individuals direct the course of the complexities of their lives, offering support and encouragement along the way.

As a spiritual guide, I seek to illuminate the path to self-discovery, encouraging others to embark on a campaign of introspection and growth. Through wisdom and compassion, I assist them in uncovering their true selves and connecting with their innermost desires and aspirations.

For me, mentoring and life coaching go beyond mere instruction—they are opportunities to inspire and empower individuals to reach their full potential. By fostering a nurturing and supportive environment, I enable others to cultivate their talents, overcome obstacles, and achieve their goals with confidence and determination.

Through my writing, counseling, spiritual guidance, or mentoring, I strive to uplift and empower those around me, guiding them toward a life of fulfillment, purpose, and joy.

My challenge lies in distilling these multifaceted roles into a cohesive message that speaks to the universal human experience. It's about crafting statements that resonate, inspire, and guide others toward their paths of self-discovery and fulfillment.

In this endeavor, I understand the importance of authenticity and sincerity, recognizing that genuine connection is critical to making a lasting impact. Through my writing, counseling, and guidance, I strive to create a space where individuals feel seen, heard, and understood.

I believe that by sharing my exploration and insights, I can offer hope and encouragement to those struggling or seeking direction. Each word I pen, each session I conduct, is an opportunity to make a positive difference in someone's life, to help them unlock their potential and live their most authentic selves.

Continuing to evolve, I remain dedicated to serving others and spreading light in a world that sometimes feels dark and uncertain. With compassion and determination, I seek to empower individuals to embrace their uniqueness, pursue their passions, and create lives filled with meaning and purpose.

My message also continues to evolve. Each interaction, counseling session, and written piece contributes to refining this message—a message that seeks to uplift, empower, and inspire others on their quests for freedom and self-realization.

With every step forward in my pilgrimage of personal growth and professional development, I gain new insights and perspectives that enrich the message I share with the world. Through my dedication to authenticity and vulnerability, I connect deeply with others, fostering a sense of trust and understanding that lays the foundation for meaningful transformation.

As I hone my craft and deepen my understanding of human nature, I remain committed to serving as a beacon of light for those sailing the problematic life. Whether through my words, counseling sessions, or presence as a guiding figure, I strive to provide support and encouragement to all who seek it.

My message is one of hope, resilience, and the unwavering belief in the inherent potential of every individual to create a life of meaning and fulfillment. As I continue to evolve and grow, so does the impact of my message, resonating ever more deeply with those ready to embark on their sojourn of self-discovery and empowerment.

In the grand collage of life, my story intertwines with countless others, creating a collective record of growth, resilience, and the pursuit of a harmonious reality. And so, my adventure continues, each step a deliberate act of creation, each moment an opportunity to share the wisdom that emanates from a life dedicated to finding and packaging a message that transcends the boundaries of individual experience.

With each encounter and shared experience, I add new threads to the rich fabric of human existence, contributing to the ever-evolving story of humanity. My commitment to self-discovery and personal growth fuels my desire to impart knowledge and insight to others, guiding them toward enlightenment.

While navigating the twists and turns of my quest, I remain steadfast in my belief in the transformative power of connection and shared wisdom. Through my words and actions, I seek to inspire and uplift those around me, fostering a sense of unity and purpose in our collective expedition toward a more harmonious reality.

In this way, I continue to weave my story into the more extensive variety of life, leaving behind a legacy of hope, inspiration, and profound insight for generations to come.

2

Growing Up

---

*I*n the genesis of my existence, the canvas of my early life was painted with the hues of family, surroundings, and experiences that would mold the contours of my identity. Born into the embrace of a family deeply rooted in traditions, my earliest memories echo with the laughter of relatives and the warmth of shared moments. This familial backdrop, a drapery woven with the threads of heritage, became the nurturing soil from which the seeds of my identity sprouted.

Growing up in the embrace of my family, each member contributed brushstrokes to the portrait of who I would become. The values instilled by my parents, the anecdotes shared by grandparents, and the camaraderie with siblings and cousins all played pivotal roles in shaping the early chapters of my life. These were not just individuals but architects crafting the foundation upon which I would stand.

Wandering through the chapters of my upbringing, the backdrop of my community painted another stroke on the canvas of my life. The streets I roamed, the school I attended, and the friends I made offered diverse viewpoints that enriched my perception of the world. Childhood companionships and joint escapades contributed to the combinations of my identity, offering glimpses into the person I was evolving into. We kicked soccer balls, staged plays in our makeshift dramatic society, and organized festive gatherings during holidays like Christmas, Easter, and community celebrations.

These shared experiences wove threads of camaraderie and belonging into the fabric of my being, shaping my understanding of community and connection. Through the laughter and challenges, I discovered the value of cooperation, empathy, and shared joy. Whether playful or profound, each interaction left an indelible mark on my soul, influencing the path I would eventually tread. Reflecting on those formative years, I recognize the profound impact of my community in sculpting the person I have become.

However, as with any masterpiece, shadows began to emerge. Challenges and adversities cast their forms on the canvas, adding depth and complexity to the evolving portrait.

Struggles within the family, societal expectations, and personal dilemmas became integral components, painting shadows that mingled with the vibrant colors of joy and success.

In the migration through life's ever-changing tides, I understood that identity is not a fixed point but a dynamic force, evolving with each passing moment. The lessons ingrained in me during my formative years served as the bedrock upon which I built my sense of self. Like a sturdy ship sailing turbulent waters, my upbringing gave me the tools to weather life's storms and bask in its sunny skies.

In the ebbs and flows of existence, I discovered that resilience and adaptability are essential companions on self-discovery. The trials and tribulations I encountered served as refining fires, tempering my character, and fortifying my spirit. Conversely, moments of triumph humbled me, reminding me of the interconnectedness of all beings and the importance of gratitude.

As I charted my course through life's labyrinth, I found solace in knowing that my identity was not set in stone but rather a fluid notion of experiences, beliefs, and aspirations. Each chapter of my progress added new brushstrokes to the canvas of my soul, painting a portrait of resilience, courage, and growth.

In the grand symphony of existence, I learned to embrace the ever-changing melody of life, knowing that each note, whether sweet or discordant, contributed to the rich blends of my being. I handle the currents of change, finding strength in the unwavering truth that my identity is not defined by external circumstances but by the depth of my inner being.

Through the prism of my family's background and early experiences, I discovered the contours of my beliefs, the roots of my passions, and the source of my resilience. The foundation established during those formative years continues to influence my choices, values, and relationships, reminding me that the shadows in the rain are an integral part of the masterpiece that is my identity.

In the chapters of my early life, pain became a teacher, unveiling lessons that would shape the person I was becoming. Both sunlight and storms marked the seasons of my life, each leaving an indelible mark on the canvas of my existence.

Pain, a universal experience, became a chapter in my story. It taught me resilience in the face of adversity and the art of transforming struggles into stepping-stones. The shadows in my rain were not just moments of discomfort; they were invitations to introspection, to find strength in vulnerability, and to emerge from the storm with newfound wisdom.

Burrowing more profound into the recesses of my shadows, I discovered the intricate dance between pain and growth. The struggles that once seemed impossible became the catalysts for transformation. In those moments, I realized that pain was not my enemy but a guide leading me toward self-discovery.

The shadows in my rain also cast light on the importance of introspection. Amidst life's challenges, I found solace in reflecting on the shadows that colored my experiences. This introspection became a compass, guiding me through the labyrinth of emotions and unveiling the layers of my resilience.

Who am I in the face of pain? This question echoed through the corridors of my identity. The shadows did not define me; they refined me. Each trial became a mirror, reflecting the strength I possessed within. The chronicle of my pain became intertwined with the narrative of my growth, creating a harmonious symphony.

Amid life's shadows, I found the courage to confront my vulnerabilities. The storms within me echoed the storms around me, creating a synergy that propelled me forward. The Shadows in My Rain became a tale of adversity and a testament to the human spirit's capacity to endure, adapt, and emerge stronger.

Embracing the complexities of my own story, the shadows ceased to be ominous. They became companions on the adventure of self-discovery, revealing facets of my character that sunlight alone could not illuminate. In the shadows, I discovered resilience, empathy, and an unwavering belief in the possibility of growth.

Thus, the history of my early life, family background, and the shadows in my rain became an intricate rainbow. It showcased the vivid colors of joy and success and the subtle shades of pain and resilience. The canvas of my identity was painted with the strokes of a life well-lived, embracing both the sunlight and the shadows in my rain.

Embracing the title of an explorer, I've cultivated a restless spirit that propels me forward, constantly seeking change and variety. This inclination toward a free-spirited lifestyle has taught me a crucial lesson: to live the adventures I create. Recognizing that a lack of proactive engagement in my life might result in unnecessary drama, I've become intentional about meeting new people, trying new things, and relentlessly pursuing answers to life's questions driven by an insatiable curiosity.

Looking back on my path toward completeness and contentment, I uncovered a heavy burden that had weighed me down for years. Recognizing this burden sparked a transformative shift as I realized I could transmute it into joy and fulfillment. Internally, I embarked on a quest for self-betterment, striving to cultivate inner peace and abundance. However, I yearned for this inner transformation to reflect in my external world, fostering a seamless harmony between my inner and outer realities.

This passage of self-discovery led me to confront the obstacles that stood in the way of my happiness. I faced my fears, challenged my limiting beliefs, and embraced vulnerability as a path to growth. Through introspection and reflection, I unearthed the deep-rooted patterns and conditioning that had kept me bound, gradually shedding the layers of doubt and insecurity that clouded my self-perception.

Armed with this newfound understanding, I embarked on a pilgrimage of self-empowerment and transformation. I reclaimed my agency and embraced my inherent worthiness. I learned to set boundaries, prioritize self-care, and cultivate meaningful connections. As I nurtured a more profound sense of self-love and acceptance, I found the courage to pursue my passions and dreams unapologetically.

During my college years, a profound longing stirred me to probe deeper into my spiritual odyssey. This inner calling led me to seek out the Catholic faith, where I embarked on a transformative path of spiritual growth. One significant milestone in my expedition was my baptism into the Catholic

Church, a considerable experience that marked the beginning of my formal commitment to my faith.

A year later, I underwent the sacrament of confirmation, reaffirming my dedication to my newfound spiritual path. This sacred ritual was pivotal in my sojourn, solidifying my connection to the Catholic community and deepening my understanding of Catholic teachings and traditions.

Inspired by a genuine desire to serve God and humanity, I decided to pursue a vocation to the priesthood. This decision led me to enter the seminary, where I embarked on a rigorous exploration of theological study, spiritual formation, and personal development.

Over the next decade, I immersed myself in the various stages of seminary training, each phase contributing to my growth and preparation for a life dedicated to serving others. From academic studies in theology and philosophy to pastoral work and spiritual direction, I embraced every opportunity to deepen my knowledge and strengthen my spiritual foundation.

My time in the seminary was a profound spiritual awakening and self-discovery. It was a time of introspection, prayer, and discernment as I sought to discern God's will for my life and cultivate the virtues necessary for a life of service and ministry.

Though my progress in the seminary was not without its challenges and uncertainties, it was ultimately a deeply enriching and fulfilling experience. It was a time of profound transformation and growth, shaping me into who I am today and laying the groundwork for my continued spiritual drive.

Continuing to dive deeper into my studies and immersed myself in the Catholic faith's rich traditions, I became increasingly drawn to the teachings of Jesus Christ and the principles of compassion, love, and service that defined His ministry—each day presented new opportunities for spiritual growth and self-reflection, as I grappled with complex theological concepts and sought to apply them to my life and vocation.

Throughout my time in the seminary, I was blessed with the guidance and support of mentors and fellow seminarians who walked alongside me on this faith excursion. We shared moments of prayer, fellowship, and discernment, offering each other strength and encouragement as we sail the challenges and joys of seminary life.

One of the most profound aspects of my seminary experience was the opportunity to engage with diverse communities and cultures, both within the seminary itself and in the broader world. Through immersion experiences, pastoral placements, and outreach initiatives, I gained invaluable insights into the complexities of human knowledge and the universal call to love and serve all God's children.

Progressing through the stages of formation and discernment, I remained steadfast in my commitment to God and His Church, trusting in His divine plan for my life. Though the path to priesthood was not always easy, I remained grounded in faith, knowing that God's grace would sustain me through every trial and challenge.

Looking back on my expedition through the seminary, I am grateful for the countless blessings and opportunities that have shaped me into who I am today. While my path ultimately led me in a different direction, the lessons and experiences I gained during my formation continue to inform and inspire my ongoing spiritual quest.

Approaching the culmination of my seminary training, I felt a deep sense of anticipation and readiness to embark on the next phase of my passage. With my mentors' support and my community's prayers, I embraced the call to serve God and His people with humility and dedication.

After completing my studies and receiving the sacrament of Holy Orders, I was ordained as a deacon, marking a significant milestone in my spiritual adventure. As a deacon, I found fulfillment in serving the Church and ministering to those in need through preaching, teaching, or acts of charity.

Throughout my diaconal ministry, I witnessed firsthand the transformative power of God's love and mercy in the lives of individuals and communities. From comforting the sick and grieving to advocating for social justice and reconciliation, I sought to embody the Gospel's message in both word and deed.

As I continued to discern God's will for my life, I remained open to His guidance and direction, trusting He would lead me where I needed most. While the path ahead was uncertain, I found solace in knowing that God's grace would accompany me every step of the way.

With a heart filled with gratitude and a spirit of obedience, I embraced the challenges and opportunities ahead, confident that God's plan for me was unfolding according to His divine wisdom. As I thoroughly prepared to embrace my vocation as a priest, I looked forward to serving God and His people with unwavering faith and devotion.

I transitioned into the priesthood and felt a profound sense of responsibility and privilege to shepherd God's flock and minister to His people, of the sacred trust placed upon me and the immense privilege of being called to serve as a mediator between God and His children.

As a priest, I embraced my pastoral duties with humility and dedication. Whether presiding over Mass, administering the sacrament of reconciliation, or offering spiritual guidance and counsel, I sought to be a beacon of hope and compassion to all who crossed my path.

I immersed myself in the parish's daily life and witnessed firsthand the faithful's joys and struggles. From baptisms and weddings to funerals and moments of crisis, I walked alongside my parishioners, offering comfort, encouragement, and support in their faith itinerary.

Despite the challenges and demands of ministry, I found strength and inspiration in God's unwavering love and grace. Through prayer, reflection, and ongoing formation, I continued to deepen my relationship with Christ and grow my understanding of what it means to be a servant leader in the Church.

In reflection on my expedition thus far, I marveled at how God had guided and sustained me through every season of my life. From the initial stirrings of my vocation to the challenges and blessings of the priesthood, I recognized His hand at work in all things, shaping me into the person He intended me to be.

With a heart filled with gratitude and a spirit of humility, I looked ahead to the future, eager to continue serving God and His people with joy and devotion. I embraced the sacred calling of the priesthood, praying for the grace to remain faithful to my vocation and always seek God's will in all things.

At a pivotal juncture in my vocational hike, I confronted a profound decision that would shape my life. After much reflection and soul-searching, I made the difficult choice to step away from the priesthood, recognizing the need to embark on a path of personal development and self-fulfillment.

Leaving the priesthood was not a decision I made lightly. It involved complex emotions, including doubt, uncertainty, and a deep sense of loss. Yet, amidst the turmoil, I felt a stirring within my soul—a call to explore new horizons, discover new facets of myself, and pursue a more authentic expression of my faith and purpose.

As I head towards this transition period, I embarked on a tour of self-discovery and introspection. I looked into various avenues of personal growth to uncover my passions, talents, and aspirations. I immersed myself in literature, art, and philosophy, drawing inspiration from the wisdom of poets, thinkers, and spiritual guides who had traversed similar transformation paths.

Even with uncertainty, I found solace in the support of friends, mentors, and loved ones who stood by me with unwavering encouragement and understanding. Their presence provided a steady anchor amidst the tumult of change, offering reassurance that I was not alone on this adventure of self-exploration and renewal.

While venturing into uncharted territory, I encountered new opportunities and challenges that tested my resilience and resolve. I embraced each experience as an opportunity for growth, viewing setbacks as stepping-stones to self-discovery and fulfillment.

With each passing day, I felt myself evolving—shedding old layers of identity and embracing the fullness of my being with renewed clarity and purpose. Though the road ahead was uncertain, I embraced the trek with an open heart and a steadfast determination to live authentically and passionately, guided by the inner compass of my soul.

Leaving the priesthood was not the end of my spiritual exploration; instead, it was a new beginning—a chance to redefine my relationship with God, faith, and community on my terms. As I ventured into the unknown, I carried with me the lessons and blessings of my time in the priesthood, grateful for the experiences that had shaped me and eager to embrace the boundless possibilities ahead.

I stepped into this new chapter of my life, embracing the freedom to explore my beliefs, values, and spirituality more expansively and inclusively. I sought diverse spiritual communities, engaging in dialogue and reflection with individuals from different backgrounds and traditions.

Amid this exploration, I discovered a deep sense of connection and belonging that transcended the confines of any single religious institution. I found solace in the shared campaign of seeking truth and meaning, recognizing many faith traditions' inherent beauty and wisdom.

As I immersed myself in this rich mosaic of spiritual inquiry, I encountered profound insight and revelation that deepened my understanding of myself and the world around me. I embraced practices of meditation, prayer, and contemplation, finding solace and inspiration in moments of stillness and silence.

In the middle of life's challenges and uncertainties, I found refuge in the sanctuary of my inner sanctuary—a sacred space where I could commune with the Divine and draw strength from the wellspring of grace and wisdom within.

Through this expedition of self-discovery and spiritual exploration, I realized that true fulfillment and wholeness could only be found by embracing the full spectrum of my humanity—the light and the shadow, the joy and the sorrow, the certainty and the doubt.

I continued to operate the ever-changing landscape of my spiritual adventure, remaining open to the mysteries of life and the unfolding of divine grace in unexpected ways. I embraced the beauty of the present moment, recognizing that each step of the travel held its unique gifts and blessings.

In the end, I understood that the essence of spirituality lies not in rigid dogma or doctrine but in the boundless capacity of the human heart to love, seek, and connect with the sacred in all its myriad forms. And so, I walked forward with faith and humility, trusting in the guiding hand of the Divine to lead me ever closer to the truth of who I am and the purpose for which I was created.

As I burrow deeper into this exploration of spirituality, I was drawn to the teachings of various mystics, philosophers, and sages from across cultures and eras. Their profound insights into the nature of existence and the human experience resonated deeply within me, offering new perspectives and pathways for growth.

In the quiet moments of reflection and contemplation, I encountered a sense of profound interconnectedness—a recognition that all beings are intricately woven into the fabric of the universe, each one a unique expression of divine love and creativity. This realization sparked a profound shift in my understanding of spirituality, moving beyond the confines of organized religion to embrace a more expansive and inclusive worldview.

Continuing to explore the depths of my inner landscape, I unearthed layers of conditioning and belief systems that no longer served me. I began questioning long-held assumptions and societal norms, daring to chart a course that felt authentic to my inner guidance.

While in the middle of this process of self-discovery and transformation, I encountered moments of resistance and uncertainty. Old fears and insecurities bubbled to the surface, challenging me to confront them with courage and compassion. Yet, with each step forward, I felt a growing sense of liberation and empowerment—a recognition of my inherent worth and dignity as a human being.

In steering the twists and turns of my spiritual adventure, I was surrounded by a community of kindred spirits—souls who, like me, sought to awaken to the truth of their divine nature. Together, we shared stories, insights, and practices that nurtured our souls and deepened our connection to the sacred.

Ultimately, I realized that spirituality is not a destination to be reached but a journey to be lived. It is a continuous soul unfolding, a dance of light and shadow, joy and sorrow, love and loss. In embracing the fullness of this exploration, I discovered a profound sense of peace and purpose that transcended all boundaries and limitations.

Looking back on my spiritual odyssey, I am grateful for the richness and depth of the experiences that have shaped me. Each encounter and revelation have been a sacred gift—a stepping-stone to wholeness and fulfillment. And as I continue to walk this path, I do so with an open heart and a deep sense of reverence for the mystery and wonder of life.

Each step forward made me feel lighter, more accessible, and more aligned with my true essence.

The expedition was not without its challenges, but I embraced the process wholeheartedly, trusting in the wisdom of my inner guidance. As I continued to walk the path of self-discovery, I discovered a newfound sense of purpose and fulfillment that transcended my wildest dreams.

Exploring further along the path of personal growth and self-discovery, I encountered a formidable obstacle that seemed to thwart my progress at every turn. This obstacle, known to experts as "mind gravity," exerted a powerful influence over my thoughts, feelings, and actions, pulling me into a state of inertia and resistance.

At first, I struggled to identify the source of this invisible force, feeling frustrated and defeated by its relentless hold on my psyche. However, as I looked deeper into my inner landscape, I began to recognize the subtle ways in which external influences had shaped my perception of reality.

I realized that much of my conditioning and belief systems had been imposed upon me by society, family, and culture, creating a mental gravity that kept me tethered to old patterns and ways of thinking. I saw how these influences had instilled shame, guilt, and unworthiness, leading me to doubt my abilities and potential.

In a moment of clarity, I understood that this burden of shame and guilt was not mine to bear alone. It was a product of external conditioning, a subtle manipulation of the mind imposed upon me from an early age. With this realization came a sense of liberation—a lifting of the weight that had been pressing down upon me for so long.

In an act of radical self-forgiveness, I chose to release myself from the grip of shame and guilt, recognizing that holding onto these negative emotions only served to perpetuate the cycle of suffering. Instead, I embraced the truth that my attention shapes my reality in real time and that I could choose where to focus my energy and awareness.

This newfound awareness empowered me to take control of my mind and internal world, reclaiming my sovereignty and agency in the process. I began to practice mindfulness and presence, learning to observe my thoughts and emotions without judgment or attachment.

While letting go of the past and surrendered to the present moment, I discovered a profound sense of peace and freedom that transcended all limitations. I realized that every experience was a product of my focus and attention and that by shifting my perspective, I could transform my reality from one of limitation to one of possibility.

In embracing this truth, I opened myself to new opportunities and possibilities for growth and expansion. I learned to trust in the wisdom of my inner guidance, knowing that I held the key to unlocking my fullest potential. As I continued my adventure, I did so with a renewed sense of purpose and passion, knowing that the power to create my reality lay within me.

While continuing my self-discovery and personal growth adventure, I realized overcoming mind gravity was just the beginning. I began to explore more profound layers of my consciousness, uncovering long-held beliefs and conditioning ingrained within me from childhood.

I recognized that many of these beliefs were rooted in fear and scarcity, leading me to perceive the world through a lens of limitation and lack. I saw how these beliefs had shaped my thoughts, emotions, and behaviors, holding me back from fully embracing my true potential.

With this newfound awareness, I embarked on inner alchemy, transforming the lead of limiting beliefs into the gold of expansive possibility. I challenged myself to question the validity of these beliefs, asking myself whether they were serving my highest good or holding me back from living a life of fulfillment and abundance.

Confronting these limiting beliefs head-on, I began to see them for what they indeed were—imaginary constructs of the mind, devoid of any natural substance or truth. I realized

I could dismantle these beliefs and replace them with ones supporting my growth and evolution.

In doing so, I opened myself up to a new way of being—a way of being that was grounded in love, abundance, and possibility. I cultivated a mindset of positivity and optimism, focusing on life's inherent goodness rather than dwelling on its perceived shortcomings.

With each step forward, I felt lighter and more liberated, as if a weight had been lifted from my shoulders. I no longer felt bound by the constraints of fear and limitation but embraced the boundless potential within me.

I continued to unravel the layers of conditioning that had held me captive for so long, feeling deeply grateful for the exploration that had brought me to this point. I knew challenges would be ahead, but I also knew I had the inner resources and resilience to face them head-on.

Armed with this newfound sense of self-awareness and empowerment, I stepped boldly into the unknown, ready to embrace whatever the future held. I knew the path ahead would be filled with twists and turns, but I also knew I had the strength and courage to handle it gracefully and efficiently.

And so, with each passing day, I continued to expand my consciousness and deepen my connection to the limitless wellspring of creativity and possibilities within me. I knew the exploration was far from over, but the destination was infinite potential and boundless joy.

Having shed the burden of guilt and resentment, I found myself in a state of clarity and inner peace, ready to embark on a tour of more profound connection with others. It became evident that to cultivate fulfilling relationships with others, I needed to develop a sense of contentment and fulfillment within myself.

This realization was the cornerstone of my relationship approach – that true happiness and harmony in our connections with others can only blossom from a place of inner peace and self-acceptance. I understood that I needed to be at peace with my own life, choices, and identity before I could fully share myself with another person.

With this understanding, I began to prioritize my well-being and self-care, nurturing my physical, emotional, and spiritual health, continuing to find solace in practices such as mindfulness, meditation, and self-reflection, which helped me to deepen my connection to myself and cultivate a greater sense of inner peace.

As a result, I noticed a profound shift in my relationships with others. I could approach interactions with greater openness, authenticity, and compassion. Rather than seeking validation or fulfillment from external sources, I could derive joy and contentment from within, which allowed me to show up more fully in my relationships.

In my partnerships and friendships, I became more attuned to the needs and desires of others and more capable of offering support, understanding, and empathy. I learned to communicate more effectively, to listen more attentively, and to lead through conflicts with grace and compassion.

As a result, my relationships began to flourish, imbued with a sense of mutual respect, trust, and love. I was surrounded by people who uplifted and inspired me, accepted me for who I was, and brought joy and meaning into my life.

In my romantic relationships, I discovered a newfound depth of intimacy and connection as I learned to share my authentic self with vulnerability and honesty. I found that embracing my inner peace and self-acceptance could create a safe and nurturing space for love to flourish and grow.

Ultimately, I realized that the key to building happy and fulfilling relationships lies in cultivating a solid foundation of self-love and self-acceptance. When we are at peace with ourselves, we are better equipped to give and receive love and create meaningful connections that enrich our lives and bring us lasting happiness.

Much of my life was spent enduring circumstances, but this realization became a turning point. Armed with self-awareness, forgiveness, and an understanding of the power of my attention, I pilot life as an explorer with a renewed sense of purpose. My pilgrimage is no longer marked by endurance but by the active creation of a fulfilling and harmonious reality.

My exploration towards wholeness has been a revelation, unraveling the intricacies of my personality and demonstrating how each facet contributes to shaping the person I am today. Through this process, I've discovered how to embrace and love every part of myself, recognizing the unique strengths that define me. These strengths have become the foundation for building a successful and fulfilling tomorrow.

Understanding my weaknesses has been an integral part of this exploratory mission, and while overcoming them is ongoing, I've gained valuable insights that guide my continuous self-improvement. Every challenge becomes a stepping-stone, propelling me forward on the path to becoming the best version of myself.

This introspective voyage of exploration has been like turning on a light in a dark room, revealing the true desires of my heart and providing a clear roadmap for their realization. With this newfound understanding, success is no longer a far-off fantasy but a tangible reality.

The lessons I've learned from my failures have become stepping-stones, firmly anchored in the past and no longer holding me back. Instead, they propel me forward, guiding my steps toward the bright future I now envision.

In the depths of my aspirations, a profound yearning for freedom pulses at my core. Yet, along the way, I've learned that true freedom isn't free. It demands a price—one that extends far beyond the realm of material possessions.

In the previous chapter I asked, 'What is the cost of freedom for me?' It's a question that reaches into the depths of my soul, exploring the territories of self-discovery and personal evolution. For me, the cost of freedom entails shedding the shackles of limiting beliefs, breaking free from self-imposed constraints, and embracing the weighty responsibility that accompanies genuine autonomy.

It's a expedition of letting go, releasing the fears and doubts that hold me back, and stepping boldly into the vast expanse of possibility that lies before me. And though the road may be challenging, I know that the rewards of true freedom—of living authentically and fully—will far outweigh the sacrifices made along the way.

While making my way across this complex mission to explore, I've grasped that freedom isn't something handed to me on a silver platter—it's a decision I must actively make. It demands ongoing dedication, a deep understanding of myself, and the bravery to defy the norms imposed by society.

My unwavering commitment to authenticity quantifies the price of this freedom, my willingness to chase after my passions, and my determination to surmount any obstacles that stand in my way.

It's a quest where each step forward requires me to shed the layers of conformity, strip away the expectations placed upon me by others, and embrace the true essence of who I am. And though the path may be daunting at times, I know that the liberation found in living authentically is worth every ounce of effort expended.

Pursuing freedom, I am carving out a trail that resonates with my innermost essence. This adventure towards completeness has not only peeled back the layers of my identity but has also furnished me with the instruments to shape a life brimming with meaning and genuineness.

Pressing onward, the price of freedom morphs into an investment in the life I yearn to inhabit—one characterized by self-compassion, accomplishment, and the relentless chase of my most profound aspirations.

With each step along this path, I am reminded that true freedom isn't merely the absence of constraints but the presence of alignment with my deepest values and desires. It requires courage to confront the barriers that stand in the way, resilience to persevere through challenges, and self-love to embrace the exploration with open arms.

As I continue negotiating this intricate terrain, I am filled with purpose and determination. The sacrifices made along the exploration are insignificant compared to the profound fulfillment of living true to myself. And so, I press onward, fueled by the vision of a future where freedom reigns supreme, and my soul dances freely in the light of its truth.

I reject the label of "conventional" because I find no solace in the safety of the familiar. Instead, I am drawn to the thrill of taking risks and shun the monotony of routine. While I acknowledge that risk may lead to unintended consequences, I see it as a deliberate avenue for opportunity—a calculated embrace of the unknown in my quest for freedom.

Embracing risk is not about reckless abandon but rather a systematic approach to managing the uncertainties of life. It's a mindset that allows me to embrace challenges head-on, knowing that each risk is a step closer to realizing my aspirations. By stepping outside my comfort zone and venturing into the unknown, I open myself up to new experiences, growth, and fulfilling my deepest desires.

My knack for influencing others and my talent for inspiring them naturally make me an ideal candidate for roles in sales or marketing. Yet, my unconventional spirit propels me towards a different career trajectory that resonates with my aversion to the mundane. Professions with a strong emphasis on travel are a perfect match, providing a vibrant atmosphere that shields me from the dullness of routine often found in other fields.

In these roles, I find fulfillment in the ever-changing landscapes and the diverse encounters with each expedition. The thrill of exploring new places and cultures fuels my passion, while the challenges of handling unfamiliar territories sharpen my adaptability and problem-solving skills.

While the conventional path may offer stability and predictability, I thrive in the unpredictable and dynamic nature of a career that embraces travel. It allows me to break free from the confines of the ordinary.

The thought of being trapped in a repetitive or mundane job fills me with a restless energy. The strict structure of a nine to five job, where answering to someone else becomes routine, doesn't match my vision of a satisfying and liberated career. Instead, I crave positions that enable me to chart my course, venture into unknown realms, and embrace the excitement of breaking free from the conventional mold.

I yearn for roles that offer flexibility and autonomy, where creativity and innovation are valued over adherence to rigid schedules and protocols. In these unconventional paths, I find the freedom to shape my destiny and the exhilaration of forging new paths that others may fear to tread.

While the allure of stability may tempt some, I am drawn to the thrill of the unknown and endless possibilities beyond traditional employment's confines. True fulfillment lies in pursuing adventure, growth, and the unbridled freedom to chart my course.

For me, the quest for freedom isn't merely a belief; it's a driving force that influences my career decisions. I excel in environments where I can push boundaries, embrace calculated risks, and forge a distinct path that mirrors my identity as a nonconformist striving for fulfillment beyond the confines of the ordinary.

I find purpose and excitement in these environments that propel me forward. The opportunity to challenge the status quo and blaze my trail fills me with profound satisfaction. While others may seek comfort in the familiar, I am drawn to the thrill of charting new territories and pushing the limits of what is possible.

True fulfillment lies in the freedom to express myself authentically and pursue my passions without constraints. I am driven by the belief that life is too short to settle for anything less than extraordinary, and I am determined to carve out a career that reflects this philosophy in every aspect.

Versatility has always shaped my career trajectory, allowing me to explore many professional avenues. The longing to chart my course as an entrepreneur has remained a constant aspiration, fueled by a deep-seated desire for autonomy and the flexibility to go along life on my terms. However, amidst this pursuit lies a profound challenge—a struggle to embrace stillness and a palpable fear of being confined, whether to a specific location or within the confines of a relationship.

This inherent tension between the craving for independence and the fear of confinement has led me on a quest for self-discovery and introspection. It's a delicate balance between the allure of freedom and the comfort of stability. Yet, I am committed to confronting this challenge head-on, embracing the discomfort as an opportunity for growth and transformation.

This intricate dance between autonomy and attachment causes me to remain open to life's lessons. I strive to find harmony in the ebb and flow of change, recognizing that true freedom lies not in escaping constraints but in transcending them with grace and resilience.

Sometimes, the burden of limiting beliefs has held me firmly in place, tethering me to a symbolic ground. Understanding that my beliefs shape my reality, I've wrestled with the challenge of breaking free from these mental constraints. To some degree, these beliefs have restricted the full expression of my adventurous nature and impeded my pursuit of the inherent desire for autonomy.

But I refuse to be defined by these limitations. With each passing day, I am learning to challenge and dismantle these beliefs, replacing them with empowering thoughts that fuel my sense of exploration and independence. It's a quest of self-discovery and self-liberation as I strive to embrace the boundless possibilities that lie beyond the confines of my mind.

I continue to shed the shackles of limiting beliefs, reclaiming my agency and forging a path that honors my true desires and aspirations. With each step forward, I am reclaiming my adventurous spirit and embracing the freedom to chart my course, unencumbered by the doubts and fears that once held me back.

While my passion for freedom extends beyond my desires to include a genuine concern for the autonomy and well-being of others, I grapple with the dichotomy of my dual nature. Despite my deep compassion, my intense focus on adventure and curiosity may occasionally lead me to overlook the feelings of those around me inadvertently.

This internal conflict between my desire for independence and empathy for others is a constant balancing act. I am committed to finding harmony between these two aspects of myself, striving to be mindful of how my actions may impact those around me while honoring my need for exploration and self-discovery.

It's an adventure of self-awareness and growth as I move along the complexities of human relationships and endeavor to cultivate a deeper understanding of myself and the people in my life. With each interaction, I am learning to strike a better balance between my adventurous spirit and my compassion for others, ultimately striving to create a more harmonious and fulfilling existence for myself and those around me.

Furthermore, my constant pursuit of the next adventure has sometimes left my life aimless. This lack of a defined path has, at times, resulted in feelings of discontent and frustration. While seeking out new experiences is exhilarating, it can also foster a sense of restlessness and a longing for something deeper and more enduring.

The relentless quest for novelty can be like chasing after fleeting shadows, leaving me craving a sense of purpose and direction. It's a delicate balance between embracing the excitement of the unknown and finding stability in the steady rhythm of everyday life.

Piloting this dynamic tension has taught me to appreciate the beauty of spontaneity and structure. By cultivating mindfulness and intentionality, I strive to infuse each moment with meaning and significance, finding fulfillment not only in the thrill of new experiences but also in the depth of meaningful connections and the fulfillment of long-term goals.

As I tread the fine line between freedom and connection, I acknowledge the significance of confronting and transcending my limiting beliefs. This expedition is self-exploration and perpetual evolution, where the thrill of adventure harmonizes with the quest for direction and meaningful relationships. Embracing this challenge, I strive to forge a path that not only satiates my innate longing for freedom but also fosters authentic, lasting connections and imbues life's pilgrimage with purpose.

This intricate dance of balancing freedom and connection teaches me to unravel the constraints of my own beliefs and embrace the boundless possibilities that lie ahead. It's a mission to explore filled with both excitement and introspection, where each step forward brings me closer to understanding myself and my place in the world.

While steering this path, I am discovering the importance of cultivating meaningful relationships and finding purpose in my interactions with others. While the call of adventure beckons me to explore new horizons, I am also grounded by the desire to forge deep, authentic connections that enrich my life and the lives of those around me.

Ultimately, I aim to create a life rich in experiences, meaningful connections, and a sense of fulfillment by aligning with my true self. In embracing the challenge of balancing freedom and connection, I am paving the way for an adventurous and deeply fulfilling exploration.

A Journey of Transformation:
The Healing Power of Self-Forgiveness

Not too long ago, I embarked on a transformative voyage of self-exploration, dedicating myself to looking into the depths of my inner being. This odyssey of introspection unveiled the heavy burden of past hurts and grievances that I had been carrying, burdens that were gradually wearing me down. Through this process of deep reflection, a pivotal revelation emerged – the imperative need for forgiveness.

Confronting the scars of past wounds and the weight of unresolved resentments, I realized that forgiveness was not merely a gift I could offer to others but a healing balm for my soul. It was a recognition that holding onto anger and bitterness only imprisoned me in the past, preventing me from moving forward and embracing the fullness of life.

In releasing the grip of resentment and extending forgiveness to those who had wronged me, I experienced a profound sense of liberation and inner peace. It was a transformative mission that allowed me to let go of the burdens of the past and embrace a future filled with hope, compassion, and renewed vitality.

I understood the vital importance of forgiveness, not only for those who had wounded me but also for myself—for the mistakes I had made and the pain I had caused myself and others. This realization carried profound significance in shaping the course of my life, like a radiant beacon illuminating my path with divine clarity.

Embracing the power of self-forgiveness, I felt the weight of guilt and shame gradually lift from my shoulders, allowing me to step into a new chapter of my life with renewed purpose and freedom. A campaign of healing and redemption transformed my inner landscape and set me on a course toward greater self-awareness and compassion.

In forgiving myself, I found the strength to acknowledge my humanity and embrace my imperfections with grace and humility. It was a profound act of self-love and acceptance, laying the foundation for a future filled with greater peace, joy, and fulfillment.

In the face of trials that tested me physically, emotionally, and spiritually, I discovered an inner reservoir of strength and resilience that enabled me to forgive. This capacity to offer forgiveness became a blessing from above, a celestial acknowledgment that I had weathered my share of tribulations and that the moment for love and healing had finally come.

With each act of forgiveness, I felt the burdens of resentment and pain slowly melt away, replaced by a profound sense of peace and liberation. It was as if the heavens were bestowing me a divine reward for my courage and perseverance in adversity.

Embracing the transformative power of forgiveness, I felt a renewed sense of connection to the world around me and a deepened appreciation for the beauty of life. It was a testament to the resilience of the human spirit and the boundless capacity for love and compassion within each of us.

The celestial enlightenment I received convinced me that I could bring my deepest desires to fruition despite my trials and setbacks. Like precious gems waiting to be unearthed, these desires offered the prospect of healing my wounded heart after enduring countless tribulations.

I also felt a sense of hope and resilience by embracing this newfound belief in my power to manifest my dreams. It was as if the universe had whispered words of encouragement, urging me to trust in the inherent magic of my existence.

With each passing day, I felt renewed purpose and determination to pursue my aspirations with unwavering faith and perseverance. The challenges I had faced no longer seemed impossible but instead stepping-stones to realizing my deepest desires.

In the light of this divine illumination, I embarked on a pursuit of knowledge of self-discovery and transformation, guided by the unwavering belief that I could shape my destiny and create a life filled with abundance, joy, and fulfillment.

Yet, amidst my newfound happiness, a looming "shadow" appeared. This metaphorical obstacle stood in my path, thwarting my efforts. It served as a barrier, holding me back from crossing potential pitfalls and from stepping into the abundant and fulfilling life that, by all rights, should have been mine from the start.

Despite the brightness of my newfound joy, this shadow lingered ominously, casting doubt and uncertainty over my path forward. It was a constant reminder of the challenges and setbacks I had endured, threatening to overshadow the beauty and abundance that awaited me.

Yet, I refused to let this shadow define or dictate my future. With determination and resilience, I confronted the obstacles that stood in my way, refusing to be held back by fear or self-doubt. I embraced the quest for discovery ahead with courage and optimism, trusting that I had the strength and wisdom to overcome any challenges.

In the face of adversity, I remained steadfast in my belief that my dreams were within reach and that I would emerge victorious with perseverance and unwavering faith.

And so, I pressed on, determined to banish the shadow and step boldly into the radiant light of my destiny.

As I find myself on the brink of this profound understanding to explore transformation, I am faced with the daunting task of dispelling this looming shadow. I recognize that achieving a life of fulfillment and prosperity demands more than just forgiveness—it requires the bravery to conquer internal barriers. Guided by divine insight, I stand prepared to steer this intricate path, eager to welcome the love and fulfillment I know is mine.

With each step forward, I draw upon the strength of my convictions and the wisdom gained from past experiences. I refuse to be held captive by doubts or insecurities, knowing that I possess the resilience and determination to overcome any obstacle that stands in my way.

As a result of embarking on this undertaking to explore, I am filled with a sense of purpose and clarity, guided by the unwavering belief that I deserve all the blessings life has to offer. With each passing day, I move closer to realizing my dreams, fueled by the inner fire of my aspirations and the unwavering support of the Divine.

In the face of adversity, I stand tall, unwavering in my commitment to creating a life filled with love, abundance, and fulfillment. And with each triumph over adversity, I am reminded that the shadow may cast its presence, but it can never extinguish the radiant light that shines within me.

The moment has arrived for me to take the reins of my destiny, to bask in the abundant and indulgent life that fate appears to have set before me. I've come to understand that my destiny is nothing less than extraordinary, and now, I am determined to make decisions that harmonize with this remarkable adventure. With unwavering resolve, I step forward, ready to embrace the grandeur and abundance that await me. Each decision is a deliberate step towards fulfilling my destiny, which promises richness and fulfillment beyond my wildest dreams.

My attention is now centered on nurturing my emotional wellness, yearning for a life filled with joy and carefree bliss. Along this path, I've understood that manifestation flows effortlessly when I embrace a state of openness, surrendering myself to trust in the mysterious forces at play in life. Armed with clear intentions and a renewed sense of empowerment, I stand prepared to make choices that will sculpt the destiny I envision for myself. It's a voyage that celebrates the richness of existence, reveling in the luxury and delights that rightfully belong to me.

As I explore the unknown, I am guided by the belief that abundance is my birthright, and I am determined to claim it with open arms. With each step I take, I immerse myself in the joy of the present moment, trusting that the universe will conspire in my favor to bring my desires to fruition.

I feel a sense of liberation and empowerment like never before in this state of alignment and trust. No longer shackled by doubt or fear, I move forward with confidence, knowing that I am co-creating my reality with the divine forces of the universe.

With gratitude and a spirit of adventure, I embrace the expedition to seek ahead, ready to embrace the luxuries and pleasures that await me. For I know that my destiny is one of abundance, and I am worthy of all the blessings that come my way.

Acknowledging the necessity for profound healing, I've chosen to mend relationships with family and friends who have drifted apart. I recognize that this step holds the key to unlocking profound healing, a quest for new horizons my soul yearns for. I aim to cultivate authentic connections with the Divine, trusting it to lead me toward meaningful relationships filled with love and blessings. As I embark on this pioneering expedition of forgiveness, I sense the burden of guilt lifting, clearing the path for a life liberated from pain, anger, and resentment.

With each step toward reconciliation, I feel a sense of lightness and clarity over me, as if a weight has been lifted from my shoulders. I am filled with hope and optimism for the future, knowing that by embracing forgiveness, I am opening myself up to a world of boundless possibilities and deep, meaningful connections.

Even as I yearn for a life of harmony, I recognize a peculiar struggle to attain it. I sense that this challenge stems from an imbalance within myself. The reassuring truth is that I am not alone on this adventure to investigate. There exists an opportunity to uncover the necessary tools to confront this pressing issue and bring equilibrium back into my life.

With determination and openness, I commit to exploring the root causes of this imbalance, seeking guidance and support from those who can offer insight and assistance. I understand that this process may require courage and vulnerability. Still, I will embrace the discomfort to achieve lasting transformation and a renewed sense of harmony.

Digging further into my inner self, I've started to tune in to the voice of my inner child, recognizing the wounds and tending to the neglected parts of myself. By aligning with the divine, I harness this healing energy inward, laying the groundwork for a more harmonious and balanced life. Through this odyssey of self-exploration and connection with the divine, I discovered the tools necessary to reshape my life, ushering in a period of healing, forgiveness, and a deeper comprehension of the influences that shape my existence.

With each step on this transformative path, I feel a profound sense of liberation and empowerment as I release old wounds and embrace the fullness of my being. I am grateful for the opportunity to heal and grow, knowing that with each moment of self-discovery, I am moving closer to a life of true fulfillment and inner peace.

Indeed, the time had come to mend the bridges with my loved ones, whether through virtual connections or in-person encounters. This endeavor goes beyond repairing external relationships; it is a vital step toward my inner integration. This moment has culminated in a pursuit of knowledge through shadow work, cultivating self-love, and setting healthy boundaries to reach where I am now.

Embarking on this scouting trip of reconciliation and self-discovery has filled me with purpose and determination. I approach each interaction with openness and humility, recognizing that true healing requires vulnerability and authenticity. Through this process, I am repairing past wounds and strengthening the foundation of my self-awareness and resilience.

Reflecting on my exploratory expedition thus far, I am filled with awe at the road I have traveled, recognizing the obstacles I have conquered and the personal growth I have experienced to reach this point. It's a time for self-appreciation, a moment to commend myself and acknowledge that I truly deserve the blessings unfolding for me, my family, and my relationships.

With each milestone reached and every challenge overcome, I am grateful for the lessons learned and the strength gained along the way. As I celebrate my expedition to seek, I am reminded of my resilience and determination, knowing that I have the power to create the life I desire and deserve.

My main focus is to delight in the present happiness surrounded by my loved ones. It's a moment to cherish the joyous present and welcome the love and brightness that fills my life. The mission to explore has been challenging, but it has brought me to this beautiful chapter where I can relish the richness of relationships and revel in the blessings bestowed upon me by life. Here's to more love and brightness, embracing the beauty of the here and now with gratitude and happiness.

I continue to immerse myself in the warmth of the present moment, continually feeling a deep sense of contentment and fulfillment washed over me. Surrounded by the love and support of those closest to me, I am reminded of the abundance surrounding me daily. This beautiful chapter of my life is a testament to the resilience of the human spirit and the power of love to transcend any obstacle. With each passing moment, I am filled with gratitude and joy, eager to embrace whatever the future may hold with open arms.

3

Seasons of My Life

Born on a Tuesday, according to Hausa tradition, and I could have been named "Tatu," symbolizing a male child born on that specific day. In Hausa culture, a famous saying echoes: "suna linzami," meaning 'your name leads you.' This adage encapsulates the profound belief that an individual's name holds significant sway over their personality and ultimate destiny.

Furthermore, the Qur'an, a guiding light for many, underscores the importance of a name in shaping one's character. It emphasizes the need to select names that embody positive qualities and aspirations. According to Islamic teachings, names carry a profound weight, influencing an individual's life trajectory. Thus, naming a child is not merely a cultural tradition but a sacred responsibility, reflecting the parents' hopes and aspirations for their offspring.

The Bible also addresses the concept of naming in several significant ways, reflecting its importance in the spiritual and cultural context of the scriptures. In summary, names in the Bible carry deep significance, reflecting character, destiny, divine promises, and spiritual transformations. They serve as markers of identity and purpose, deeply intertwined with the individuals' lives and relationships with God.

As a child born on a Tuesday, I emerged into the world enveloped in a sense of profound significance and grace. My arrival was not just a moment but a culmination of centuries of tradition and ancestral legacy. The ceremony to name me was not merely a formality but a sacred ritual for my future.

In many cultures, naming a child is a deeply symbolic and meaningful event, steeped in tradition and imbued with spiritual significance. It is a moment when the child's identity is formally recognized and celebrated, and the hopes and dreams of generations are bestowed upon them.

In the rich traditions of the Isoko tribe of the Niger Delta, as well as in the diverse cultural melting pot of Nigeria, the act of naming a child is far more than a mere formality—a significant ritual imbued with meaning, history, and a connection to the spiritual world. Among these communities, a name is not just an identifier but a narrative that reflects the undertaking to explore the child has already begun, even from the moment of conception.

Names in these traditions are often chosen based on the unique circumstances of the birth, whether they are fortunate or challenging. If a child is born after a long waiting period or amidst great joy, their name might show the family's gratitude and blessing for their arrival. For instance, names like "Oghenekevwe" (God has done it) in Isoko or "Nkechi" (What God has given) in Igbo are expressions of divine favor, encapsulating the happiness and relief of parents who may have prayed for the child's safe arrival.

If difficulties mark the birth—perhaps a struggle in labor or losing an earlier child—the name given might bear the weight of that experience as a reminder of the trials endured and the strength found in overcoming them. In such cases, names like "Omokhudu" (The child has been tested) or "Osaro" (God's time is the best) are imbued with resilience and the acknowledgment of the challenges faced, reflecting a deep understanding that life, even from its earliest moments, is a complex blend of joy and sorrow, trial and triumph.

These names, rooted in the linguistic and cultural traditions of the people, are often passed down through generations, carrying with them the stories of ancestors, the

59

hopes of parents, and the dreams for the future. They are more than mere words; they are living connections to the past, present, and future, serving as constant reminders of the circumstances of one's birth and the expectations placed upon them as they drive through life.

In this way, the tradition of naming in the Isoko tribe and other Nigerian ethnic groups transcends the simple act of choosing a name. It becomes a profound statement of identity, purpose, and destiny—a declaration that each individual's story is unique, shaped by the circumstances of their arrival into the world and the cultural heritage they are born into.

These naming customs reflect the culture's deeply ingrained beliefs and superstitions, serving as a form of protection and warding off negative energies. They illustrate the profound significance of names within the community, shaping the individual's identity and perceived destiny.

Reflecting on these cultural traditions, I am reminded of the intricate shade of beliefs and customs that shape our identities from birth. The stories behind our names remind us of the rich heritage and spiritual significance permeating every aspect of our lives.

In embracing my name, I am also embracing the legacy of my ancestors and the wisdom passed down through generations. It reminds me of the resilience and strength that runs through my veins, guiding me through life's challenges and triumphs.

Exploring the epistemological roots of my birth name offers more than just a mere identifier; it unveils a story about my character, temperament, and possibly even the trajectory of my life. It links to cultural customs, beliefs, and the profound importance of names in defining one's place within the diverse mosaic of Nigerian societies.

Probing into the origins of my name allows me to unravel layers of heritage and tradition, shedding light on the values and principles cherished by my ancestors. It is a testament to the enduring legacy passed down through generations, guiding me as I grapple with the issues of modern life while honoring the wisdom of those who came before me.

As I research deeper into the significance of my name, I uncover a report that resonates with my exploration mission of self-discovery and personal growth. It serves as a reminder of the cultural richness that shapes my identity and informs my understanding of the world around me.

With each revelation about the origins of my name, I am inspired to embrace the values and traditions woven into its fabric over generations. It empowers me to forge my path while remaining rooted in the wisdom and heritage of my ancestors.

The name "Omomaro" in the Isoko tradition carries profound meaning, rooted in the epistemology of the culture and its deep connection to the experiences and realities of life. In the Isoko language, "Omomaro" translates to "child of goodness" or "child of kindness," encapsulating the essence of benevolence, grace, and the innate goodness believed to reside within the bearer of this name.

The Isoko people, like many other ethnic groups in Nigeria, believe that names are more than just labels—they are reflections of the soul, expressions of destiny, and markers of the circumstances surrounding one's birth. A name like Omomaro is often given to a child whose arrival brings peace, joy, or healing to their family or community. The name signifies the embodiment of positive qualities and the expectation that the child will grow up to personify the virtues of kindness, compassion, and generosity.

Carrying the name Omomaro impacts me profoundly as a person. It is a constant reminder of the expectations that come with such a name—expectations not only from my family and community but also from myself. The name encourages me to strive for goodness in all I do, approach life with a heart full of kindness, and spread positivity in every interaction. It shapes my identity, guiding my actions and decisions and pushing me to live up to the ideals that my name represents.

In a world that can often be harsh and unforgiving, the name Omomaro is a beacon, urging me to remain faithful to the values it embodies. It reminds me that no matter the challenges I face, I must respond with kindness and goodness, staying aligned with the essence of my name. It is both a blessing and a responsibility—a reminder of my legacy and the impact I am meant to make.

The name Omomaro also connects me to my roots and the rich cultural heritage of the Isoko people. It anchors me in a tradition that values the power of names and the stories they tell. It reminds me that I am part of a larger narrative that stretches back through generations and that my life continues the hopes and dreams of those who came before me. My name is a link to my ancestry, a bridge between the past, present, and future, and a testament to the enduring power of goodness in shaping the world.

Ultimately, being named Omomaro is a daily call to live with integrity, to be a source of light in the world, and to honor the legacy of kindness that my name represents. It is a name that shapes not how others see me but how I see myself—constantly challenging me to embody the goodness that the Isoko tradition envisions in every "child of goodness."

Each utterance of my name reminds me of the values and virtues that define me. It serves as a beacon of pride and identity, guiding me on my expedition through life with a sense of purpose and belonging.

As I direct the world around me, I carry the weight of my name with honor and reverence, knowing that it represents not just who I am but also the legacy of my ancestors and my family's aspirations. In every interaction, my name speaks volumes about my heritage, values, and cultural identity richness as an Isoko indigene.

I have always strived to live up to my name, Omomaro. From a young age, I understood the significance of the name bestowed upon me—"child of goodness"—and felt a deep sense of responsibility to embody the virtues it represents. This name is not just a label; it is a call to action, a reminder that in every choice I make and interaction, I am expected to reflect the kindness and compassion that my name signifies.

Throughout my life, I have prioritized approaching others with empathy, offering help when needed, and contributing positively to the lives of those around me. Whether in small acts of kindness or more significant ways, I have endeavored to ensure that my actions align with the ideals that my name upholds.

Living up to the name Omomaro is not always easy. There have been moments of challenge, times when the pressures of life tested my ability to remain faithful to the goodness that my name suggests. But even in those difficult times, I have been guided by the understanding that my name carries a more profound meaning—a purpose that transcends personal struggles and speaks to a higher calling.

Reflecting on my quest for new horizons, I believe that I have lived up to my name, not because I have been perfect, but because I have continually sought to align my life with the values it represents. In moments of doubt, I have drawn strength from the knowledge that my name is a reminder of the goodness within me that I am called to nurture and share with the world.

For my parents, selecting my name was a purposeful and profound decision beyond a simple label or an easy identifier. In the Isoko Niger-Delta cultural framework, naming holds significant weight, symbolizing the family's values, hopes, and frequently shared identity. The timeless African proverb states, "The child's possession of a goat is as superficial as the color of its fur, for when it comes time to sell or slaughter the goat, no one consults the child," underscores the notion that naming a child is a responsibility beyond mere aesthetics; it reflects familial values and aspirations, shaping the child's identity and influencing their exploratory mission through life.

In choosing my name, my parents sought to imbue it with significance and purpose, ensuring that it would be a source of pride and connection to our cultural heritage. It reflects their hopes and dreams for me and their desire to instill a strong sense of identity and belonging within our tribal community.

As I grow and mature, I carry the weight of this naming agreement with me, recognizing the importance of honoring the values and traditions passed down to me. My name is a constant reminder of the love and care that went into its selection, guiding me as I survive the hardship of the world around me.

From the moment a child is born, careful consideration is given to their name selection. It is not a decision made lightly but reflects their family's hopes, dreams, and aspirations. Each name carries a story, a tale that speaks to the unique qualities and attributes of the individual, as well as their place within the broader social fabric.

Within this cultural context, the importance of names is deeply ingrained in everyday life. From birth ceremonies to social interactions, names are revered and honored, a constant reminder of the interconnectedness of individuals within the community.

In times of celebration and sorrow, in moments of triumph and defeat, a name is a constant companion, a beacon of hope, and a source of strength. It reminds us of the resilience of the human spirit and the enduring bonds that unite us all.

Firstborn Child

When I entered the world as the firstborn child of my parents, I became the embodiment of their hopes, dreams, and aspirations. My arrival brought an overwhelming sense of pride and joy into their lives, marking the beginning of a new chapter filled with endless possibilities and adventures.

As the firstborn, I carried the weight of responsibility and expectation, destined to pave the way for my siblings and set an example for future generations. My parents admired me, seeing in me the promise of a bright future and the fulfillment of their deepest desires.

From the moment I took my first breath, I was surrounded by love and affection, nurtured and cherished in ways only a firstborn child could understand. Every milestone I achieved, and every obstacle I overcame was met with cheers of encouragement and unwavering support from my parents.

Together, we embarked on countless adventures, exploring the world around us with wide-eyed wonder and excitement. From playful days in the playground to quiet evenings spent sharing stories by the fireside, each moment was a precious treasure, etched into the fabric of our family history.

As the firstborn, I served as a bridge between the past and the future, carrying forward the traditions and values instilled in me by my parents while forging my path in the world. With each passing year, I grew in wisdom and maturity, guided by the love and understanding of those who came before me.

Though the earliest exploration was not always easy, filled with challenges and obstacles, I knew I was never alone. My parents stood by my side, offering guidance and support as I direct the course of life's twists and turns, helping me become who I am today.

As the firstborn child of my parents, I was not just a source of pride and joy; I was the beacon of hope and the promise of a brighter tomorrow. As I undertake to explore through life, I carry the lessons and memories of those early days, forever grateful for the love and blessings surrounding me.

As I matured, I began to understand the significance of my role as the firstborn in my family. I was not just a sibling; I was a leader, a protector, and a source of guidance for my younger brothers and sisters. My parents looked to me to set an example with pride and honor.

With each passing year, I embraced my responsibilities with determination and resolve, striving to be the best role model for my siblings. I took on the challenges that came my way with courage and resilience, knowing that my actions would shape my future and influence the paths of those who looked up to me.

Through it all, my parents stood by my side, offering encouragement and support as I address the problems of growing up. They instilled in me values of hard work, integrity, and compassion, guiding me in making decisions that would benefit not only myself but also my family and community.

As the firstborn, I learned the importance of sacrifice and selflessness, putting my family's needs above my desires. I embraced my role with pride, knowing I was part of something greater than myself, a legacy that would endure long after I was gone.

Today, as I reflect on my passage of exploration as the firstborn, I am grateful for the opportunities and experiences that have shaped me into the person I am today. Though the road may have been challenging, I am proud to have laid the foundation for my family's future and honored to have been entrusted with such a significant role.

When my parents bestowed upon me my name, it wasn't a decision made in haste or without careful consideration. Instead, it was a process infused with deep meaning and profound significance. Their choice was guided not only by cultural traditions but also by their personal beliefs and values.

Their name for me wasn't just a label; it reflected their aspirations and hopes for my future. It carried within it the essence of their philosophy of wealth and prosperity, symbolizing their desire for abundance and success in my life.

However, the naming process had a spiritual dimension beyond the material realm. My parents believed that the name they gave me would shape my destiny, influencing my life in ways both seen and unseen. They imbued the name with blessings and prayers, invoking divine guidance and protection for my exploratory mission.

In choosing my name, my parents sought to bestow upon me a legacy, a name that would carry me through life with strength, purpose, and resilience. It was a name that spoke to their deepest hopes and dreams for me, a name that would resonate with the very core of my being.

Destiny

External circumstances, such as socioeconomic status, cultural background, and environmental influences, can all play a role in shaping the trajectory of our lives. These external forces interact with our internal desires, ambitions, and innate qualities to mold our path. While our names may provide a symbolic roadmap, our actions, choices, and perseverance ultimately determine how closely we align with our destined path.

The concept of destiny intertwined with our names reminds us of the intricate dance between fate and free will. While our names may set the stage for our crossing, our agency and determination enable us to experience life's changes, ultimately shaping our destinies.

Tackling the problem of destiny can feel like roaming a maze, where unforeseen events and the strength of our desires interplay to shape our paths. However, amidst this intricate dance, a formidable challenge emerges from the barrage of resistant thoughts that populate our minds daily. These thoughts, deeply entrenched by years of external influences and neurological barriers, pose significant obstacles to realizing our life's aspirations.

Imagine each resistant thought as a brick in a mental fortress, fortified over time by societal norms, past experiences, and self-imposed limitations. These barriers hinder the flow of positive energy and impede the manifestation of our deepest desires. Whether doubts about our abilities, fears of failure, or ingrained beliefs about our worthiness, these mental barricades stand as formidable impediments on the track toward our destined paths.

71

Overcoming these barriers requires a concerted effort to dismantle the walls of resistance and cultivate a mindset of empowerment and possibility. It entails rewiring our thought patterns, challenging limiting beliefs, and fostering a sense of self-belief and resilience. By cultivating a mindset aligned with our highest aspirations, we can chip away at the mental barriers that obstruct our path, clearing the way to realize our true destinies.

Reflecting on the inception of my destiny, I'm intrigued by the question of when the universe began orchestrating energies on my behalf. Was it during my formative years in school that I began to develop the ability to make personal choices? Or did it unfold gradually as I transitioned into adulthood? I've recognized that destiny has been at play for much longer than I initially realized.

Looking back on my life, I can see the subtle threads of fate weaving through every experience, shaping the trajectory of my expedition to seek. From the earliest moments of my childhood to the challenges and triumphs of my adult years, the universe has quietly guided me, nudging me toward my destined path.

Each decision I've made, every obstacle I've overcome, and every success I've celebrated has been a part of the intricate material of my destiny. Even when I couldn't see the bigger picture, the universe worked behind the scenes, aligning circumstances and opportunities to lead me toward my highest purpose.

This realization fills me with awe and gratitude, knowing I am part of something greater than myself. It reminds me to trust in the unfolding of my scouting trip and to embrace the guidance of the universe as I continue to cope with altering life circumstances.

Examining deeper into my destiny, I realize that its crystallization is a multifaceted process that extends far beyond the moment of my birth. My contemplation on when the universe began orchestrating energies on my behalf is thought-provoking, and I can't help but wonder if the answer lies in a time even before my conception.

Contemplating the intricate dance between identity, destiny, and the cosmic energies at play, I am struck by the profound significance of my name. It is a powerful acknowledgment of the depth and continuity of my passage through life. In recognizing the role of my name, I understand that orchestrating my destiny is a lifelong process, stretching back to the time before my birth and extending into the unfolding chapters of my life.

From the moment I was given my name, it became a vessel through which the universe could channel its energies, guiding me along the uniquely mine path. Each syllable of my name carries a resonance, a vibration that harmonizes with the cosmic forces shaping my existence. It reminds me that my expedition is not confined to the present moment but is part of a larger, ongoing narrative that spans time and space.

As I manage changing life dynamics, I am constantly reminded of the interconnectedness of all things and the role that my name plays in this grand scheme of existence. It is a source of comfort and guidance, reminding me of the infinite possibilities and the boundless potential within me.

In this way, my name becomes more than just a label; it reflects my true essence, a testament to the continuity of my path, and a reminder of the divine forces at work in my life. With each passing day, I embrace the unfolding of my destiny, knowing that my name carries the promise of a life filled with purpose, meaning, and fulfillment.

Looking into the significance of my name and the precise details of my birth, I'm struck by the profound insights they offer into my life's progress. Exploring these aspects through practices like astrology and numerology reveals much information about my traits and talents in this lifetime. It's as if these details serve as a unique key, unlocking the door to a deeper understanding of myself and my path.

Yet, as I ponder the implications of these revelations, I find myself grappling with questions about destiny and personal agency. On the one hand, there's a sense of awe and wonder at the intricate web of forces shaping my existence, from the cosmic alignments at the moment of my birth to the resonance of my name. These factors seem to point towards a predetermined path, a script already written in the stars.

Personal agency refers to an individual's ability to make choices, set goals, and take action to exert control over their own life and circumstances. It encompasses the sense of empowerment, autonomy, and self-determination that enables people to shape their destinies and achieve desired outcomes.

Personal agency involves a combination of self-awareness, self-efficacy, and self-control. It entails recognizing one's strengths, weaknesses, values, and beliefs and understanding the impact of one's actions on oneself and others.

Individuals with a strong sense of personal agency typically exhibit the following characteristics:

1. **Self-awareness:** They have a clear understanding of their strengths, weaknesses, interests, and values, which enables them to make informed decisions aligned with their goals and aspirations.

2. **Self-efficacy:** They believe in their ability to overcome challenges, solve problems, and achieve desired outcomes through effort, perseverance, and

resilience. This confidence in their capabilities fuels motivation and goal attainment.

3. **Self-control:** They demonstrate the ability to regulate their thoughts, emotions, and behaviors by their long-term goals and values. They can resist impulsive actions, delay gratification, and focus on essential tasks despite distractions or setbacks.

4. **Autonomy:** They value independence and freedom of choice, preferring to take responsibility for their actions and decisions rather than relying on external influences or circumstances.

5. **Proactivity:** They proactively seek opportunities, take initiative, and set challenging goals. They are not passive bystanders but actively engage in shaping their future.

6. **Adaptability:** They are flexible and open-minded, willing to adapt to changing circumstances, learn from experiences, and adjust their strategies as needed to achieve success.

Personal agency empowers individuals to cope with altering life circumstances, pursue meaningful goals, and create positive change in their lives and the world around them. It is crucial in fostering personal growth, resilience, and well-being.

However, alongside this recognition of destiny's influence, there's also a stirring of something else within me: a sense of autonomy, of the power to shape my fate. It's a reminder that while the universe may set the stage, it's ultimately up to me to play my part in the unfolding drama of life. I realize that destiny and personal agency are not mutually exclusive but coexist in a delicate balance, influencing the other in profound and mysterious ways.

While I may not completely control the events, I can choose how to respond. I can embrace the opportunities that come my way, cultivate my strengths, and chart a course that aligns with my deepest desires and aspirations.

So, as I continue on my venture, I do so with a newfound appreciation for the complexity of destiny and the boundless potential of personal agency. I am both a product of cosmic forces and a co-creator of my destiny, weaving my story into the rich drapery of existence with every choice I make.

Contemplating the extent of my control over my destiny leads me into a labyrinth of thought, where the lines between creation and circumstance blur and intertwine. It's a movement through the complexities of existence, where the truth reveals itself in shades of gray rather than black and white.

On one hand, there's the undeniable influence of circumstance. From the moment of my birth, I've been shaped by the myriad forces of the world around me—my upbringing, my environment, the people I've encountered, and the events that have unfolded in my life. These factors have undoubtedly left their mark, molding me into the person I am today and influencing the path I've walked thus far.

Yet, amidst the stream of circumstance, there's also the thread of creation—the power within me to shape my destiny. While I may not have control over every event or situation that arises, I do have agency in how I respond to them. I can meet adversity with resilience, seize opportunities with courage, and pass-through life's maze with grace and determination.

In this way, destiny becomes a co-creation between myself and the world around me. It's a dance between fate and free will, where the steps I take and the choices I make ripple outwards, shaping the course of my life in ways both seen and unseen. And while I may not have complete control over the outcome, I hold the power to influence it—to write my own story, one chapter at a time.

So, as I ponder the question of destiny and control, I find solace in the understanding that while circumstances may shape the path before me, it's ultimately up to me to determine the direction in which I walk. I am both a product of my environment and a creator of my destiny, wielding the power of choice to craft a life that reflects my deepest values, aspirations, and dreams.

Exploring Astrology and Numerology

Exploring astrology and numerology has been a fascinating spin, offering glimpses into the intricate brocade of my life path. I've seen these tools not as rigid predictors of fate but as invaluable guides, illuminating the hidden corners of my pursuit of knowledge with their cosmic insights.

Astrology, with its celestial maps and planetary alignments, paints a vivid picture of the energies at play in my life. By studying the positions of the stars and planets at birth, astrologers can uncover patterns and themes that shape my personality, relationships, and experiences. It's like peering into a cosmic mirror, reflecting my unique essence and the path I'm meant to walk.

Similarly, numerology investigates into the mystical language of numbers, revealing the underlying vibrations that reverberate throughout my life. Each number carries its energy and significance, influencing everything from my personality traits to my life's purpose. Through numerology, I've gained a deeper understanding of the strengths and challenges that define my campaign, helping me to handle them with clarity and insight.

However, perhaps the most powerful aspect of these tools is how they empower me with self-awareness. By shining a light on the hidden dimensions of my being, astrology, and numerology invite me to investigate the depths of my soul and embrace the fullness of who I am. They reveal not only my potential but also the paths that lie before me, offering guidance as I adapt to life changes.

In essence, astrology and numerology are not meant to dictate my destiny but to illuminate it—to offer me a roadmap of possibilities and empower me to chart my course. With their guidance, I can progress forward confidently, knowing that I am not alone but supported by the wisdom of the cosmos.

I may have outsourced some of my responsibility to external factors like astrology and numerology. While these practices can provide insights and guidance, I recognize that they are not meant to dictate my destiny. Instead, they serve as tools to illuminate possibilities and empower me to make informed choices.

I may inadvertently diminish my agency and accountability by relying too heavily on astrology and numerology to shape my decisions or justify my actions. It's important to remember that I am the ultimate architect of my life. While these practices can offer valuable insights, they should not override my intuition, reasoning, and free will.

Rather than passively accepting the predictions or interpretations offered by astrology and numerology, I can use them as tools for self-reflection and personal growth. By understanding the patterns and influences in my life, I can make more conscious and intentional choices that align with my values and aspirations.

Ultimately, I am responsible for the direction of my life and the outcomes of my decisions. By recognizing the limitations of external influences like astrology and numerology, I can reclaim my agency and take proactive steps to shape my destiny.

Searching deeper into astrology and numerology, I appreciated the delicate balance between fate and free will. While external circumstances certainly shape my experiences, I've realized that I can shape my responses and decisions. It's a dynamic interplay between destiny and personal agency, where I am both a product of my circumstances and an active participant in creating my reality.

By embracing this duality, I've learned to leverage the insights from astrology and numerology to my advantage. Armed with a deeper understanding of my strengths, weaknesses, and potential challenges, I can make more informed choices and take proactive steps to manifest my goals. Rather than feeling powerless in the face of adversity, I approach challenges with a sense of resilience and determination, knowing I can shape my destiny.

In essence, astrology and numerology are potent tools for self-discovery and empowerment. They provide me with a roadmap of possibilities and opportunities, allowing me to cope with life shifts confidently and clearly. With each decision I make, I become an active co-creator of my destiny, shaping my reality in alignment with my highest purpose and aspirations.

Covering life's ever-changing landscape, I recognize the intricate dance between fate and free will. While certain expedition elements seem predetermined, I understand that I am not merely a passive observer but an active participant in shaping my destiny. It's a collaborative effort between the circumstances I encounter and the choices I make in response to them, each influencing the trajectory of my life in a personal way.

Astrology and numerology are invaluable for self-discovery and guidance in this dynamic interplay. Rather than rigid roadmaps dictating my every move, they act as mirrors reflecting the possibilities available to me. Armed with this knowledge, I can make conscious choices that align with my most authentic self and the life I envision.

It's important to remember that destiny is not set in stone but fluid and adaptable. By embracing the wisdom offered by these tools, I am better equipped to endure life transitions of my quest with grace and intention. Each decision I make becomes a brushstroke in the canvas of my life, contributing to creating a description that is uniquely mine. In this way, I step into the role of a co-creator, actively shaping my reality in alignment with my deepest desires and highest aspirations.

Reflecting on the unique traits and talents that I carry within, I find myself empowered by the realization that they are not just passive attributes but powerful tools that can shape my pilgrimage. Each trait, creativity, resilience, or empathy, holds the potential to help me achieve my goals, overcome obstacles, and unlock new opportunities.

However, what truly resonates with me is the understanding that possessing certain traits does not confine me to a predetermined path. Instead, I am reminded that choice is a constant companion on my adventure, offering me the freedom to embrace or change my circumstances at any moment. This recognition fills me with a sense of agency and possibility, empowering me to chart my course and pursue my desired life.

The agency is the heartbeat of your existence—the pulsating rhythm that drives you forward and instills a deep sense of purpose within your soul. It is the guiding force behind your capacity to shape your destiny, mold your thoughts and actions according to your will, and confront the myriad challenges life throws.

In the quilting of your being, the agency is the vibrant thread that weaves together resilience and adaptability. It is the bedrock upon which your psychological stability rests, providing the anchor to weather storms of conflict and change with grace and poise.

But agency is more than just a concept—it is a lifeline that tethers you to the essence of your existence and empowers you to soar to new heights. It is the unwavering belief in your capabilities, the steadfast faith that you possess the strength and wisdom to tackle any task or situation that comes your way.

In moments of doubt and uncertainty, your sense of agency whispers words of encouragement, urging you to take the reins of your life and steer it towards the shores of your dreams. The beacon of light guides you through the darkest nights, illuminating the path ahead with the promise of hope and possibility.

So, cherish your sense of agency, nurture it, and let it flourish within the depths of your soul. The key unlocks the door to your true potential, propelling you toward a future filled with promise and purpose. Embrace, embody, and let it guide you through life's wondrous drapery.

With every step you take, feel the pulse of agency coursing through your veins, infusing you with courage, determination, and resilience. Embrace the challenges that come your way, knowing you possess the power to shape your destiny and overcome any obstacle.

In moments of uncertainty, trust in your innate ability. Draw strength from the depths of your being, tapping into the wellspring of agency within you. For it is in these moments of adversity that your true character shines brightest, illuminating the world with the brilliance of your spirit.

As you sojourn forward, remember that agency is not just a fleeting sensation—a steadfast companion. This guiding light accompanies you through every construct of your exploration. Hold it tightly; the beacon leads you to fulfill your deepest desires and aspirations.

Then, whenever you are faced with moments of doubt or fear, remember that agency is not about controlling every outcome but rather about embracing the uncertainty of life with courage and resilience. Trust your heart's wisdom, listen to your soul's whispers, and know you can achieve greatness beyond your wildest dreams.

Agency is the vibrant thread that weaves together the moments of joy, the challenges, and the triumphs. Embrace it with open arms, for it is the essence of your being, the heartbeat of your existence.

With agency as your compass, cross the seas of life with confidence and conviction. Let it guide you towards the shores of your dreams, where the possibilities are endless, and the expedition is filled with adventure and discovery.

Ultimately, it is not the destination that matters most but the adventure itself—the pilgrimage of self-discovery, growth, and transformation. And with the agency as your faithful companion, every step of the way becomes a testament to the power of the human spirit and the boundless potential that resides within us all.

With each decision I make, I am reminded of the infinite possibilities that lie before me. Whether I lean into my strengths, examine new avenues, or challenge myself to grow, I am actively shaping my reality and forging a path that aligns with my values and aspirations. This tour of self-discovery and empowerment is a testament to the boundless potential within each of us, waiting to be unleashed through the power of choice.

Scrutinizing deeper into the understanding of the energies and traits I possess, I found that they serve as a compass, guiding me through the intricacies of life's quest. Rather than confining me to a predetermined path, this awareness offers clarity and insight into my choices.

With each decision, I draw upon this knowledge as a valuable resource, allowing me to conquer the difficulty of life with greater ease and confidence. I am better equipped to make informed decisions that align with my values and aspirations by recognizing my strengths and understanding how they influence my actions.

The Wisdom of Self-Awareness And Freedom

Moreover, understanding my energies and traits enables me to anticipate potential challenges and pitfalls, helping me proactively address them before they become obstacles. It empowers me to chart a course that is not only aligned with my goals but also conducive to my growth and well-being.

In essence, this knowledge serves as a guiding light, illuminating the path ahead and empowering me to face life's twists and turns successfully with grace and resilience. It is a valuable asset that allows me to move forward with clarity, purpose, and confidence.

I am the architect of my campaign. While certain inherent traits and talents may predispose me to specific paths, the freedom to choose and adapt is ever-present. It's a dynamic dance between the intrinsic qualities I carry and the choices I make in response to the evolving circumstances of life.

Recognizing this balance empowers me to embrace my unique gifts and the opportunities that come my way. I understand that while my inherent traits may influence my inclinations, preferences, flexibility, and resilience, they do not determine my destiny in a rigid sense. Instead, I am constantly shaping my path through the decisions I make and the actions I take. I become the master of my fate, charting a course that reflects my authentic self and leads to fulfillment and growth.

Acknowledging my control over my life is empowering, means taking a proactive approach, where I don't just react to circumstances but actively shape and mold them according to my aspirations. This mindset boosts my resilience and fosters a sense of empowerment and ownership over my life's story.

I recognize that I can influence my circumstances and take charge of my destiny. I become the driver of my exploration, making intentional choices and taking decisive actions that align with my goals and values. This sense of agency allows me to confidently maneuver challenges, knowing I can overcome obstacles and create my desired life.

Embracing this proactive mindset transforms challenges into opportunities for growth and transformation. Instead of feeling helpless in the face of adversity, I see setbacks as temporary setbacks that I can overcome through determination and perseverance. This shift in perspective empowers me to turn setbacks into stepping-stones toward success and fulfillment.

Ultimately, embracing control over my life's account enables me to live with purpose and intention. I take ownership of my decisions and actions, knowing they shape my life's course. This sense of empowerment fuels my drive to pursue my dreams and create the life I envision.

The Balancing Act of Self-Awareness

As I hike through life, I allow myself to be constantly guided by the wisdom of self-awareness and freedom. My life is like a canvas, and the traits and talents I possess are the colors I can blend and rearrange to create a masterpiece that reflects my true essence.

Each choice I make is an opportunity to express myself authentically and to move closer to my goals and aspirations. I embrace the quest of self-discovery, recognizing that it's not about reaching a destination but embracing growth and evolution.

Self-awareness allows me to understand my strengths, weaknesses, and values, empowering me to make decisions that align with my authentic self. It's a quest of self-discovery and acceptance, where I embrace all aspects of myself and use them to inquire into life's twists and turns.

With this awareness comes the freedom to shape my circumstances according to my desires and aspirations. I recognize that I have the power to create the life I want. I see challenges as opportunities for growth and transformation and approach them with optimism and resilience.

As I paint the canvas of my life, I embrace creativity and experimentation, knowing that each brushstroke contributes to the masterpiece I am creating. I trust my intuition and follow my heart, allowing my true essence to shine through in everything I do.

In the end, my progress is a reflection of my innermost desires, values, and aspirations.

In the vast expanse of my story, I find myself mitigating the intricate life cycle of conflict. The tale begins with a boy's aspirations, a yearning to unravel the world's mysteries and understand where he fits into the lush patterns of existence.

As a boy driven by dreams, I was eager to explore the depths of knowledge and experience what life had to offer. However, my aspirations were not isolated; they were intricately entwined with my family dynamics. Our family dynamic was sometimes exoteric and wild, filled with complexities and challenges.

Growing up, I found myself between the desire to pursue my dreams and the responsibilities and expectations placed upon me by my family. This internal conflict shaped my expedition, leading me down paths filled with uncertainty and self-discovery.

At times, the conflicting desires within me created tension and confusion. I struggled to balance my aspirations with the needs and expectations of those around me. Yet, amid the turmoil, I also found moments of clarity and growth, where I began to understand the interconnectedness of my journey with that of my family.

The conflicts I faced served as catalysts for personal growth and transformation. Through adversity, I learned valuable lessons about resilience, empathy, and the importance of communication and understanding within familial relationships.

Amid conflict, I discovered the power of compassion and forgiveness for myself and those around me. Each challenge became an opportunity for introspection and

91

growth, leading me closer to understanding my place in the world and my role within my family.

I learned to embrace the conflicts that arise, knowing they were integral to my campaign toward self-discovery and fulfillment. With each challenge, I emerged more muscular, resilient, and deeply connected to myself and those I love.

However, a question still lingered in the recesses of my mind—am I merely living within the euphoria of my perceptions, or am I grounded in the nuances of my subconscious reality? The adventure into the symbolic Wild Wild West introduced me to a realm with vast possibilities, but the path to accomplishment is singular — to think for myself.

In the Wild, Wild West, I entered a realm brimming with untapped potential and daunting obstacles. This symbolic space wasn't just a backdrop but a vivid portrayal of the campaign I was embarking on — a mission where individuality and self-reliance would reign supreme.

So, armed with nothing but my dreams and the echo of their call, I set out into the unknown, ready to embrace whatever adventures awaited me. Ultimately, I knew it was about reaching a destination and the journey itself — a voyage of self-discovery, growth, and fulfillment.

Exploring this Wild, Wild West of my existence was like embarking on an adventure into the unknown. It was an expedition filled with excitement, uncertainty, and the constant quest for truth and authenticity.

In this symbolic landscape, the possibilities seemed endless, stretching out before me like the vast expanse of the American frontier. Yet, amidst the excitement of exploration, there was also a sense of isolation and vulnerability. The path to accomplishment was unclear, and I had to rely on my instincts and intuition to handle the challenges ahead.

While walking along this path, I encountered obstacles and detours, moments of doubt and uncertainty. Yet, with each step, I found strength I didn't know I possessed and courage I never thought I had. Each challenge became an opportunity for growth, a chance to push beyond my limits and discover the depths of my potential.

I soon realized that the key to success lay in my ability to think for myself. I had to break free from the constraints of societal expectations and norms, forging my path based on my own beliefs, values, and desires.

Fundamentally, the Wild, Wild West became a metaphor for the tumultuous nature of life itself — a place where conflicts arose, choices had to be made, and growth was inevitable. I emerged on the other side with a newfound sense of clarity and purpose, ready to face challenges with courage and determination.

Sequentially, my exploration into the Wild Wild West is a testament to the power of self-discovery and self-reliance. It was about embracing the unknown, trusting in myself, and daring to venture into uncharted territory to pursue my dreams and aspirations.

The Act of Thinking

Thinking is more than just a mental exercise; it's a quest into the depths of the self, where inner thoughts find their voice and are brought to life through external expression. This intricate interplay between the internal and external worlds holds immense power and significance in shaping our reality.

While reflecting on the act of thinking, I understood that perception plays a crucial role in how we interpret and highjack the world around us. Our thoughts and beliefs color our experiences, shaping how we perceive reality and interact with others.

This realization brings comfort, especially during the tumultuous enterprise of growing up. It reminds me that while life may be filled with challenges and uncertainties, I can shape my reality through thinking and perceiving the world.

By embracing the power of thought, I discovered a wellspring of strength and resilience. It enabled me to master life's challenges with clarity and purpose, understanding that my thoughts hold the key to shaping my reality and guiding me through the twists and turns of the responsibility ahead.

Despite the tumultuous terrain of adolescence, I was confronted by profound questions that reverberated within the corridors of my mind. Questions of identity, purpose, and the overwhelming fear of failure and anger loom large, casting shadows over my journey.

I've realized that adolescence is a time of immense internal conflict. It's a period marked by the relentless pursuit of self-discovery amidst the swirling difficult situation, and each day brings new challenges and uncertainties, leaving me to wrestle with the ever-present fear of failure and the daunting specter of anger.

The fear of failure weighed heavily on my shoulders, casting doubt on my abilities and clouding my vision of the future. I found myself constantly questioning whether I was capable of achieving my dreams or if I would fall short of expectations. The pressure to succeed was palpable, driving me to push myself harder and strive for perfection in everything I did.

Similarly, the fear of anger loomed large, haunting me with its unpredictable power. I feared the consequences of expressing my emotions, worried that my anger might spiral out of control and cause irreparable damage to myself and those around me. It was a constant battle to keep my emotions in check, to maintain a façade of composure even when I felt as though I was unraveling inside.

But amidst the chaos and uncertainty, I knew that this journey of adolescence was essential for my growth and development. It was a time of exploration and self-discovery, where I would learn valuable lessons about the power of resilience and perseverance. Though the path was fraught with challenges, I was determined to control the course with courage and conviction, knowing that each hurdle I overcame would bring me one step closer to understanding myself and my place in the world.

A profound realization began to dawn on me — perception is the architect of reality. This understanding, while initially daunting, became a beacon of light amidst the stormy seas of life. It granted me a sense of agency, a tool to ride the tide.

Amid the chaos and confusion, I understood how I perceived the world around me shaped my reality. The lens through which I viewed my experiences, my reality. This revelation was empowering and daunting, placing the responsibility for squarely shaping my reality in my hands.

Yet, this newfound understanding became a source of solace amid uncertainty. It gave me a semblance of control over its unpredictable twists and turns. Armed with this knowledge, I realized that I could influence my reality by choosing how I perceive and respond to the events unfolding around me.

Existence here refers to the state or fact of being honest, tangible, or having objective reality. It encompasses the presence or occurrence of something in the physical world or the realm of abstract concepts. Existence implies that something is present, whether a physical object, a living being, a thought, or an idea. It encompasses the entire spectrum of being, from the smallest particles to the vast expanses of the universe and includes both observable phenomena and intangible aspects of reality. Existence is fundamental to our understanding of reality and forms the basis of our perception and experience of the world.

Like a lantern illuminating the darkness, this realization guided me through the struggles and challenges of adolescence. It reminded me that while I may not control external circumstances, I can control how I perceive and resolve them. With this newfound perspective, I felt a sense of clarity and purpose, ready to face whatever obstacles came my way with courage and determination.

As an adult, I find myself drawn to the art of self-discovery in a uniquely poetic manner. In composing a poem, I unearthed a profound catharsis, a journey of externalizing and comprehending the inner tumult that resides within.

Crossing the Threshold:
A Journey into Adulthood

In the twilight of innocence, we roam,
Unaware of the weight of time's tome,
But as the sun sets on our youth's abode,
We embark on the journey to adulthood's road.

With each passing day, we shed our childlike guise,
As responsibilities and challenges arise,
We trade in our carefree laughter and play,
For the burdens and duties that come our way.

We stumble and falter, uncertain and scared,
As we ride out a world that seems unprepared,
But with each stumble, we gain strength anew,
Learning and growing, as adults do.

We forge our path through trials and strife,
Carving our destiny with each choice and life,
And though the road may be steep and long,
We emerge resilient, brave, and strong.

For adulthood is not just a state of age,
But a journey of wisdom, earned page by page,
So let us embrace the journey, come what may,
And become the adults we're meant to be, day by day.

— Omomaro Okekaro

In the quiet moments of introspection, I find solace in personifying anger through the strokes of my pen. Each word becomes a brushstroke, painting a vivid portrait of the emotions that swirl within me. Through this creative expression, I began to unravel the complexities of my inner world, peeling back the layers to reveal the raw essence of my being.

Yet, amidst the chaos of emotion, a key revelation emerges — the realization of the interconnectedness of pain, problems, and purpose. In crafting this poem, I understood that anger is not merely an isolated emotion but a symptom of deeper underlying issues. It serves as a messenger, signaling areas of my life that need attention and healing.

Through the lens of poetry, I gained clarity and insight into the intricate web of my experiences. Each verse became a stepping-stone to self-discovery, guiding me toward a deeper understanding of myself and my place in the world. As I continue to inspect the depths of my emotions through artistic expression, I embrace the transformative power of poetry as a tool for healing and growth.

Analyzing deeper into the labyrinth of self-discovery, I uncovered a profound truth that reshaped my perspective on adversity. I no longer view pain and problems as obstacles blocking my path; instead, I see them as integral threads woven into the fabric of my purpose.

This shift in perception transformed the narrative of my life. What were once struggles now become stepping-stones, guiding me toward personal growth and resilience. Each challenge I face is a crucible in which I forge my inner strength and fortitude.

With this newfound insight as my compass, I traverse not only through the tough times but also beyond them. It became a guiding light that illuminated the darkest corners of my journey, revealing hidden truths and deeper meanings.

Embracing this realization, I embodied a beacon of light, radiating resilience and wisdom born from the crucible of self-discovery. My expedition is no longer defined by hardship alone but by a profound connection to my inner self and a sense of purpose that transcends adversity.

ANGER

I am Anger. Who are you?
Who am I? What is that to you?
Ho! Ho! Do you question my authority?
Lest you get carried away, face reality.

I am Anger. Who are you?
Ha! That sounds familiar, but no, not you.
Come on, friend, face reality.
Oh! Anger, is this your existential reality
Hey! What do you mean, who are you?

Reality Hmm. What is reality?
Anger? You lock me in your jail…. Called reality
Where I was afraid, ashamed, and guilty
Where I feel broken and confronted with my vulnerability

I am anger and I belong to this world.
Oh, talking about this world
What do you know about this world?
Oh yes, welcome to my world
Yes, I recognize you anger, you're valuable to my world.

You give me power, comfort, and protection.
You help me hide beyond recognition.
You put out guilt and shame with no absolution.
Befriending you anger, there is no demolition.

My anger has a passion.
The passion of fireworks, NO!
The passion of burning coal, Yes!
The passion of anger! NO
The anger of passion, Yes
Oh, what a fantastic passion

101

My anger has a boundary.
The boundary has a balance.
The balance has a passion.
The passion has transcendence.
The transcendence has an identity.
The identity is holy anger.
Anger, Oh anger! You are my actual world.

— *Omomaro Okekaro*

4

Education

---

*E*ducation has played a pivotal role in shaping the foundation of my life's adventure. From the earliest stages of my upbringing, it has been a guiding light, illuminating my path and instilling a sense of purpose and direction. Like a sturdy cornerstone, education has provided the solid footing upon which I have built my knowledge, beliefs, morals, and social skills.

My educational odyssey began as a child when I was introduced to the fundamental principles of learning. It was a pilgrimage beyond the classroom walls, encompassing everything from social interactions to personal experiences. Through it all, education served as a guiding light, illuminating the path ahead and providing me with the tools necessary to understand the complexities of society.

At its core, education was about fostering intensive and critical thinking. It encouraged me to question the world, seek new ideas and perspectives, and challenge my assumptions. This process of intellectual growth was both empowering and transformative, helping me to develop a deeper understanding of myself and the world around me.

But education wasn't just about academics and moral and social development. It taught me the importance of empathy, compassion, and integrity, instilling a strong sense of ethics and responsibility. These values became the foundation upon which I built my relationships and grapple with the issue of society.

Throughout my formative years, I was privileged to receive a well-rounded education that extended beyond academic learning. This holistic approach nurtured both my intellect and my character. From engaging classroom lessons to diverse extracurricular activities, I was exposed to a broad spectrum of experiences that fostered critical thinking, creative problem-solving, and meaningful engagement with the world.

Education was more than just accumulating knowledge; it was about cultivating the skills and mindset necessary to confront our challenges. It gave me the tools to assess situations, make informed decisions, and communicate effectively. This foundation has prepared me for continuous learning and growth, enabling me to adapt to changing circumstances and embrace opportunities for personal and professional advancement.

Education instilled in me a strong sense of responsibility to positively impact society. It taught me the importance of empathy, compassion, and social responsibility, guiding me to use my knowledge and skills to benefit others. These lessons enhance my life and enable me to uplift and inspire those around me.

The hybrid nature of my education, combining the rich traditions of African heritage with the structure of a Eurocentric academic system, provided me with a unique and multifaceted learning experience. This blend allowed me to appreciate the wisdom of African traditions, emphasizing community, respect, and interconnectedness while also benefiting from a structured curriculum that sharpened my analytical thinking and problem-solving skills. This approach has broadened my perspective, enabling me to deal with diverse challenges and opportunities. It has fostered a deep appreciation for diversity and inclusivity, crucial for building a more harmonious society.

Education instilled in me resilience and adaptability, teaching me to view challenges as opportunities for growth rather than setbacks. Through perseverance and grit, I learned the importance of overcoming fears to achieve my goals. My educational expedition shaped my personal development and laid a strong foundation for my future, empowering me to overcome obstacles confidently and honestly. It has also equipped me with the tools and confidence to address social issues, advocate for change, and contribute meaningfully to my community, guiding my ongoing personal and societal development campaign.

A key lesson from this blended educational experience was the value of adaptability. Life is full of uncertainties, and adjusting to changing circumstances is essential. Whether confronting academic challenges or personal hardships, I learned to develop my resilience and emerge stronger. This holistic education equipped me not only for life's successes but also for its inevitable setbacks, instilling in me confidence and self-reliance, knowing that I possess the knowledge and skills to get a grip on any challenge that comes my way.

Reflecting on my educational adventure, I am deeply grateful for the diverse perspectives and experiences shaping my worldview. The fusion of traditional wisdom and modern knowledge has prepared me for academic success and enriched my life beyond the classroom.

This dual foundation has been crucial in my ability to foster social cohesion and bridge cultural divides. By integrating traditional African wisdom with Eurocentric knowledge, I have developed a unique perspective that enables me to tackle concerns of various cultural frameworks quickly. It continues to shape my identity and influence my role in society, guiding me through life's complexities like a path where ancient wisdom harmonizes with the demands of modernity.

Moreover, this education has equipped me with the skills to engage in meaningful dialogue and constructive problem-solving. Understanding others' perspectives and my diverse background have empowered me to facilitate discussions and initiatives that promote mutual understanding and cooperation.

I believe that my education is not just about personal growth but also about contributing to the greater good. Through my interactions and engagements, I aim to create a ripple effect of positive influence, inspiring others to embrace diversity and work towards a more inclusive society. In essence, my dual educational foundation has empowered me to be a catalyst for social change and progress. I am committed to building bridges and fostering a more cohesive and harmonious world. As a result, I can now transcend geographical boundaries and embrace diversity in all its forms. This mindset has been invaluable in my personal and professional endeavors, allowing me to connect with people from different cultures and backgrounds more deeply.

One of the critical aspects I learned was successful decision-making. Early on, I knew that my choices didn't just affect me, they had consequences that extended to the broader community. This taught me to consider the welfare of others in addition to my gain, instilling in me a sense of responsibility toward the community.

Continuing this quest, I am reminded that education is not just a destination but a lifelong pursuit. It's a quest of self-discovery, a constant interplay between the wisdom of the past and the present challenges. With each step forward, I confidently stride into an ever-evolving future with the knowledge and insights gleaned from this rich and diverse experience.

I am grateful for the opportunities it has afforded me and the person it has helped me become. It has laid the groundwork for a lifetime of learning and growth, empowering me to impact the world positively. It was a cornerstone of my development as a member of society. It gave me a solid foundation to build my understanding of the world and my role within it.

Looking back, as I connect the dots, I can see how my relentless pursuit of learning played a crucial role in shaping the person I am today. It has provided me with the skills and values necessary to positively impact the world around me, empowering me to contribute to the welfare of society in meaningful ways.

To succeed in life, I understand it's essential to nurture and develop various types of education beyond the formal learning structures. Each type of education plays a distinct role in shaping an individual's growth, adaptability, and ability to thrive in different areas of life. Below is an expanded explanation of the five key types of education.

1. Formal Education

Formal education is the traditional, structured system of learning that takes place in schools, colleges, universities, and other academic institutions. It is designed to provide foundational knowledge in mathematics, language, science, and humanities.

This is important as formal education builds essential intellectual skills like critical thinking, problem-solving, and analytical reasoning. It creates a solid foundation of knowledge that is often required for many career paths. Formal qualifications such as degrees and certifications usually serve as a passport to professional opportunities.

The limitation is that while formal education is essential, it is insufficient. Success in life often requires additional forms of learning and experiences that go beyond the confines of a classroom.

2. Informal Education

Informal education refers to self-directed learning that happens outside formal institutions. This includes life experiences, hobbies, reading, online courses, and mentorship. It is driven by curiosity and a desire to acquire new skills or knowledge.

Moreover, this matters in that informal education fosters creativity, adaptability, and a sense of curiosity. It allows individuals to check up on interests at their own pace, encouraging lifelong learning. With the rapid changes in technology and industry, informal education is critical for staying current and relevant in one's field.

Examples:

Learning a new language through an app, picking up coding skills through online tutorials, or developing soft skills through real-life experiences.

3. Emotional Education

Emotional education, often called emotional intelligence (EQ), involves understanding one's emotions, managing them effectively, and developing empathy toward others. It also includes building healthy relationships, practicing self-awareness, and developing resilience.

The significance here is that emotional education is crucial for personal well-being and professional success. Individuals with high emotional intelligence can better resolve stressful situations, work collaboratively, and lead others. Emotional education enhances communication, builds trust, and is vital for leadership and conflict resolution.

The applications in the workplace are that emotional education helps manage team dynamics, provide effective feedback, and motivate others. It improves personal relationships with friends, family, and partners, fostering harmony and mutual respect.

4. Financial Education

Financial education equips individuals with the knowledge and skills to manage their finances effectively. It includes understanding concepts such as budgeting, saving, investing, managing debt, and planning for the future.

It is worth noting that financial literacy is vital for long-term stability and wealth creation. Individuals who understand managing their finances are better prepared to make informed decisions, avoid financial pitfalls, and achieve personal goals like buying a house, planning for retirement, or starting a business.

Some critical components of financial education encompass knowledge of personal finance (e.g., budgeting, credit scores), investments (stocks, bonds, real estate), and economic principles. It also involves understanding taxes, insurance, and ways to build multiple income streams.

5. Social and Cultural Education

Social and cultural education refers to learning about society's values, traditions, norms, and diversity. It encompasses understanding different cultures, developing social skills, and learning how to interact effectively with people from various backgrounds.

Why it matters? In a globalized world, social and cultural awareness is essential for building relationships, working in diverse teams, and understanding different perspectives. It helps individuals adapt to various environments, both professionally and personally. It also fosters respect for cultural differences and opens international collaboration and networking doors.

The real-world relevance is that social and cultural education helps develop networking skills crucial to career advancement. It also aids in dealing with the difficulty of modern social structures and contributes to building a sense of belonging and inclusion in a multicultural world.

In conclusion, these five types of education form a comprehensive framework for personal and professional success. Formal education provides the intellectual foundation, while informal education keeps individuals adaptable and innovative. Emotional education is the cornerstone of interpersonal success; financial education ensures stability and independence, and social and cultural education broadens perspectives and enhances adaptability in a global environment. By embracing all five types of education, individuals can manage predicaments, seize opportunities, and achieve holistic success.

The five types of education have been instrumental in shaping my personal growth and development, guiding me through life's challenges and opportunities. Reflecting on how each has influenced my expedition gives me a deeper appreciation of the holistic nature of learning and the paths I've chosen.

1. Formal Education

A formal education gave me the foundation to understand the world and discover my passions. From early school to advanced studies, it instilled in me the critical thinking and analytical skills that have become the backbone of my personal and professional life. I learned discipline, perseverance, and the importance of structured knowledge.

My formal education shaped my curiosity and taught me how to approach problems methodically. It helped me acquire the qualifications I needed to open doors in my career. However, I've understood that education is a lifelong process, and what I learned in the classroom was just the beginning.

2. Informal Education

Outside the classroom, my thirst for knowledge has never waned. Whether through self-study, pursuing hobbies, or exploring new ideas on my own, informal education has allowed me to grow beyond the boundaries of formal learning. I've developed skills by following my passions, diving into books and online courses, and learning from mentors.

Informal education has made me more adaptable and resourceful. It's where I find inspiration and innovation. Whether learning a new skill for personal fulfillment or exploring fresh ideas in my field, informal education keeps me open to growth and continuous improvement.

3. Emotional Education

Over the years, I've realized the importance of understanding and managing my emotions. Emotional education has been a pivotal part of my development, teaching me resilience, empathy, and the power of vulnerability. By working on my emotional intelligence, I've become more in tune with my feelings and those of others, which has enhanced my relationships and leadership abilities.

Learning to manage emotions has helped me find balance in my personal and professional life. It allows me to handle stress more effectively and approach conflicts calmly and compassionately. This education has been crucial in building meaningful connections and fostering a supportive environment for growth.

4. Financial Education

Understanding my finances has been a critical lesson in independence and long-term planning. As I've grown older, I've realized that financial education goes beyond knowing how to save or invest—it's about building a foundation for future security and freedom.

I've worked hard to become financially literate, making informed budgeting, saving, and investing decisions. This education has given me confidence and control over my financial future, allowing me to pursue personal goals with a clear sense of purpose and direction. It's about creating a stable environment where I can continue to thrive.

5. Social and Cultural Education

As someone who values diversity and inclusivity, I believe social and cultural education is fundamental to a complex, interconnected world.

This form of education has helped me engage with people from all walks of life, enhancing my communication skills and empathy. It has allowed me to appreciate the richness of cultural diversity and develop a sense of belonging in a global society. This knowledge has also contributed to my evolution, reminding me that growth often comes from embracing different viewpoints and experiences.

Conclusion

These five types of education have formed a balanced framework for my personal growth and development. Each has shaped who I am today—an individual constantly learning, evolving, and striving for fulfillment in every area of life. By integrating formal education, informal learning, emotional intelligence, financial literacy, and cultural understanding, I have laid the foundation for continued success, resilience, and meaningful contribution to the world.

Education and African Traditional Values

African traditional education is deeply rooted in communal values, practical learning, and the passing down of wisdom from generation to generation. It's an approach that goes beyond the confines of formal schooling and integrates life skills, moral values, spiritual understanding, and a deep connection to nature and the community. Reflecting on the five types of education through the lens of traditional African education, I see how this holistic approach aligns with modern personal development concepts.

1. Formal Education and African Tradition

Formal education in many African societies was not based on written texts or classrooms but on practical instruction within the community. Elders, parents, and skilled artisans were the teachers, imparting knowledge through storytelling, observation, and participation in daily activities. The traditional apprenticeship system—learning by doing—mirrors the principles of formal education today.

Growing up in my community, the knowledge passed down by my elders was our version of formal education. Whether learning how to farm, make tools, or determine the direction of traveling the natural world, the lessons were structured, practical, and aimed at preparing us for life. In modern times, while I engaged with formal schools and universities, I cannot forget the importance of those foundational lessons that continue to guide my professional adventure.

2. Informal Education in the African Context

Informal education is woven into the fabric of African life. There is no strict separation between learning and living; knowledge is gained through every experience, from how elders address problems to how celebrations are conducted.

I learned many lessons as a child by observing and participating in my community's daily life. Whether it was the way my mother prepared food or the rituals that marked the changing seasons, these informal moments were profound sources of education. In today's world, I continue to carry this mindset of learning from every situation and finding wisdom in unexpected places.

3. Emotional Education and Communal Life

African traditional education places significant emphasis on emotional intelligence. The values of respect, humility, patience, and compassion are instilled from an early age. Children are taught to manage their emotions and understand their place within the larger community, fostering a sense of responsibility and empathy for others.

The teachings of my community shaped my emotional education. I was taught to honor my emotions but also to balance them with the needs of others. The wisdom of the elders taught me that emotional resilience is not just about individual strength but also collective support. This lesson resonates with me as I tread through personal and professional relationships.

4. Financial Education in Traditional African Societies

In many African communities, wealth was measured by material possessions and one's contributions to the community. Livelihood was based on sustainability, reciprocity, and collective welfare. People learned how to manage resources through farming, trading, and communal sharing, ensuring the community thrived.

I remember my grandparents teaching me the value of sharing and saving, not in terms of money, but in how we managed the harvest or helped each other in times of need. In today's world, where financial independence is critical, I apply those early lessons of resourcefulness and cooperation. I've learned to see wealth in personal gain and how it benefits those around me.

5. Social and Cultural Education: The Heart of African Tradition

African traditional education is deeply tied to social and cultural identity. From oral histories to rites of passage, individuals are taught who they are and where they come from. This education fosters a strong sense of belonging, instilling pride in one's heritage while encouraging an understanding of other cultures.

The stories told by my elders helped me understand my place in the world, grounding me in the knowledge of my ancestors and their struggles. As I continue to grow, I cherish the lessons of my cultural heritage. It informs my sense of identity and connection to others, reminding me that education is not just about personal success but about carrying forward the values of my people.

Conclusion

African traditional education, in many ways, prefigures the five types of education we recognize today—formal, informal, emotional, financial, and social. It emphasizes the individual's holistic development in intellectual terms and emotional, spiritual, and communal growth. As I move through life, I remain grounded in the traditional teachings that continue to shape my personal and professional development, weaving together the wisdom of my ancestors with the tools of the modern world.

Blend Of Cultural Influences

Growing up, I was immersed in the rich traditions of my African heritage. I learned the importance of community, respect for elders, and the value of storytelling to pass down wisdom from one generation to the next. These teachings formed the foundation of my cultural identity, instilling a deep sense of pride and connection to my roots.

At the same time, I was exposed to the principles of a Eurocentric educational system. I studied subjects like math, science, and literature, learning about historical events and scientific discoveries that shaped the modern world. I was taught the value of experiential learning and practical skills from a young age. Whether it was through hands-on projects, internships, or real-world simulations, I was encouraged to apply what I learned in the classroom to real-life situations.

This emphasis on practical learning has prepared me for an independent future. It has equipped me with the skills and confidence to face the world's complexities independently. From managing finances to problem-solving and decision-making, I had a solid foundation to build my life.

But perhaps more importantly, my blended education (a mosaic—a beautiful dosser woven from threads of traditional wisdom and modern knowledge) has taught me that failure is not the end but an opportunity for growth and learning. I have learned to think critically, analyze information, and communicate effectively in challenging situations.

I have been equipped with the tools to understand an increasingly interconnected world while grounding me in the values and traditions that are the foundation of who I am.

Indeed, my education has played a significant role in shaping my beliefs and worldview. Growing up, the interplay between my home environment and my experiences at school shaped my understanding of culture and identity in profound ways. While my parents, both educators, imparted a deep appreciation for our family's cultural heritage, the multicultural environment of our school presented a different perspective.

At home, cultural preservation was paramount. My parents emphasized the importance of embracing our family's traditions and customs, instilling in me a strong sense of pride in our heritage. This emphasis was particularly significant given our nomadic lifestyle, which often meant moving between different communities and environments.

Despite emphasizing our family's culture at home, each move brought us to new cultures and traditions. This exposure to multicultural environments enriched my understanding of the world and broadened my perspective and appreciation for cultural diversity. I became accustomed to adapting to new surroundings and embracing different ways of life, fostering a sense of openness and inclusivity. Despite this exposure, I was still linguistically challenged, limiting my primary language to English, the country's official language in government and education.

However, my school experiences exposed me to many cultures and perspectives. Despite my parents' profession as educators in a diverse setting, the reception of cultural diversity within our home was sometimes at odds with the multicultural exposure I encountered at school. While my parents valued cultural preservation, the school environment encouraged accepting and appreciating diverse backgrounds.

This paradox created a unique dynamic in my upbringing. While my parents sought to maintain our family's cultural identity, my experiences at school fostered an openness to different cultures and ways of life. This duality encouraged me to operate the nuances of local culture with curiosity and an open mind, ultimately shaping my beliefs and worldview in profound ways.

In contrast to the emphasis on cultural preservation at home, my experiences at school, secondary, and post-secondary schools opened my eyes to various cultures, each with its unique practices, beliefs, and traditions. I immersed myself in a rich diversity drapery, becoming a student of cultural pluralism.

The multicultural environment of my school encouraged an appreciation for diversity and the importance of embracing different cultural perspectives. It was a melting pot of traditions, languages, and customs, sparking my curiosity and igniting a desire to understand the world beyond the confines of my family's cultural norms.

The hope that this exposure was from a non-biased perspective further fueled my curiosity. I yearned to explore and engage with the various cultures represented in my school community, eager to learn from each unique perspective.

The irony of my parents, both educators, working in an environment rich in cultural diversity added complexity to my upbringing. While one might expect a seamless merging of these two worlds—home and school—the reality underscored the challenges many face in the delicate balance between preserving one's cultural roots and embracing the richness of a multicultural society.

The delicate balance between preserving my family's cultural heritage at home and being exposed to diverse cultures at school was pivotal in shaping my evolving beliefs and identity. My parents were the guardians of our family's traditions and values at home. They placed great importance on instilling a strong sense of belonging and pride in our heritage.

Our home was a sanctuary of our cultural identity, filled with the sounds of traditional music, the aromas of our native cuisine, and the language that carried the weight of generations. My parents clarified that these aspects of our heritage were not just relics of the past but living parts of who we were. They taught me to respect and uphold the customs passed down through our family, ensuring that I sincerely appreciated the wide variety of traditions that defined our lineage.

Yet, as I stepped outside the walls of our home and entered the broader world of school, I was introduced to a multitude of cultures, beliefs, and ways of life that were different from my own. The diversity of the school environment was a stark contrast to the cultural homogeneity of my home life. I encountered classmates and teachers from various backgrounds, each with unique perspectives, traditions, and values. This exposure was enlightening and challenging, forcing me to reconcile the differences between my upbringing and the world around me.

Mitigating these dual influences required a delicate balancing act. I had to learn to honor and preserve my family's cultural identity while being open to and respectful of the diverse cultures I encountered at school. This process was not always easy. There were moments of tension, confusion, and even conflict as I struggled to find my place within these two worlds. However, it was through this exploration that I began to develop a more nuanced understanding of identity and belonging.

I realized that my cultural heritage did not separate me from others but rather a foundation from which I could engage with the world. My family's traditions and values gave me a strong sense of who I was, allowing me to approach new experiences and perspectives with confidence and curiosity. At the same time, my exposure to diverse cultures at school broadened my horizons and challenged me to think critically about my beliefs. It taught me that identity is not static but evolves, shaped by our roots and experiences.

Ultimately, the juxtaposition of these two influences—preserving my cultural heritage at home while engaging with diverse cultures at school—allowed me to develop a multifaceted sense of self. I learned to appreciate the richness of my culture while embracing the beauty and diversity of the world around me. This exploration has shaped my beliefs, values, and worldview, making me proud of where I come from and excited about the endless possibilities of who I can become.

Coordinating between these two spheres—home and school—was not always easy. At times, I grappled with reconciling the importance of preserving my family's cultural heritage with the openness and inclusivity fostered by the multicultural environment at school. However, this dichotomy ultimately contributed to the complexity and depth of my worldview.

Through this dual influence, I learned to appreciate the beauty of cultural diversity while also cherishing the

127

traditions and values passed down through generations in my family. It taught me the importance of honoring my roots while remaining open-minded and respectful towards others' beliefs and practices. This cultural exploration and self-discovery adventure continues to shape my identity and enrich my perspective on the world around me.

The juxtaposition between the cultural cocoon of my home and the kaleidoscope of diversity at school created a dynamic tension within me. While my family instilled a deep sense of pride in our cultural roots, the multicultural environment of the school setting broadened my horizons and challenged my perspectives. This interplay between the familiar and the unfamiliar catalyzed personal growth, fostering empathy, understanding, and a genuine appreciation for the richness of human culture.

The interplay between the cultural teachings within the confines of my home and the multicultural exposure I received at school undoubtedly played a pivotal role in shaping my understanding of diversity. It was a delicate dance between the microcosm of familial culture and the expansive vistas of global perspectives. This intersection of influences, influenced by familial traditions and educational experiences, has undoubtedly left a profound imprint on my beliefs. As a result, I have learned to critically question and appreciate the nuances of diverse cultural practices while honoring my heritage.

Over time, I developed a nuanced understanding of diversity that transcended mere tolerance and embraced the richness of varied perspectives. The interplay between my upbringing in a culturally rich home environment and my exposure to diverse cultures at school laid the foundation for my beliefs. This pattern continued into my post-secondary education, leading me to experience multiple college campuses.

Each transition to a new school brought fresh experiences and cultural exposure. I immersed myself in diverse environments, where classmates hailed from myriad backgrounds and traditions. These interactions broadened my perspectives and enriched my understanding of the world.

Attending different educational institutions also taught me invaluable lessons in adaptability and resilience. Each new environment presented challenges, from adjusting to teaching styles to forging new friendships. Yet, with each transition, I honed my ability to adapt and thrive in diverse settings.

Decision-Making And Identity Formation

The varied educational settings I experienced played a pivotal role in shaping my decision-making process and defining my sense of self. Transitioning between various schools and colleges exposed me to multiple viewpoints and social contexts, cultivating adaptability and a sharp skillset for maneuvering through diverse environments.

Morals and responsibilities were emphasized throughout my upbringing, at home, and in school. However, the interpretation of these values varied across the different educational settings I experienced. Despite the diversity of perspectives, the core principles taught by my teachers remained steadfast and universal.

Joggling these varied moral teachings gave me a nuanced understanding of ethical considerations. It taught me to critically evaluate different viewpoints and discern the underlying principles that guide moral behavior. Ultimately, this exposure helped shape my identity and reinforced the importance of integrity and empathy in my voyage.

Progressing through my educational adventure, I encountered many challenges and opportunities that tested my resilience and determination. The diverse experiences I gained from attending different schools and colleges enriched my perspective and broadened my horizons, preparing me for the complexities of adulthood.

Despite the ever-changing educational landscapes, the values instilled in me by my parents remained constant pillars of support. Their guidance and teachings, rooted in our family's cultural heritage, gave me a solid foundation to commandeer the diverse environments I encountered.

Moving forward, I approach life with a sense of curiosity and openness, eager to continue learning and growing from the rich patterns of experiences that lie ahead. Armed with the lessons learned from my educational adventure and the values instilled in me by my upbringing, I embrace the future with optimism and resilience.

Respecting others and their ideas and refraining from making fun of different cultures, religions, families, and appearances were fundamental principles instilled in me from a young age. These values were not just rules to follow but core beliefs that shaped how I interacted with the world around me. Growing up, my parents emphasized the importance of treating everyone with dignity and kindness, regardless of our differences.

This commitment to basic principles of respect and acceptance extended beyond the confines of my home and into the educational environments I inhabited. Whether elementary, middle, high, or college, I understood that diversity should be celebrated, not ridiculed. I sought to create and nurture an inclusive atmosphere where everyone felt valued and accepted.

The emphasis on respect and understanding in my upbringing laid the foundation for a solid moral compass that guides my actions. It taught me the importance of empathy, compassion, and open-mindedness, which transcend cultural and geographical boundaries. I continue to strive to uphold these principles and contribute to building a more tolerant and harmonious society.

Acknowledging the diversity of moral perspectives and a steadfast commitment to fundamental values has been a cornerstone of my educational expedition. It's a recognition that while individuals may hold different beliefs and principles, certain universal truths transcend cultural and ideological boundaries.

This understanding underscores the importance of a universal ethos rooted in empathy, tolerance, and respect. These values are the bedrock of a cohesive and inclusive society where individuals from diverse backgrounds can coexist harmoniously.

Throughout my upbringing, I've witnessed firsthand the power of embracing diversity and fostering an environment of mutual understanding and acceptance. Through this lens, I approach interactions with others, striving to cultivate empathy and respect in all my relationships.

As I continue on my personal development quest, I remain committed to upholding these values and contributing to creating communities where everyone feels valued, heard, and respected.

Opportunity To Form New Friendships

The start of each school year was always filled with anticipation and excitement for me. It began a new chapter in my academic quest and the chance to immerse myself in a fresh environment. One of the most exciting aspects of this time was the opportunity to form new friendships.

However, these relationships always had a unique aspect that colored them with a hint of uncertainty. This came from the awareness that my family might relocate again by the end of the year. While I looked forward to building meaningful connections with my classmates, a lingering sense of impermanence accompanied each new friendship.

Despite this uncertainty, I embraced the opportunity to forge bonds with my peers, cherishing the time we spent together and the memories we created. Each new friendship brought unique experiences and perspectives, enriching my life in ways I could not have imagined. The transient nature of my family's lifestyle taught me the importance of living in the present moment and cherishing the relationships I formed. While some friendships may have been fleeting, their impact on my life was lasting, shaping me into the person I am today.

The awareness of potential relocation significantly influenced the dynamics of my relationships, leading to a delicate balance between forming meaningful bonds and guarding against emotional attachment. With the looming possibility of separation, I grappled with the need to protect myself from the inevitable emotional turmoil accompanying any departure.

As a result, I tended to maintain a certain level of emotional distance in my relationships, subconsciously bracing myself for the possibility of saying goodbye. While I cherished the connections I formed, there was always a lingering sense of apprehension, knowing that our time together might be cut short.

This uncertainty became a recurring theme throughout my formative years, leaving an indelible mark on how I approach connections, even in adulthood. While I value deep and meaningful relationships, I instinctively hold back, wary of investing too much emotionally in fear of potential separation.

Despite these challenges, I've learned to appreciate the beauty of fleeting connections and the lessons they impart. No matter how brief, each interaction has contributed to my growth and understanding of human connections, shaping me into the resilient and adaptable individual I am today.

As an adult, the mindset cultivated during my formative years influenced my approach to friendships and emotional investment. The patterns established out of necessity have become deeply ingrained in my relational blueprint.

The capacity for emotional intimacy may carry a cautious undertone, shaped by the adaptive strategies developed during a youth marked by the constant flux of arrivals and farewells. While I value connections deeply, there's often a lingering awareness of their transient nature, leading me to approach them guardedly.

This isn't to say that I can't form deep and meaningful relationships. Instead, it acknowledges the challenges of dealing with life's uncertainties. Each friendship is cherished, but there's a subtle understanding that circumstances may change, requiring a certain level of emotional resilience.

Despite the lingering echoes of this mindset, I strive to embrace the present moment and cultivate authentic connections with those around me. While impermanence may linger in the background, I am committed to fostering genuine bonds that enrich my life and those I encounter.

This dichotomy became particularly pronounced as I transitioned into adulthood. While I cherished the bonds I formed, there was always a lingering sense of detachment, a subconscious defense mechanism against the potential pain of separation. Despite this guardedness, I remained open to cultivating meaningful connections, understanding that each encounter, no matter how fleeting, had the potential to enrich my life. I've learned to strike a balance between vulnerability and self-protection. While the specter of impermanence continues to influence my approach, I remain committed to embracing the beauty of connection and the richness it brings to my assignment.

Education served as a personal and social growth conduit, with teachers serving as beacons of inspiration and guidance. Their influence continues to resonate in my life, shaping how I approach relationships, crisscross challenges, and strive for excellence in all endeavors.

Teachers

From my earliest days in school, teachers were pivotal in guiding my development, serving as mentors and role models who imparted academic knowledge and valuable life lessons. They fostered an environment where every voice was heard and every opinion valued, instilling a sense of empathy and understanding for those around me. I honed my social skills through group projects, discussions, and extracurricular activities and learned to cut across diverse social dynamics.

Beyond the academic curriculum, teachers offered insights into the ramifications of life, sharing personal anecdotes, wisdom, and guidance that transcended textbooks. Their mentorship extended beyond the confines of the classroom, as they provided support and encouragement during both triumphs and challenges.

As I progressed through my educational adventure, I realized teachers' profound impact on my personal growth and development. Their dedication, passion, and commitment to nurturing young minds made an indelible mark on my character and outlook. They equipped me with the knowledge and skills needed to succeed academically and instilled in me the values and principles to guide my interactions with others and contribute positively to society.

Throughout my educational transmigration, I was fortunate to encounter many teachers who went beyond the traditional curriculum to impart valuable life skills. While their primary focus was on academic subjects, they recognized the importance of equipping students with practical skills that would serve us well beyond the classroom.

These teachers were not content with delivering lectures and assigning homework; they took the time to engage us in discussions about real-world scenarios, teaching us how to problem-solve, communicate effectively, and make informed decisions. Whether through role-playing exercises, interactive projects, or guest speakers from different professions, they ensured that we received a well-rounded education beyond the confines of textbooks.

These teachers also impacted my understanding of existence and purpose. One such experience occurred during high school when my English teacher introduced me to existential literature. Through the works of authors like Albert Camus and Jean-Paul Sartre, I grappled with questions of meaning, freedom, and the absurdity of human existence.

In college, my philosophy professor challenged my preconceived notions about reality and pushed me to question the fundamental nature of existence. Engaging in lively debates and philosophical discussions, I probed deeper into existentialism and its implications for personal identity and moral responsibility.

Reflecting on these experiences, I realize that my teachers catalyzed intellectual growth and self-discovery. Their guidance and mentorship enriched my academic pursuits and deepened my understanding of the human condition. Through their teachings, I gained valuable insights into the complexities of existence and emerged with a renewed sense of purpose and curiosity about the world around me.

One of the most valuable lessons I learned from these teachers was the importance of time management and organization. They taught us how to prioritize tasks, set goals, and create schedules to ensure we could juggle multiple responsibilities effectively. These skills have proven invaluable in my personal and professional life, enabling me to meet deadlines, manage my workload, and maintain a healthy work-life balance.

Additionally, many of my teachers emphasized the importance of critical thinking and problem-solving. They challenged us to think analytically, question assumptions, and approach challenges with creativity and resilience. Through hands-on activities and open-ended assignments, they encouraged us to view different perspectives and develop innovative solutions to complex problems.

Furthermore, my teachers nurtured our interpersonal skills and emotional intelligence. They taught us how to communicate assertively, resolve conflicts diplomatically, and empathize with others' perspectives. These skills have been instrumental in building strong personal and professional relationships and going through social situations with confidence and empathy.

My teachers' commitment to holistic education enriched my academic experience and equipped me with the practical skills and competencies necessary for success in all aspects of life. Their dedication to our development as well-rounded individuals left a lasting impression on me, shaping how I approach challenges, interact with others, and strive for personal and professional growth.

Strong Faith-Based Orientation

Growing up within the Nigerian educational system, I encountered a curriculum deeply intertwined with religious teachings, predominantly centered around Christianity and Islam. This emphasis on faith-based education presented a unique challenge, particularly considering the blend of African traditional values and Eurocentric educational principles that shaped my upbringing. Understanding this multifaceted landscape required delicacy as I straddled the intersections of belief systems and cultural norms.

The expectation to embrace the predominant religious teachings was palpable, creating situations where conformity was encouraged and often implicitly required. As a result, there were moments when I felt compelled to acquiesce, even if it meant suppressing my beliefs or conflicting with my authentic self. This internal conflict, while subtle, underscored the complexity of reconciling diverse influences within the educational sphere.

Furthermore, this dual exposure to religious and cultural values necessitated a nuanced approach to understanding and interpreting the world around me. I grappled with questions of identity, morality, and belief, seeking to reconcile the teachings of my upbringing with the broader educational framework imposed by the curriculum. In doing so, I embarked on a migration of introspection and self-discovery, striving to forge a cohesive understanding of my place within the intersecting spheres of religion, culture, and education.

Despite the challenges posed by this juxtaposition of influences, it also presented opportunities for growth and enlightenment. I learned to evaluate complex social dynamics, engage with differing perspectives, and cultivate a sense of tolerance and respect for diverse beliefs. Through this process, I developed a deeper appreciation for the richness of Nigeria's cultural blend and the interconnectedness of faith and education in shaping individual and collective identities.

My experience within the Nigerian educational system underscored the intricate interplay between religion, culture, and education. It challenged me to reconcile conflicting values and beliefs while fostering a greater sense of empathy, understanding, and resilience. By coping with this terrain's

141

obstacle, I developed a deeper understanding of myself and the world around me, enriched by the diverse influences that shaped my educational sojourn.

Growing up under the dual influence of the Nigerian educational system and the cultural values instilled by my family posed significant challenges, especially during the crucial formative years of cognitive development. The collision of these two distinct systems created a complex and sometimes conflicting internal landscape, shaping what I now understand as a hybrid mentality. This fusion of cultural and educational influences continues to be a source of growth and struggle, even well into adulthood.

Throughout my formative years, I grappled with the discordance between the cultural values instilled within my family and local community and the ideologies propagated within the educational system. Raised in a household deeply rooted in traditional African customs and beliefs, I immersed myself in a rich fabric of cultural heritage and spiritual practices. However, as I embarked on my academic exploration, I encountered a contrasting narrative that leaned heavily towards a Eurocentric worldview, often influenced by Christian or Islamic teachings.

These divergent influences became particularly pronounced as I transitioned from the Northern region, where Islamic traditions dominated, to the Southern part of the country, where Christian values held sway. This geographical shift exposed me to a spectrum of religious beliefs and intensified the internal conflict stemming from the clash between my familial upbringing and the prevailing educational ethos.

Upon entering tertiary education in Abuja, the new Federal Capital Territory, I immersed myself in a melting pot of cultures and ideologies, further complicating my struggle to reconcile the teachings of my upbringing with the perspectives espoused within academic discourse. This dichotomy frequently thrust me into moments of confusion and introspection.

My campaign through various educational environments was a crucible, and I grappled with the tension between tradition and modernity, spirituality and academia. Each encounter with contrasting ideologies challenged me to forge a path that honored my cultural heritage and the pursuit of knowledge, ultimately profoundly shaping my identity and worldview.

As I matured, the complexities of this hybrid mentality became more apparent. While I developed a deep respect for both systems and the values they imparted, reconciling their differences remained a persistent challenge. The cognitive dissonance caused by this intersection of cultural and educational influences profoundly shaped my perceptions, beliefs, and behaviors, influencing everything from my decision-making process to my interpersonal relationships.

Even in adulthood, the struggle to make sense of this amalgamation persists. The dynamic interplay between diverse perspectives and values continues to shape my worldview, challenging me to constantly reevaluate and adapt my understanding of the world around me. While this ongoing process can be daunting at times, it also serves as a source of growth and self-discovery, pushing me to embrace the richness of my cultural heritage while remaining open to the insights offered by alternative perspectives.

While the challenges posed by this intersection are ongoing, they have also fostered resilience, empathy, and a deep appreciation for the interconnectedness of diverse perspectives and experiences.

In my quest, I've encountered a profound disconnect between my indigenous culture and the knowledge systems imposed by development planning experts. Despite this challenge, I've remained committed, turning failures into opportunities for success. My path has been marked by a sensitivity to a religion that, while not authentically African, has been deeply ingrained in my upbringing – a Judeo-Christian faith tainted by Eurocentric influences.

Blessed with a keen intellect and sharp wit, I possess an innate ability to perceive and evaluate the skills of others.

Yet, my source of knowledge is a hybrid, a blend of traditions that has enriched me and caused moments of identity crisis. I am grateful for its creativity but wary of its potential pitfalls.

The phrase "the devil is in the details" resonates deeply with me. It reminds me of the intricate complexities woven into every aspect of life, from religion to culture. While profound in its implications, it also highlights the danger of overlooking the nuances and intricacies that define our existence.

This nuanced understanding has led me to approach life with appreciation and skepticism. I've learned to bridge the intricacies of my hybrid knowledge system, recognizing its strengths while remaining vigilant against its potential to obscure deeper truths.

I've realized the importance of pondering beyond surface-level interpretations to grasp these complexities. It's not enough to accept things at face value; proper understanding requires a willingness to rummage into the depths and unravel the underlying intricacies.

Through introspection and exploration, I've begun to unravel the layers of my identity, embracing the richness of my heritage while critically evaluating the influences that shape my worldview. This ongoing expedition of self-discovery is empowering and humbling, offering glimpses into the complexity of human experience.

I am often reminded of the importance of embracing ambiguity and uncertainty, for it is within these liminal spaces that proper growth and understanding usually emerge. These moments of discomfort, development, and enlightenment often emerge, guiding me toward a deeper understanding of myself and the world around me.

My story is a lush pattern woven with threads of diverse influences, each contributing to the intricate pattern of my experiences. At its core lies the rich drapery of my indigenous culture and knowledge systems, which have often been overlooked or misunderstood in development planning. The prevalence of Eurocentric perspectives has led to dismissing these invaluable traditions, relegating them to the sidelines of discourse.

Despite these challenges, I have embraced my heritage with a deep commitment and pride. Rather than succumbing to the pressures of assimilation, I have sought to reclaim and celebrate the wisdom embedded within my indigenous culture. It is a culture steeped in tradition, resilience, and deep-rooted connections to the land and community.

Through it all, I have emerged with a profound intellect and a quick wit, attributes that have served me well in evaluating the intricacies of my hybrid knowledge system. While I am grateful for the creativity it has sparked within me,

I remain cautiously skeptical of its potential to obscure deeper truths.

My account is a testament to the richness and complexity of the human experience, a pilgrimage marked by resilience, introspection, and an unwavering commitment to authenticity.

5

The Disruption of Our System

I've always been drawn to the thrill of travel, the excitement of adventure, and the endless possibilities of meeting new people. With a curiosity akin to that of a cat, I yearn to discover every corner of life and embrace every opportunity that comes my way. Making friends comes naturally to me, and I've been told that my magnetic personality tends to leave a lasting impression on those I meet.

Unlike many others, I find myself thriving amidst change and uncertainty. I see these moments as opportunities for growth and discovery rather than reasons for apprehension. However, there have been instances when unexpected disruptions to my daily routine have left me feeling vulnerable and unsettled. In those moments, I've had to confront my insecurities and guide the challenges with courage and resilience.

Reflecting on Blaise Pascal's timeless words, "Somewhere, something incredible is waiting to be known," I couldn't help but feel a pang of longing for that elusive sense of discovery. There have been moments in my life when it seemed like the essence of that incredible something was beyond my reach, especially when life felt like it was slipping through my fingers.

In those moments, I found myself in a peculiar state of limbo, where the lines between certainty and ambiguity blurred, and the things I once held dear lost their significance. It was as if I was suspended in a timeless void, where the past no longer held sway and the future uncertain.

When looking at my life, the liminal space, with its uncertainty and anticipation, serves as a crucial juncture. It's a threshold where the familiar fades into the background, making way for transformation and change to take center stage. In this space, I find myself grappling with the tension between what was and is yet to come, reflecting on the lessons learned and eagerly awaiting the promise of new beginnings.

Rather than allowing the liminal space to be a void of waiting and uncertainty, I choose to imbue it with purpose and intention. It becomes a canvas for introspection, a sanctuary for reflection, and a fertile ground for growth. Here, amidst the swirling currents of change, I cultivate harmonious energies of love, joy, and inspiration, infusing the space with the essence of my best self.

With each moment spent in this liminal space, I strive to remain anchored in my worth and deservingness. It's a conscious effort not to lose sight of my inherent value and the boundless potential that awaits on the other side of transformation. In embracing the liminal space with open arms and an open heart, I pave the way for a future filled with love, joy, and boundless possibilities.

Amid the uncertainties of the liminal space, resilience emerges as my steadfast companion, guiding me through the upheavals and disruptions that challenge my sense of routine and stability. Despite the prolonged disruptions to my daily life, I find solace in my innate love for diversity and adventure.

I thrive on actively engaging in various projects and pursuits, constantly seeking new experiences and growth opportunities. This inclination towards embracing novelty and diversity fuels my resilience, empowering me to adapt and thrive in the face of change.

My flexibility and adaptability are invaluable assets, enabling me to skip the shifting tides of uncertainty with grace and resilience. Rather than being overwhelmed by the unpredictability of the liminal space, I embrace it as an opportunity for growth and exploration.

With each construct in the expedition, I remain open to new adventures and experiences, allowing them to shape and enrich my history. Through this mindset of openness and adaptability, I continue with resilience and determination, ready to embrace whatever the future may hold.

Undoubtedly, my yearning for freedom surpasses all other desires, propelling me to break free from any constraints that threaten to tether me down. Though some may label me as impulsive or extreme, attributing my actions to a "wild child" spirit, it's simply a testament to the vibrant free spirit that resides within me. Over the past five years alone, I've likely encountered more adventures and experiences than many do in a lifetime.

Blessed with the rare gift of uplifting and motivating others through my rich combination of experiences and words of wisdom, I am confident I am effortlessly fulfilling my Life Path potential. Yet, every compelling narrative is woven with conflict; mine is no exception.

My story unfolds in the liminal space between worlds, never fully belonging to any realm. This fluidity, this in-betweenness, imbues my memories with depth and resonance. I oscillate between worlds, finding fleeting comfort in each but ultimately feeling most at home in the space in between.

Gratitude serves as the lens through which I manage this ambiguous terrain, allowing me to appreciate the need for

151

support and encouragement amidst the inherent tensions of my existence. This internal conflict, this perpetual dance between worlds, lies at the heart of my story, shaping its contours and imbuing it with a richness that begs to be shared.

My tale unfolds along a trajectory that seems destined to intersect with the will of fate itself. In the hanging of life, I've understood that I bear responsibility for what I allow to shape my path. Yet, amidst the ebb and flow of existence, I've grappled with a profound identity crisis, questioning whose will truly governs the trajectory of my destiny.

The inevitable clash can be tumultuous and tense when multiple wills converge on a collision course. Like two mighty elephants locked in battle, their conflict reverberates throughout the surrounding landscape, leaving devastation in its wake. As the old African adage wisely observes, 'the grass and the ground beneath bear the brunt of their struggle.'

In this collision of wills, I am caught in the crossfire with the tumultuous terrain of conflicting desires and competing agendas. Yet, amidst the chaos, I remain steadfast in my quest for clarity and purpose, seeking to align my will with the higher forces that guide the unfolding of my destiny.

I find solace and strength in the belief that my quest is guided by the benevolent hand of Divine Intelligence, weaving its intricate swag of fate with wisdom and purpose. In moments of doubt and uncertainty, the gentle whispers of divine wisdom serve as my guiding light, leading me toward resolving the identity conflict that shadows my path.

The creative essence of Divine Intelligence illuminates the profound capabilities of the human mind, serving as a conduit through which our deepest aspirations manifest into reality. Within the vast expanse of our consciousness lies the boundless potential to conceive ideas and translate them into tangible outcomes. This innate power bestowed upon us by Divine Intelligence reflects our divine essence and underscores our role as custodians of creation.

With each word from the Divine Intelligence, I am reminded of the profound interconnectedness of all things and the harmonious balance between individual agency and cosmic will. While I am the architect of my destiny, I am also a vessel through which the divine will expresses itself, infusing my existence with purpose and meaning.

Embracing this divine guidance, I face the complexities of existence with clarity and purpose, knowing that my journey is guided by forces greater than myself. In surrendering to the flow of divine wisdom, I find liberation from the shackles of uncertainty and embrace the creative power within me.

Central to this creative process is the remarkable faculty of the mind to serve as both architect and observer of our thoughts and actions. Through introspection and self-awareness, we harness the transformative potential of our thoughts, shaping our reality in alignment with our deepest desires. This ability to consciously direct the course of our lives distinguishes us as beings made in the image of Divine Intelligence.

As stewards of this divine gift, we wield the power of memory to construct the framework of our existence, weaving together the threads of past experiences to inform our present choices and shape our future endeavors. By cultivating mindfulness and embracing the observer's role, we unlock our minds' full potential to orchestrate profound personal transformation and address the problem of life's crusade.

The essence of Divine Intelligence embodies a profound sense of self-reflection and intentionality, guiding us to transcend mere impulsivity and embrace conscious awareness in all facets of our being. Through my responsibility of growth and self-discovery, I've recognized the subtle nuances of my thoughts, emotions, and behaviors, shedding light on previously unconscious patterns that governed my actions.

By cultivating a practice of self-observation and mindfulness, I've gained invaluable insight into the underlying triggers and impulses driving my responses to life's stimuli. This heightened awareness has empowered me to break free from self-sabotaging behaviors and repetitive cycles that hindered my progress and stifled my potential.

With each moment of introspection, I forge a deeper connection with the essence of Divine Intelligence within myself, aligning my intentions and actions with a higher purpose. Through this deliberate practice of self-reflection, I embrace the transformative power of conscious awareness, paving the way for greater fulfillment, authenticity, and success in my crusade of personal evolution.

Identity Crisis

I firmly believe in the transformative strength of resilience, interpreting setbacks not as roadblocks but as chances for progress and triumph. This perspective shapes my proactive outlook on life, where obstacles serve as stepping-stones rather than barriers. It's a dedication to converting adversity into opportunity, showcasing my resolve and fortitude.

Yet, within the fabric of my identity lies a complex interweaving of cultural and religious influences. My traditional African background, rich in heritage and wisdom, stands juxtaposed with the imposition of a Judeo-Christian religion tainted by Eurocentric influences. This collision of worlds has added complexity to my sense of self, challenging me to reconcile disparate belief systems and cultural paradigms.

Understanding and successfully applying this hybrid knowledge system has demanded intellectual prowess and emotional resilience. On the one hand, I am deeply grateful for the richness and diversity it has brought into my life, broadening my understanding of the world and enriching my cultural heritage. On the other hand, I approach this amalgamation with cautious skepticism, recognizing the potential for distortion and manipulation inherent in blending diverse traditions.

My expedition is a testament to the power of introspection and critical thinking as I continually interrogate the assumptions and biases embedded within my hybrid identity. It's a delicate balance between honoring the traditions of my ancestors and challenging the narratives imposed upon me by external forces.

In embracing this complexity, I find strength and clarity, for true self-discovery and growth often occur within the depths of ambiguity. My narrative is one of resilience, intellectual curiosity, and a relentless pursuit of authenticity in a world filled with competing voices and conflicting truths.

Traveling over the intricate weave of diverse influences, I am reminded of the value of embracing complexity and considering beyond superficial interpretations. This ongoing operation is characterized by exploration, introspection, and a profound appreciation for the subtle nuances that shape my identity and inform my interactions with the world.

Journey of Self-Discovery and Reconciliation

This ongoing journey of self-discovery and reconciliation fuels my growth and evolution as an individual. It challenges me to confront biases, expand my perspective, and cultivate empathy for differing viewpoints. Despite the inherent complexities and occasional struggles, I find solace and strength in the richness of my heritage and the diversity of experiences that have shaped me.

Moving forward, I embrace the duality of my identity with openness and curiosity, recognizing that I can fully understand and appreciate the depth of my own story by embracing the intricacies of my cultural, religious, and intellectual background. Each encounter, each challenge, and each moment of introspection contributes to the ongoing memoirs of my life, shaping me into a more resilient, compassionate, and self-aware individual. As I continue to explore the complexities of my identity, I am reminded of the profound interconnectedness of humanity and the endless potential for growth and transformation within each of us.

In my indigenous culture, the strong influence of Western civilization has led to widespread Christianization, with a significant Islamic population in the Northern States and some parts of the Western States. Despite these religious influences, African traditional worship still thrives among my people. Our philosophy revolves around the belief that death is not the end of life, nor does it sever the bonds between individuals and their families and loved ones.

In our culture, death is viewed as a transition from a physical existence to a spiritual one. We believe in the continuity of life beyond the physical realm, with death marking a shift rather than an endpoint. This understanding forms the basis of ancestral veneration, a practice deeply rooted in the belief that life follows a cyclical rather than a linear course. While our ancestors may no longer be physically present, we believe they continue to exist in a different spiritual realm, exerting influence and guidance in the lives of the living.

This worldview underscores the interconnectedness of past, present, and future generations, emphasizing the ongoing relationship between the living and the deceased. It shapes our rituals, traditions, and daily practices, providing comfort and guidance as we comprehend life's challenges and milestones. In embracing this perspective, we honor the wisdom and legacy of those who came before us, recognizing their enduring presence in our lives and communities.

In my family lineage, I was fortunate to have known my maternal great-grandfather personally before he transitioned into the next life at 110 years old. He is one of my revered ancestors, and his wisdom inspires me.

Remarkably, my ancestors possessed insights into the natural rhythms of the earth and upcoming cosmic events long before they occurred. This innate connection to the Universe allowed my ancestors to live with a deep sense of harmony and wisdom. They didn't rely on modern instruments or scientific methods but turned to the natural world for guidance and knowledge. Their ability to synchronize with the cosmic order speaks volumes about their intuitive understanding of the interconnectedness of all things. Their intimate relationship with the cosmos speaks to a deeper understanding of our place in the universe—a perspective that transcends the boundaries of time and space.

As I carry their legacy forward, I am inspired to reconnect with the natural world and embrace the wisdom of the ages. Their knowledge was not static but dynamic, evolving in response to the ever-changing patterns of the cosmos. They observed the stars, the moon, and the changing seasons with reverence and awe, recognizing them as guides in life's adventure. Reflecting on their legacy fills me with awe and reverence, reminding me of the profound wisdom that surpasses modern science and technology. My ancestors' ability to interpret the subtle signs of the cosmos is a testament to the depth of human understanding and the enduring strength of ancient knowledge. Their mastery was not just a skill but a way of life—an expression of their deep connection to the natural world and the spiritual realm, embodying a wisdom that has stood the test of time.

Reflecting on their legacy, I am reminded of the importance of honoring and preserving traditional wisdom in a rapidly transforming world. In today's society, where technology and scientific progress dominate, it is easy to lose sight of the timeless knowledge handed down through generations. Yet, in this fast-paced, digital age—where we are often disconnected from nature—the lessons of my ancestors carry profound meaning. They urge us to slow down, to listen to the whispers of the wind, and to reconnect with the rhythms of the earth, reminding us of what truly sustains and grounds us.

In doing so, I honor my ancestors and the rich fabric of human experience that spans millennia. Theirs is a legacy of resilience, intuition, and reverence for the mysteries of existence. This legacy continues to guide me on my obligation of self-discovery and spiritual growth.

As I reflect on their wisdom, I am struck by the depth of their knowledge and the humility with which they approached the mysteries of existence.

By embracing ancestral wisdom, I strive to cultivate a deeper connection with the natural world and the cosmos, honoring the legacy of those who came before me and paving the way for future generations to walk in harmony with the universe.

The phrase "in sync with the Universe" encapsulates a profound understanding and alignment with the natural rhythms and cosmic harmonies that govern existence. It signifies a state of attunement where one is deeply connected to the cyclical patterns of nature and the cosmic forces that shape the universe. This attunement is not merely a passive observance but an active participation in the dance of life, where one becomes attuned to the ebb and flow of the cosmos.

For my ancestors, being "in sync with the Universe" was more than just a poetic notion; it was a way of life deeply rooted in their cultural and spiritual heritage. It involved a combination of keen observation of the natural world, the transmission of ancestral wisdom through generations, and a profound spiritual worldview that recognized the interconnectedness of all things.

Their ability to discern the subtle language of the cosmos allowed them to sail through life with a sense of harmony and balance. They understood that they were part of a more extensive cosmic web, where every action and event was interconnected and influenced by cosmic energies.

This attunement to the Universe permeated every aspect of their existence, from agriculture and weather prediction to spiritual rituals and daily life. It was a holistic approach that recognized the interconnectedness of the physical, spiritual, and cosmic realms.

As I reflect on the wisdom of my ancestors, I am inspired to cultivate a deeper connection with the natural world and the cosmic forces that shape our lives. By aligning myself with the rhythms of nature and honoring the interconnectedness of all things, I seek to embody the essence of being "in sync with the Universe" in my own life.

The remarkable longevity of my great-grandfather, living to the age of 110, adds a fascinating dimension to our family's narrative. His advanced age is more than just a statistical anomaly; it embodies a profound testament to the practices and wisdom of his time. It suggests that his life was not only shaped by the passage of years but also by a deep alignment with the rhythms of nature.

In many cultures, longevity is often associated with a life lived in harmony with the natural world. It implies a balance of physical health, mental well-being, and spiritual alignment. For my great-grandfather, this harmony with nature likely played a significant role in his remarkable longevity.

His ability to live such a long and fulfilling life could be attributed, in part, to the lifestyle practices and wisdom passed down through generations. These could include dietary habits, physical activity, stress management techniques, and spiritual practices—all of which may have contributed to his overall well-being and longevity.

Moreover, my great-grandfather's longevity symbolizes resilience and adaptability in facing life's challenges. Living through decades of societal changes, technological advancements, and personal trials, he faced the complex world with grace and wisdom, drawing upon the timeless principles of his cultural heritage.

As I reflect on his life and legacy, I am reminded of the importance of living in harmony with the natural world and cultivating practices that promote holistic well-being. His story inspires me to embrace the wisdom of the past while conquering the difficulty of the present, guiding me toward a life of balance and fulfillment.

In a rapidly changing world where technology often takes center stage, there's a timeless wisdom in honoring and preserving the ancient ways of understanding the world. The ability of my ancestors to interpret the subtle language of the cosmos serves as a poignant reminder of the depth of indigenous knowledge and their profound connection to both the Earth and the celestial realms.

Their capacity to read the signs of the cosmos speaks volumes about the richness of their cultural heritage and their innate understanding of the interconnectedness of all things. Rather than relying solely on modern advancements, they looked to the natural world for guidance, drawing upon centuries-old practices and traditions passed down through generations.

In today's fast-paced society, where many are disconnected from the rhythms of nature, there's much to be learned from the wisdom of indigenous peoples. Their reverence for the Earth, their ability to live in harmony with the natural world, and their deep respect for the cycles of life offer valuable lessons for negotiating our increasingly complex world.

My ancestors' legacy reminds me of the importance of preserving and honoring indigenous knowledge. Their teachings provide a blueprint for sustainable living, fostering a deeper appreciation for the interconnectedness of all life forms and the need to steward the Earth with care and respect. Despite the march of time, it's a heritage that continues to offer profound insights and inspiration for living in harmony with the natural world.

My ancestors possessed a profound mastery in connecting with the Divine, a skill honed through generations of reverence for nature and the cosmos. They understood the intricate relationship between humanity and the Universe, recognizing that harmony could be achieved by syncing with the flow of Universal energy. Rather than relying on modern-day tools, they turned to ancient resources embedded in their cultural heritage.

When I need to deepen my spiritual connection, I find myself drawn to the practices and wisdom of my ancestors. Their ability to listen to nature and interpret the subtle cues of the cosmos is a testament to their profound understanding of the interconnectedness of all things.

In today's fast-paced world, where technology often dominates our lives, there's a timeless wisdom in returning to the ancient ways of connecting with the Divine. By tapping into the practices passed down by my ancestors, I can align myself with the natural rhythms of the Universe, finding solace and guidance in the flow of Universal energy.

This connection to ancient wisdom guides my spiritual pilgrimage, offering a pathway to deeper understanding and inner peace. It reminds me that despite the advancements of modern society, there is immense value in preserving and honoring traditions.

By following in the footsteps of my ancestors and embracing their practices, I can cultivate a sense of harmony and alignment with the Divine. Their teachings resonate with me profoundly, providing inspiration and guidance in helming life's complexities.

In essence, the wisdom of my ancestors serves as a beacon of light in a world filled with noise and distraction. It reminds me to slow down, listen to the whispers of nature, and trust in the ancient rhythms of the cosmos. Through their teachings, I find strength, clarity, and a deep connection to something greater than myself.

In the assortment of my ancestral wisdom, the emphasis on syncing with the universe's energy emerges as a profound insight into the nature of success and fulfillment. It speaks to a dynamic relationship with the spiritual and natural forces that permeate our existence. For my ancestors, this attunement wasn't just a survival strategy; it was ingrained in the very fabric of their daily lives.

Their understanding of cosmic energies went beyond mere observation; it was a deeply intuitive connection to the universe's rhythms. They recognized that by aligning themselves with these energies, they could harness a source of guidance and inspiration that transcended the limitations of individual effort.

In essence, syncing with the energy of the Universe was a way of life—a philosophy that permeated every aspect of their existence. It shaped their decisions, interactions, and understanding of the world around them. Doing so paved the way for a profound sense of harmony and fulfillment that continues to resonate through the generations.

In my lifework to deepen my connection with the Divine, I am drawn to ancient resources rather than modern tools. This choice reflects a profound reverence for the timeless wisdom passed down through generations. It's an acknowledgment that despite the advancements of the contemporary world, there is a depth of knowledge embedded in traditional practices that remains unmatched.

Turning to ancestral practices underscores a belief in the enduring power of age-old rituals and teachings. These practices have stood the test of time, offering insights into the mysteries of existence that transcend the limitations of contemporary technology. There's a sense of humility in recognizing that the wisdom of our ancestors holds the keys to understanding the intricacies of the cosmos and our place within it.

Moreover, embracing ancient resources speaks to a desire for authenticity and connection. In a world often characterized by rapid change and superficiality, pursuing our forebears' traditions provides a sense of grounding and continuity. It's a way of honoring our roots and finding solace in the timeless truths that have guided humanity for centuries.

Ultimately, I am tapping into a rich reservoir of spiritual knowledge and insight by turning to ancient wisdom. It's a calling of discovery and rediscovery as I seek to uncover the profound teachings that can transform and illuminate my path.

This calling is not merely a quest for knowledge but a profound exploration of the interconnectedness of all things. By immersing myself in the traditions and practices of my ancestors, I am forging a deeper connection with the natural world and the cosmic forces that shape our reality.

In the hustle and bustle of modern life, it's easy to lose sight of the deeper truths that anchor us to something greater than ourselves. Yet, by embracing ancient resources, I am reminded of the timeless rhythms and cycles that govern existence. A sense of awe and wonder comes from tapping into this ancient wisdom, a recognition of the beauty and complexity of the universe.

Moreover, by honoring the practices of my ancestors, I am paying homage to the resilience and wisdom of those who came before me. It's a way of celebrating their legacy and ensuring their teachings continue guiding and inspiring future generations.

My objective in ancient wisdom involves self-discovery, connection, and transformation. It's a reminder that while the world around us may change, the fundamental truths of existence remain constant. And by embracing these truths, we can find solace, guidance, and meaning in an ever-changing world.

By appraising ancient wisdom traditions, I've come to appreciate the deep-rooted understanding of the interconnectedness of all things. These traditions teach us to listen to nature's whispers, attune ourselves to the subtle energies that circulate the universe, and recognize the inherent divinity within and around us.

My exploration of ancient wisdom has been a pursuit of rediscovery—a trust back to the timeless truths that have guided humanity for millennia. It's a charge that has deepened my understanding of myself, my place in the world, and the profound interconnectedness of all existence.

My operation to deepen my connection by drawing from these ancient resources is more than a personal quest; it continues a spiritual legacy stretching back through generations. It's a recognition that within the wisdom of the ages lies a wellspring of guidance and insight that transcends the limitations of time and technology.

As I query into the teachings of my ancestors and the wisdom traditions of ancient cultures, I feel a profound connection to something greater than myself. There's a comfort in knowing that I'm walking a path that countless others have trodden before me—a path that the footsteps of seekers and sages have smoothed throughout history.

In these ancient resources, I find not only solace but also strength. They offer me a lens through which to view the world, a framework for understanding my place, and a roadmap for piloting life's challenges and uncertainties. They remind me that I am part of something much larger than myself—a cosmic fusion woven with the threads of countless lives and experiences.

In a chaotic and overwhelming world, turning to these ancient teachings gives me a sense of grounding and perspective. They remind me of the eternal truths underpinning existence—the cycles of birth and death, the interconnectedness of all things, and our inherent divinity.

My undertaking to deepen my connection is a promise of rediscovery—a drive back to the source of all wisdom and truth. As I continue to walk this path, I am grateful for the timeless legacy passed down to me and a profound sense of responsibility to honor and preserve it for future generations.

A Journey Of Self-Discovery And Empowerment

I was handed a set of numbers purporting to represent my IQ—an intelligence quotient—that was factually flawed. Standardized tests cannot accurately measure accurate intelligence, especially those rooted in Eurocentric literary traditions. This realization prompted me to ponder the fate of my ancestors, who were incredibly talented and skilled but lacked formal Eurocentric literary training.

What happened to the rich civilizations of Africa, which have contributed immensely to world history? While the ancient North African empires are relatively well-known, the legacies of civilizations like Nok in Nigeria, Kush in Sudan, and Aksum in Ethiopia are often overlooked. These cultures were pivotal in shaping human history, yet their stories remain less explored and appreciated.

The Nok civilization, known for its remarkable terracotta sculptures, flourished in Nigeria from around 1500 BCE to 200 CE. Meanwhile, the Kingdom of Kush, located in present-day Sudan, was a powerful empire that controlled vast territories and played a significant role in trade and diplomacy in the ancient world. The Aksumite Empire, centered in present-day Ethiopia, was an important player in international trade and one of the first states to adopt Christianity officially.

Despite their contributions to art, technology, trade, and governance, these ancient African civilizations are often relegated to the footnotes of history. Their stories remain hidden beneath layers of colonial bias and Eurocentric narratives. However, there is still much to be discovered and appreciated about these fascinating cultures, and efforts to uncover their histories and legacies continue to this day.

In questioning the validity of standardized IQ tests and reflecting on the overlooked achievements of ancient African civilizations, I am reminded of the importance of challenging dominant accounts and embracing diverse perspectives in our understanding of human intelligence and cultural heritage.

As I reflect on the limitations of IQ testing and the pervasive Eurocentric bias within it, I'm prompted to dig deeper into the complexities of measuring intelligence and the inherent cultural biases that influence these assessments.

Traditional IQ tests have long been criticized for their narrow focus on specific cognitive abilities, such as verbal and mathematical reasoning, while overlooking other equally valuable forms of intelligence, such as creativity, emotional intelligence, and practical problem-solving skills. This narrow definition of intelligence often fails to capture the full spectrum of human abilities and overlooks the unique strengths and talents of individuals from diverse cultural backgrounds.

Moreover, the cultural context in which IQ tests are developed and administered can influence the results. Many standardized IQ tests are based on Western cultural norms and assumptions, which may not accurately reflect individuals from non-Western cultures' experiences and knowledge systems. As a result, individuals from different cultural backgrounds may be disadvantaged by these tests, leading to inaccurate assessments of their abilities.

My contemplation on the limitations of IQ testing underscores the importance of recognizing and valuing diverse forms of intelligence. Intelligence is not a fixed, one-dimensional trait but a complex interplay of cognitive, emotional, social, and cultural factors. By acknowledging the limitations of traditional IQ tests and embracing a more inclusive and culturally sensitive approach to measuring intelligence, we can create a more equitable and accurate understanding of human abilities.

As I contemplate the flaws inherent in traditional IQ tests, I cannot help but acknowledge the significant cultural bias embedded within them. These assessments, designed to measure intelligence, often reflect a Eurocentric worldview, emphasizing skills and knowledge aligned with Western educational systems and values.

173

This Eurocentric bias is deeply concerning, particularly when considering its implications for individuals from cultures with rich histories and civilizations that diverge from the Western model. Many traditional IQ tests fail to recognize or value the unique perspectives, knowledge systems, and cognitive strengths of individuals from non-Western cultures. Instead, they prioritize specific skills, such as verbal and mathematical reasoning, that may be more heavily emphasized in Western education.

This raises fundamental questions about the validity and fairness of IQ tests as universal measures of intelligence. How can we claim to assess intelligence accurately when the criteria for intelligence are based on a specific cultural framework? By imposing Western norms and values onto diverse populations, these tests perpetuate systemic inequalities and reinforce existing power dynamics.

These issues remind me of the importance of developing more culturally inclusive and equitable approaches to measuring intelligence. We must recognize and value the diversity of human cognition, honoring the unique strengths and perspectives that individuals from different cultural backgrounds bring to the table. Only then can we move towards a more accurate and just understanding of intelligence that respects the richness and complexity of human diversity.

Reflecting on the talents and skills of my ancestors, who were not Eurocentrically literate but undoubtedly possessed valuable knowledge and capabilities, I am struck by the inadequacy of conventional IQ tests in capturing the full spectrum of human intelligence. These tests often fail to recognize or appreciate the diverse forms of intelligence in non-Western cultures, leading to a distorted understanding of intellectual ability.

The ancient African civilizations of Nok, Kush, and Aksum are prime examples of societies that thrived without conforming to Eurocentric norms of literacy and education. Their art, architecture, agriculture, trade, and governance achievements significantly influenced world history. Yet, these accomplishments are often overlooked or undervalued in traditional intelligence assessments.

Acknowledging that intelligence manifests in myriad forms beyond Western-centric criteria is essential. The skills and knowledge valued in non-Western cultures may differ from those emphasized in Eurocentric societies, but they are no less valid or valuable. By adopting a more inclusive and culturally sensitive approach to measuring intelligence, we can begin to recognize and celebrate the diverse ways in which human intelligence expresses itself.

Furthermore, expanding our understanding of intelligence to encompass a broader range of abilities and talents can foster more significant equity and inclusion in educational and societal systems. Everyone deserves to have their unique strengths and capabilities acknowledged and valued, regardless of whether they align with Western intelligence norms.

In essence, the reference to the talents and skills of my ancestors serves as a poignant reminder of the richness and diversity of human intelligence. It calls for reevaluating how we define and measure intelligence, emphasizing inclusivity, cultural sensitivity, and recognition of the full spectrum of human potential.

Indeed, there is much to be discovered and appreciated about the rich and diverse cultures that have contributed to the aggregation of human civilization. Each civilization, with its unique traditions, innovations, and cultural practices, has left an indelible mark on the collective story of humanity. By comprehensively exploring these lesser-known civilizations, we can better understand the complexities and interconnectedness of human history.

By spotlighting the achievements of civilizations like Nok, Kush, and Aksum, we can challenge prevailing documentations and foster a more inclusive and equitable approach to studying history. This broader perspective honors the legacy of these ancient cultures and enriches our collective understanding of the human experience.

As we delve into the legacies of ancient civilizations like Nok, Kush, and Aksum, we gain valuable insights into the diversity of human achievements and capabilities. These civilizations have left behind a wealth of knowledge and innovations that challenge conventional notions of intelligence and offer alternative perspectives on what it means to be intellectually gifted.

This entails recognizing the importance of creativity, adaptability, and cultural competency, which traditional intelligence tests may not adequately capture.

In essence, as we reveal and appreciate the legacies of ancient civilizations, we are reminded of the richness and diversity of human intelligence. By embracing a more inclusive and culturally sensitive approach to intelligence assessment, we can better recognize and nurture the unique talents and abilities of individuals from all backgrounds.

Africans have been historically recognized as brilliant beings. However, this perception was tarnished over time due to the deliberate destruction of our image by foreign invaders who sought to subjugate our territories. These invaders propagated negative stereotypes and created a distorted persona that came to represent all Africans, perpetuating this damaging portrayal worldwide.

In contemplating the historical portrayal of Africans and the enduring impact of external influences on our image,

177

I'm struck by the intricate interplay of identity and representation. The deliberate distortion of the African image, facilitated by invasions and the propagation of stereotypical depictions, has left deep-seated effects on our collective self-perception.

The impact of this historical manipulation of our image continues to reverberate, undermining our confidence and sense of self-worth. We need to challenge these ingrained misconceptions and reclaim our rightful place as equals in the global community, recognizing and celebrating the intelligence and contributions of Africans throughout history.

The perpetuation of negative stereotypes by foreign invaders not only distorted the perception of Africans globally but also ingrained harmful anecdotes within our communities. These false representations have seeped into our consciousness, shaping how we view ourselves and our worth in the world.

The ramifications of this manipulation extend beyond the historical context, manifesting in contemporary struggles with identity and self-esteem. Despite strides toward empowerment and reclaiming our chronologies, the echoes of centuries-old misrepresentations persist, influencing how we perceive ourselves and how others perceive us.

Cruising this complex landscape of identity and representation requires a concerted effort to challenge and dismantle entrenched stereotypes internally and externally. It's a walk of self-discovery and empowerment, reclaiming the richness and complexity of African identity and affirming our inherent worth and intelligence.

Reflecting on June 16, 1976, in Soweto, South Africa, brings to mind a pivotal moment in history when thousands of black schoolchildren took to the streets to protest against the substandard quality of their education and to assert their right to be taught in their native language. This courageous act gave birth to what is now commemorated as the Day of the African Child.

The essence of this day is rooted in the aspiration to cultivate a positive image of the African child and to facilitate a reconnection with their African heritage and identity. It symbolizes a collective endeavor to uplift and empower children of African ancestry, affirming their intrinsic value and celebrating the richness of their cultural legacy.

However, the stark reality often falls short of this ideal. Despite the noble intentions behind initiatives like the Day of the African Child, systemic barriers and ingrained prejudices continue to hinder the realization of these aspirations. Many children of African descent still grapple with discrimination, marginalization, and a distorted perception of their worth and potential.

Addressing these challenges requires a multifaceted approach encompassing educational reform, social advocacy, and cultural revitalization efforts. It necessitates a commitment to dismantling discriminatory structures, promoting inclusive education, and fostering environments where every child, regardless of their background, can thrive and embrace their heritage with pride.

When we commemorate the Day of the African Child, let us reflect on the past struggles and sacrifices and recommit ourselves to the ongoing fight for justice, equality, and dignity for all children of African descent. Through collective action and unwavering determination, we can genuinely nurture a generation of empowered and confident individuals who embrace their African identity with resilience and pride.

Indeed, the legacy of the Day of the African Child serves as a poignant reminder of the resilience and courage of young people in the face of adversity. It underscores the importance of amplifying their voices and addressing the systemic inequities perpetuating cycles of disadvantage and discrimination.

Advocating for policies and practices prioritizing inclusive and culturally responsive education is imperative. This entails recognizing students' diverse linguistic and cultural backgrounds and providing them with the necessary support and resources to thrive academically and personally.

Furthermore, efforts to promote positive representations of African heritage and identity must be embedded within educational curricula and broader societal narratives. By celebrating the contributions of African cultures to the global mosaic of humanity, we can counteract harmful stereotypes and instill a sense of pride and belonging in children of African descent.

Moreover, fostering partnerships between schools, communities, and governmental agencies is essential for creating supportive environments that nurture the holistic development of children. By working collaboratively, we can leverage collective expertise and resources to address young people's complex challenges and empower them to reach their full potential.

Ultimately, the Day of the African Child serves as a call to action—a reminder that the struggle for equality and justice is ongoing and requires sustained commitment and solidarity. As we honor the bravery and resilience of past generations, let us recommit ourselves to building a future where every child, regardless of their background, can thrive and flourish in a world that celebrates their uniqueness and embraces their heritage with dignity and respect.

Drawing parallels with the historic events in Soweto in 1976 highlights the enduring struggle for acknowledgment, dignity, and the fundamental right to education within one's linguistic and cultural framework. The inception of the Day of the African Child, catalyzed by the courageous actions of those young protestors, embodies the collective yearning to cultivate a sense of pride and belonging in children of African descent.

The resonance of this analogy extends beyond geographical boundaries, resonating with marginalized communities worldwide who continue to fight for their rights and recognition. It underscores the universal quest for equity and justice, regardless of background or circumstances.

Moreover, the Day of the African Child serves as a poignant reminder of the resilience and agency of young people in shaping their destinies and challenging systemic injustices. It emphasizes the importance of amplifying their voices and experiences, ensuring their aspirations and dreams are heard and valued.

Essentially, this analogy serves as a rallying cry for solidarity and action—a call to uphold every child's inherent dignity and rights, regardless of race, ethnicity, or social status. It underscores the imperative of building inclusive societies where every individual can thrive and contribute meaningfully to the collective drapery of humanity.

6

What Lies Within

The disparity between the envisioned ideal of nurturing a positive image and the harsh realities on the ground underscores the enduring influence of historical distortions. The journey toward reclaiming a positive identity and instilling a sense of pride in African heritage demands confronting entrenched testimonials and stereotypes that have long shaped societal perceptions.

Historical misrepresentations, perpetuated through various mediums, including media, education, and popular culture, have contributed to the marginalization and stigmatization of African identity. These reports often depict Africans in a negative light, reinforcing stereotypes of poverty, backwardness, and inferiority.

Addressing this deep-rooted issue requires a multifaceted approach that challenges prevailing versions and promotes authentic representations of African culture, history, and achievements. It involves amplifying diverse voices and narratives that celebrate the richness and diversity of African heritage, counteracting the harmful effects of historical misrepresentations.

Education plays a pivotal role in this endeavor, serving as a platform for promoting cultural pride and understanding. By integrating accurate and inclusive curriculum content that reflects the contributions and accomplishments of African societies, educational institutions can help reshape perceptions and empower individuals to embrace their heritage with pride.

Additionally, initiatives promoting cultural exchange, dialogue, and collaboration can foster greater appreciation and respect for African culture and heritage. By creating spaces for cross-cultural engagement and mutual learning, these efforts can contribute to building bridges of understanding and dismantling stereotypes.

Ultimately, the journey toward reclaiming a positive African identity is a collective endeavor that requires the commitment and collaboration of individuals, communities, and institutions. It entails challenging ingrained biases, advocating for equitable representation, and championing stories celebrating African heritage's richness and resilience. Through these concerted efforts, we can work towards a more inclusive and affirming society where everyone feels valued and empowered to embrace their cultural identity with pride.

Efforts to reshape these narratives, celebrate cultural diversity, and affirm the value of African heritage are essential to fostering a more inclusive and accurate understanding of the contributions and potential of individuals of African descent. This endeavor requires a concerted effort to challenge stereotypes, advocate for equitable representation, and embrace a case study that reflects the richness and diversity of African cultures and histories.

Challenging stereotypes involves debunking misconceptions and confronting negative portrayals that have long marginalized African identity. By highlighting African communities' achievements, innovations, and resilience, we can counteract harmful stereotypes and promote a more balanced and nuanced perception of African heritage.

Advocating for equitable representation means ensuring that African voices and perspectives are accurately and authentically represented across various platforms, including media, education, and popular culture. It amplifies diverse accounts and provides platforms for African storytellers, artists, scholars, and leaders to share their stories and insights with the world.

185

Embracing a record that reflects the richness and diversity of African cultures and histories requires recognizing and celebrating the multifaceted nature of African identity. From the vibrant traditions and customs of different ethnic groups to the dynamic contributions of African diaspora communities around the globe, a wealth of stories and experiences deserve to be acknowledged and celebrated.

By promoting cultural diversity and affirming the value of African heritage, we can create a more inclusive and equitable society where individuals of African descent feel seen, heard, and valued. This benefits individuals and communities of African descent and enriches the collective tapestry of humanity by embracing the full spectrum of human experience and expression.

The journey toward positive self-perception and recognizing the value of African heritage is a collective endeavor that requires societal awareness, educational reform, and the dismantling of ingrained biases. As individuals and as a society, we must confront the historical misrepresentations and stereotypes that have long marginalized African identity.

Acknowledging the challenges is the first step toward effecting change. It requires an honest examination of how African heritage has been misrepresented and undervalued historically and in contemporary contexts. This involves recognizing the systemic barriers and discriminatory practices that have perpetuated negative stereotypes and limited opportunities for individuals of African descent.

Educational reform is crucial in reshaping perceptions and fostering a more accurate understanding of African heritage. By incorporating diverse perspectives into curricula, providing students with opportunities to learn about Africa's rich histories and cultures, and promoting critical thinking skills, we can empower future generations to challenge stereotypes and embrace cultural diversity.

Dismantling ingrained biases requires ongoing efforts to challenge assumptions, confront prejudice, and promote empathy and understanding. It involves creating spaces for open dialogue, amplifying diverse voices, and actively challenging discriminatory attitudes and behaviors. Through education, advocacy, and allyship, we can work toward building a more inclusive and equitable society where individuals of African ancestry feel valued and respected.

Ultimately, by acknowledging the challenges and working together to address them, there is potential for fostering a sense of pride, identity, and belonging among individuals of African descent. This journey toward positive self-perception and cultural appreciation benefits individuals and communities of African ancestry and enriches the fabric of our collective humanity.

Growing up, I received an education from a system that felt foreign to my African identity. It's a perplexing reality to reconcile: Africa is a continent abundant in resources yet plagued by poverty. I've come to understand that the root of our struggles lies not in our lack of resources but in our deficient leadership.

Consider the paradox: we have banks we don't own, educational systems we don't control, and curricula we've never had a hand in shaping. Our religions, political systems, and even passports often feel like borrowed commodities designed to serve interests far removed from our own as African people.

In the guise of democracy, we find ourselves constrained by systems and structures imposed upon us by the West. Our economies are tethered to Western influence, Western standards dictate our education systems, and our access to medicine and technology, as well as our governance, is heavily influenced by external forces.

Embassies of foreign powers dot our landscapes yet wield sanctions against us. It forces one to ask the question: what kind of democracy is this, where our voices are drowned out and our autonomy undermined?

The emotions stirred within me by this reality cannot be ignored. It's a calculated exclusion, a deliberate sidelining of our agency and identity as Africans. We are left to grapple with the weight of external control while our aspirations for self-determination and true democracy remain elusive.

This reality stirs a mixture of frustration, anger, and a deep sense of injustice within me. It's a recognition that our potential as a continent is stifled by systems designed to perpetuate dependency rather than foster empowerment.

The chronicle of African leadership must shift from one of subjugation to one of sovereignty and self-determination. We must reclaim ownership of our resources, institutions, and destinies. This requires bold leadership that prioritizes the interests and aspirations of the African people above all else.

Education must be redefined to empower individuals with the knowledge, skills, and critical thinking abilities necessary to challenge existing power structures and drive meaningful change. Our educational systems should celebrate African history, culture, and achievements, instilling pride and confidence in our identity.

Similarly, economic policies must be reshaped to prioritize local empowerment, sustainable development, and equitable distribution of resources. This means fostering indigenous industries, promoting entrepreneurship, and ensuring that the benefits of economic growth are shared equitably among all citizens.

Furthermore, political systems must be reformed to reflect the will and interests of the people. Genuine democracy entails active citizen participation, transparent governance, and accountability to the electorate. It's time for African leaders to heed the voices of their constituents and work towards building inclusive, responsive, and accountable political institutions.

Ultimately, the path to true African liberation and prosperity lies in reclaiming our agency, asserting our sovereignty, and reshaping our narrative on our terms. It's a journey fraught with challenges but promises a brighter, more equitable future for future generations.

Reflecting on my journey, it's essential to acknowledge the role of emotions in shaping my experiences. While striving to maintain objectivity, I recognize the contagious nature of emotions and their impact on my path.

A subtle force has always pulled me back, hindering my progress and preventing me from fully embracing the next phase of my destiny. Breaking free from this force required courage and resilience, but once liberated, I found myself propelled toward new horizons.

Looking back, I realize that I often grappled with living up to the expectations of others rather than honoring my true self. There were moments when I wished I had summoned the courage to chart my course earlier in life, free from the constraints imposed by societal norms and external pressures.

This reflection underscores the intricate web of factors that shape the trajectory of post-colonial societies like Africa. It's a reminder of the lingering influence of colonial legacies, which continue to impact governance, economics, and social dynamics across the continent.

The mention of contagious emotions highlights these issues profoundly personal and interconnected nature. Emotions such as frustration, anger, and a yearning for liberation resonate deeply with many Africans who have witnessed their countries' persistent challenges.

The struggle to break free from the forces that hold back progress is a recurring theme in the account of African development. Whether it's external influence, corruption, or systemic inequalities, these obstacles hinder the realization of Africa's full potential.

The desire to live a life true to oneself, free from the expectations of others, reflects a universal human longing for authenticity and self-determination. It speaks to the importance of individual agency and empowerment in the quest for personal and collective liberation.

Overall, this reflection prompts us to confront the complexities of Africa's past and present while inspiring hope for a future defined by sovereignty, empowerment, and genuine progress.

This observation resonates deeply with me as it reflects a truth that has long been acknowledged but often overlooked in discussions about Africa's development. The continent indeed boasts abundant natural resources, ranging from minerals to fertile land, which hold the potential to drive economic growth and prosperity. However, the mismanagement and exploitation of these resources and ineffective governance and leadership have hindered Africa's ability to harness its full potential.

The mention of external control over critical sectors like banking, education, and even religion highlights the enduring influence of colonial powers and external actors in shaping the trajectory of African nations. This control extends beyond economic spheres to encompass cultural, political, and social domains, perpetuating a cycle of dependency and subjugation.

Moreover, the reference to Western dominance in areas such as medicine, technology, and governance raises important questions about agency and sovereignty. Despite achieving independence from colonial rule, many African nations continue to grapple with neocolonial forces that dictate policies and agendas, often at the expense of local interests and development priorities.

The narrative underscores the urgent need for African nations to assert their sovereignty, strengthen indigenous leadership capacities, and pursue policies prioritizing their citizens' well-being and empowerment. Only through effective governance, strategic resource management, and meaningful engagement with global partners can Africa overcome past challenges and realize its immense potential for growth and prosperity.

The frustration with external influence on Africa's development, including its economy, education, medicine, and technology, is deeply rooted in a desire for autonomy and self-determination. As an African, I share in this frustration, recognizing the detrimental effects of foreign interference on our nations' ability to chart their development course.

The mention of external control over critical sectors like banking, education, and medicine underscores the pervasive influence of Western powers in shaping the trajectory of African countries. This influence extends not only to economic matters but also to education and healthcare systems, where foreign agendas often dictate policies and priorities, undermining the autonomy of African nations.

The reference to Western dominance in technology highlights the unequal power dynamics that persist in the global arena. Despite efforts to promote technological innovation and development within Africa, external actors

193

hold significant sway over the direction of technological advancements on the continent.

Moreover, questioning democracy in light of external embassies, sanctions, and interference from Western powers raises significant concerns about the true meaning of sovereignty and self-governance. The presence of foreign embassies in African countries, coupled with the imposition of sanctions and other forms of coercion, undermines the principles of democracy and self-determination.

The frustration with external influence reflects a broader struggle for autonomy, agency, and self-determination among African nations. It underscores the need for greater solidarity and collaboration among African countries to assert their sovereignty and pursue policies that serve the interests of their citizens, free from external interference.

Personal Growth And Development

The personal reflection on emotional exclusion and the internal struggle to break free from restraining forces adds a poignant dimension to my account. It's an acknowledgment of the internal battles waged against societal norms and external pressures; a struggle shared by many seeking to carve their path in life.

The longing for the courage to live authentically, unencumbered by the weight of external expectations, strikes a universal chord. It speaks to the innate human desire for self-expression, autonomy, and fulfillment. Too often, we find ourselves constrained by the expectations of others, sacrificing our true selves in pursuit of societal approval or conformity.

In my journey, I've grappled with these conflicting forces, torn between the desire to please others and the yearning to honor values and aspirations. The struggle to break free from these constraints, assert my identity, and live according to my truth has been a defining aspect of my growth and development.

Ultimately, the quest for authenticity is a deeply personal and ongoing journey marked by moments of courage and self-discovery. It requires a willingness to confront external pressures, challenge ingrained beliefs, and embrace vulnerability to live a genuinely aligned life with one's innermost desires and convictions.

Reflecting on my campaign toward authenticity, I realize it's been a deeply personal and ongoing quest filled with moments of both challenge and revelation. There have been times when I've had to summon courage from the depths of my being to confront my fears and insecurities, and there have been moments of profound self-discovery that have reshaped my understanding of who I am.

One such moment I recalled several years ago when I found myself at a crossroads in my career. I had been following a path others had laid out for me, pursuing a profession that seemed practical and lucrative but didn't align with my true passions and values. Deep down, I knew that I wasn't living authentically—that I was sacrificing my happiness and fulfillment for the sake of external expectations.

It took immense courage to admit this truth to myself and others, but once I did, a weight was lifted off my shoulders. I realized that authenticity wasn't about conforming to societal norms or meeting others' expectations—it was about honoring my truth and living in alignment with my deepest desires and values.

From that moment on, I began to make choices that were true to myself, even if they were unconventional or challenging. I pursued opportunities that sparked joy and passion within me, even if they didn't necessarily lead to financial success or societal approval. And with each step I took towards authenticity, I felt a sense of liberation and empowerment that I had never experienced before.

Of course, the journey towards authenticity is far from easy, and there are still moments when I doubt myself or struggle to stay true to my path. But I've realized that authenticity is not a destination to be reached—it's a way of being, a commitment to living with integrity and alignment with my true self.

And so, I continue to embark on this commute with an open heart and a willingness to embrace whatever challenges and opportunities come my way. Ultimately, the quest for authenticity is not just about finding ourselves—it's about becoming ourselves, fully and unapologetically, in every moment of our lives.

I sincerely hope that sharing this record prompts contemplation on more prominent themes of sovereignty, autonomy, and the intricate dance between internal and external influences in determining the fates of nations. Through this reflection, I aim to shed light on the nuanced dynamics at play in the post-colonial context, where issues of governance, resource management, and foreign intervention often intersect.

Central to this story is the call for leadership that prioritizes the welfare and aspirations of the populace. It emphasizes the need for leaders committed to fostering autonomy, promoting self-reliance, and challenging systems of dependency that perpetuate inequality and hinder progress. By advocating for a more equitable distribution of resources and challenging structures that perpetuate exploitation and marginalization, we can pave the way for a future where nations are empowered to chart their destinies.

Ultimately, this narrative serves as a reminder of the agency and resilience of communities in the face of adversity. It highlights the importance of collective action, solidarity, and the pursuit of justice in overcoming systemic barriers and forging a more just and prosperous future for all.

This narrative serves as a call to action for heightened self-awareness, collective empowerment, and a critical reevaluation of systems that shape the trajectory of African nations. By engaging in these introspective reflections and constructive dialogues, there exists a profound potential for catalyzing positive change and charting paths that resonate with the authentic aspirations of the people.

It underscores the importance of individuals and communities taking ownership of their destinies, reclaiming agency, and actively participating in governance and decision-making processes. By fostering a culture of accountability, transparency, and inclusivity, African nations can transcend historical legacies of exploitation and marginalization, and forge new trajectories rooted in dignity, justice, and prosperity for all citizens.

This narrative also emphasizes the power of solidarity and collaboration on both local and international scales. By uniting across borders and mobilizing collective resources and expertise, African nations can overcome common challenges, leverage opportunities, and amplify their voices on the global stage.

Ultimately, this call to action is a testament to African peoples' resilience, ingenuity, and potential. It is a rallying cry for a renewed commitment to building inclusive, equitable, and sustainable societies that honor the continent's diverse cultures, histories, and aspirations. Through concerted efforts and unwavering determination, Africa can emerge as a beacon of hope and progress for the world.

The earth's true wealth lies beneath its surface, and only those with the courage and ingenuity to explore the depths can unlock its riches. Similarly, the wealth within me resides in the boundless potential of my mind. It is the capacity to think beyond the confines of the known, to challenge conventions, and to believe in my ability to innovate and solve problems.

Innovation is not merely about creating something entirely new; it's about seeing possibilities in the fusion of old and new ideas. It's about creatively synthesizing existing concepts to develop novel solutions to age-old and contemporary challenges. Innovation is the art of daring to venture into uncharted territory, experiment with untested methods, and push the boundaries of what is possible.

To innovate is to embrace a mindset of perpetual curiosity and exploration. It requires a willingness to question assumptions, to challenge the status quo, and to continuously seek improvement. It's about harnessing the power of imagination to envision a better future and the determination to bring that vision to life.

As I cultivate my capacity for innovation, I recognize that it's not just about generating ideas; it's about translating those ideas into tangible outcomes that positively impact the world around me. It's about embracing failure as a natural part of the creative process and using setbacks as opportunities for growth and learning.

Innovation is the driving force behind progress and transformation. This engine propels societies forward, fuels economic growth, and enhances human well-being. By nurturing my innate ability to innovate, I empower myself to shape the future and contribute meaningfully to the advancement of society.

The analogy of the true wealth of the earth lying beneath its surface resonates deeply with me. It's a profound reminder that there is often more to discover and unlock than meets the eye. In the same way, drawing a parallel between the Earth's hidden treasures and the wealth within oneself, particularly the mind, is an enlightening perspective.

Just as the Earth holds vast reserves of precious metals, minerals, and resources beneath its surface, the human mind harbors an abundance of untapped potential waiting to be unearthed. This wealth within us isn't measured in material possessions but rather in our capacity to think critically, creatively, and innovatively.

The mind is like a rich vein of ore, filled with nuggets of insight, creativity, and ingenuity. It's a reservoir of ideas, dreams, and aspirations, waiting to be mined and refined into something truly remarkable. Just as miners must dig deep to uncover the Earth's treasures, we must delve into the depths of our minds to unleash our full creative potential.

Innovation becomes excavating and refining these mental resources, transforming raw ideas into valuable solutions and inventions. It's about tapping into our inherent creativity, pushing the boundaries of what is possible, and turning imagination into reality.

By recognizing the wealth within our minds, we open ourselves up to endless possibilities for growth, discovery, and advancement. Like prospectors searching for hidden treasure, we embark on a journey of exploration and innovation, driven by the belief that the most fabulous riches are found not in the external world but within ourselves.

The notion that only those who explore the underworld can maximize the earth's wealth resonates deeply with me. It symbolizes the importance of delving into the depths, being willing to venture into the unknown, and extracting value from what may be hidden beneath the surface. This concept mirrors the essence of innovation, where the courage to explore new ideas and challenge established norms can lead to discovering novel solutions and opportunities.

Just as miners must delve deep into the earth to uncover its riches, innovators must be willing to explore uncharted territories of thought and imagination. It requires a willingness to step outside comfort zones, question assumptions, and push the boundaries of what is known.

Exploring the underworld of ideas involves delving into the depths of creativity and imagination, where groundbreaking insights and discoveries await. It's about daring to think differently, to see beyond the conventional, and to embrace the possibilities that lie beyond the surface.

Innovation thrives on the willingness to defy norms and conventions by taking risks, experimenting, pushing the boundaries of what is possible, and embracing failure as a stepping-stone to success. It's about daring to envision a future different from the present and having the courage to pursue that vision with unwavering determination.

It's a journey of exploration and discovery, where each new idea uncovered is a potential source of wealth and value.

Ultimately, exploring the underworld, whether literal or metaphorical, is a quest for knowledge, insight, and enrichment. It's a reminder that true wealth isn't always found on the surface but often lies hidden beneath, waiting to be unearthed by those bold enough to seek it out.

The emphasis on the mind as the source of true wealth resonates deeply with me, highlighting the significance of intellectual capital and creative thinking in our lives. With its boundless potential, the mind serves as a wellspring of innovation and opportunity.

At the heart of this notion lies the capacity to think beyond the known, to challenge existing norms, and to have an unwavering belief in one's ability to solve problems. It's about embracing a mindset of curiosity and exploration, always seeking new perspectives and possibilities.

Ultimately, the true wealth of the mind lies in its capacity to imagine, create, and innovate. It's a reminder that our greatest assets are not material possessions but rather the ideas, insights, and innovations we generate through our minds' power.

Central to innovation is combining old and new concepts in novel ways, drawing inspiration from diverse sources, and synthesizing ideas innovatively. It's about seeing connections where others see none and finding creative solutions to complex challenges.

Innovation, as I've come to understand it, embodies a mindset of constant exploration and experimentation. It's about daring to challenge the status quo, to question existing methods, and to envision new ways of tackling age-old problems.

At its core, innovation involves the creation, development, and application of untested approaches to problem-solving. This dynamic and forward-thinking approach is the driving force behind progress and advancement in all facets of life. Innovation fuels growth and drives positive change, Whether in science, technology, business, or the arts.

Embracing innovation means embracing curiosity— the willingness to ask "why" and "what if?" It's about being open to new ideas, perspectives, and possibilities and exploring them fully.

Creativity is another essential component of innovation. It's the ability to think outside the box, to see connections where others see none, and to find novel solutions to complex problems. Cultivating a creative mindset allows us to approach challenges with fresh eyes and uncover innovative solutions that may have previously eluded us.

Creativity has always been a driving force, guiding me to explore new ideas and perspectives others may overlook. One personal example of how creativity has fueled my innovative thinking occurred during a challenging project at work.

I was tasked with finding a solution to streamline our company's inventory management system, which had become outdated and inefficient. Initially, I approached the problem using traditional methods, relying on existing models and strategies. However, despite my best efforts, I couldn't find a satisfactory solution.

Frustrated but determined, I decided to tap into my creative mindset and approach the problem differently. I took some time to step back and brainstorm potential ideas, allowing my imagination to roam freely without limitations.

Eventually, I stumbled upon a unique idea that hadn't been considered before—a digital inventory tracking system that utilized image recognition technology. This innovative approach would allow us to automate inventory management, reducing errors and increasing efficiency.

With renewed enthusiasm, I presented my idea to the team, and my delight was met with the same enthusiasm and excitement that I had. We quickly set to work implementing the new system, and within a few months, we had successfully revolutionized our inventory management process.

This experience taught me the importance of cultivating a creative mindset in problem-solving. By thinking outside the box and embracing unconventional ideas, I

205

uncovered a solution that addressed the immediate challenge and paved the way for future innovation within our organization. It reaffirmed my belief in the power of creativity to drive positive change and propel us towards new possibilities.

But perhaps most importantly, innovation requires a pioneering spirit—a willingness to venture into uncharted territory. It's about being resilient in the face of setbacks and using them as opportunities for growth and improvement.

Ultimately, innovation is not just about generating new ideas—it's about putting them into action to create real, tangible impact. It's about harnessing the power of human ingenuity to address some of the world's most pressing challenges and to build a brighter, more sustainable future for all.

7

Whose Race Are You Running?

I felt a surge of excitement when I encountered a poster proclaiming, "When you run alone, it's called a race, and when God runs with you, it's called grace!" This reminded me of my high school days, particularly a renowned event called "Inter-House Sports." Each student belonged to one of about five "Houses" named after significant benefactors from the community.

As part of the sports preparation, a 1.5-mile "cross-country" race was held every first Saturday of the month. Participation was mandatory, especially for those in the boarding homes. The race commenced around 5:30 am, and everyone was expected to return by 7:00 am. It was a well-organized event where even less proficient runners like me received support.

In the spirit of safety, the organizers ensured that injured participants received immediate first aid and were transported in the accompanying vehicle. This race emphasized the importance of safety and empathy for the weaker and injured, highlighting that a strong sense of safety and security is crucial for thriving in life.

Participating in the cross-country race taught me valuable lessons beyond physical endurance. It mirrored life's journey, where we all embark on our unique paths, facing challenges and pushing our limits. The support and empathy demonstrated during the race underscored the significance of communal encouragement in life's pursuits.

This experience emphasized the balance between individual effort and collective support. We were not just racing against each other; we were running together, each person contributing to the overall spirit of the event. The race became a symbol of unity and shared aspirations.

As we traversed the course, the scenic surroundings became a backdrop to the more profound lessons unfolding. The sunrise painted the sky with hues of hope, signifying the promise of a new day. It reminded me that challenges are an integral part of life's journey, but we can overcome them with resilience and the support of others.

In the context of the poster's wisdom, the race was more than a mere competition; it became a venture of grace.

The communal spirit echoed the idea that our races transform into graceful strides toward a shared destination when aligned with a higher purpose and supported by others. It illuminated that life's journey is enriched when guided by grace and accompanied by kindred spirits.

Reflecting on the past, I realize that the exercise guided us to explore aspects of our lives where security, stability, and a sense of belonging may be lacking. It provided a pathway to identify and address blockages through purposeful visualizations and affirmations, encouraging us to stay present in the moment.

There were no designated winners or losers in those races, as the primary objective was to assist athletes in preparing for upcoming sporting events. The emphasis was on participation and involvement, with all students encouraged to engage in any capacity within their respective Houses. This inclusive approach fostered a sense of unity and camaraderie, transcending the traditional notions of competition and highlighting the importance of collective preparation for shared goals.

This holistic approach to preparation not only focused on physical fitness but also on the mental and emotional well-being of the participants. It created a supportive environment where individuals could address personal challenges and work collectively toward improvement.

The analogy drawn from the school's sports program, comparing running alone to a race and running with God to grace, resonates deeply. It reflects the understanding that life's journey is not merely a solo race but a journey of grace when accompanied by a higher power. This perspective encourages a shift from a competitive mindset to one that embraces divine guidance and support.

I have carried the lessons learned from those early experiences throughout my adventure. The importance of collective participation, empathy for others, and recognizing that challenges can be overcome through personal effort and divine grace. These principles shape my outlook, reminding me that life is a collaborative journey where each step contributes to a shared sense of purpose and fulfillment, no matter how challenging.

The cross-country races in high school were enjoyable until the realization set in that the school was a considerable distance away, and the return journey required a decision: either run or walk. While these races were conducted as a group effort, the ultimate objective was individual development and personal fitness, all in preparation for the grand Inter-House Sporting Event.

Reflecting on the symbolic race of life, being a member of the human race involves living life collectively, yet each life has its unique destiny. I recognize the uniqueness of my life, feeling that I was born for something extraordinary, even though it has remained elusive. Now, acknowledging that I've been holding back from sharing my gifts with the world, I am poised for a transformative change.

I've realized that life's race, like those cross-country races, is not just about running or walking but also about the individual adventure and personal development. Each person's life is distinct and has a unique purpose waiting to be fulfilled. This awareness has sparked my readiness to break free from the self-imposed limitations that have held me back from sharing my gifts with the world.

At this crossroads, I am ready to face both challenges and opportunities head-on. The path ahead may come with its share of hurdles, but I am committed to moving forward with unwavering resilience and perseverance. Just as cross-country races condition athletes for greater competitions, I view my life experiences as vital preparation for the larger purpose that lies ahead.

I am not merely running the race of life but navigating a path of self-discovery and personal growth. The finish line is not just a destination but a symbol of reaching my fullest potential and contributing my unique gifts to the world.

My journey of saying "Yes" has been battered by waves of deceit and falsehoods. During the first sixteen or seventeen years of my life, I was met with an average of four hundred "Nos" each day—years that can never be reclaimed. Even after leaving the safety of home, I faced a world that remained indifferent to what I truly deserved, and the steady assault of rejection continued.

I recall being that vibrant, appealing individual adorned with smiles and happiness. Yet, I now comprehend that the universe operates without sentimentality, guided by a rational intelligence that responds impartially to every being. It echoes back what is given to it, much like the repercussions in a valley.

In this unforgiving world, it became evident that the Universe responded to my energy, reflecting the positivity or negativity I projected. Those relentless barrage of "Nos" became a backdrop against which my resilience and determination were forged. The adversity I faced only fueled the fire within me, propelling me to defy the odds and pursue the path less traveled.

In the crucible of life's challenges, I realized that the universe, indifferent to my desires, operated on the principle of reciprocity. The energy I invested determined the echoes I received. Instead of succumbing to the weight of rejection, I decided to harness these experiences, transforming them into stepping-stones toward a destiny I was determined to shape.

The journey of a thousand "Nos" became a testament to my endurance, and with each rejection, I discovered a reservoir of strength and resilience within. My "Yes" began to echo louder, not as a mere response to external validation but as a proclamation of self-worth and an affirmation of my unique path.

As I pressed on, my life evolved from a series of rejections to a symphony of resilience and self-discovery. Each setback became a catalyst for growth, and I emerged from the crucible of rejection with an unwavering resolve to manifest my true potential.

Within the immense fabric of existence, my decision to say "Yes" served as a guiding light, lighting up the way ahead of me. The positive vibrations I sent out into the world started to come back, forming a peaceful energy that overshadowed the negativity. The unbiased but reactive cosmos mirrored my fresh determination to create a fate in harmony with the correct "Yes" inside of me.

Life is fundamentally directed by a Divine Intelligence in the vast scope of existence, encouraging me to chase the dreams in my thoughts. The vision of the future, inspired by Divine Intelligence, guides my path like a compass. According to Albert Einstein, imagination is the precursor to future manifestations in life.

Equipped with special skills, unique gifts, and inherent abilities, I stand as an individual, ready to bring my imaginative dreams to fruition. This distinctive essence within me is the

213

key to unlocking the extraordinary rewards that success promises. The Divine Intelligence has intricately programmed me to experience the bountiful fruits of my endeavors.

However, amidst this cosmic design, the trajectory of my future rewards is intricately tied to my choices. My decisions, like the brushstrokes on the canvas of life, will ultimately paint the portrait of the outcomes awaiting me. I chart the course toward realizing my envisioned future by deliberately aligning my choices with divine guidance.

Navigating the intricate collage of existence, I recognize the inherent fairness woven into the fabric of life. The Divine Intelligence orchestrates a cosmic balance that propels me to a path aligned with my mental objectives. My imagination, a powerful force fueled by the divine spark within, is a harbinger of the extraordinary possibilities awaiting manifestation.

In this grand cosmic play, I am not a mere spectator but an active participant with unique capabilities and a distinct identity. The Divine Intelligence, akin to a masterful architect, has designed me to play a crucial role in bringing forth the visions that dance within my consciousness.

The unique skills, gifts, and abilities bestowed upon me are not arbitrary; they are the tools I need to sculpt my destiny. Each decision, a brushstroke on the canvas of my life, shapes the intricate details of the masterpiece I am creating.

The divine guidance serves as a compass, steering me toward a future where the rewards of success unfold like the petals of a blooming flower.

Starting on this journey around the world, I realize that the results are not already decided but shaped by the decisions I make on purpose. The Divine Intelligence urges me to collaborate in writing the story of my life, prompting me to synchronize my choices with the universal balance that envelops and uplifts me. With every move I make, I am getting nearer to achieving my imagined future, intricately connected to the divine variety of life.

Our existence is bestowed upon us without active participation, yet our life trajectory hinges on our choices. Life doesn't necessarily unfold based on what we believe we deserve but rather on what we can effectively negotiate through our daily decisions. It took me some time to comprehend that I inhabit a just world where what I receive is not solely determined by merit but by the negotiations I engage in.

Upon introspection and a deep connection with my authentic self and ultimate source, I came to the profound realization that I am responsible for shaping my identity. Seeking my genuine self and embracing the perfection inherent in my original composition became paramount. This revelation emerged as a singular truth, shattering the metaphorical alabaster jar of my understanding.

This realization triggered the start of a connection with myself, revealing the enchanting core of who I am. Acknowledging that I am *Imago Dei* means understanding that I reflect the attributes of the Divine Intelligence as a creation of my Creator. I am a mirror of the Divine, created in the image and likeness of the supreme source of life.

Embracing this truth led me on a transformative journey of self-discovery. I delved into the depths of my being, unraveling layers of conditioned beliefs and societal expectations that obscured my authentic self. This self-exploration process was liberating and challenging, requiring me to confront insecurities, fears, and limiting beliefs.

As I navigated the intricate labyrinth of my early life, I began to understand the profound influence of my family background on the foundation of my identity. The values instilled in me during my formative years became the compass guiding my decisions and shaping my character. The roots of my identity were intertwined with the stories, traditions, and lessons passed down through generations.

The seasons of my life unfolded, marked by moments of joy, pain, and self-discovery. Each experience etched a chapter in the narrative of my existence, contributing to the complex drapes of my identity. The shadows in my rain represented the challenges and adversities I faced, casting fleeting shadows on the canvas of my life.

In the midst of turbulent weather and moments of brightness, I struggled with inquiries about my reason for existence and value. Whose race was I participating in? What is my role in the vast shade of mankind? These reflective questions motivated me to delve deeper into comprehending my individual reason for being and impact on the world.

The shadows in my rain were not mere obstacles but poignant lessons that enriched the soil of my growth. They taught me resilience, compassion, and the art of embracing imperfections. The shadows were integral to the beauty of the entire picture, revealing the contours and nuances that added depth to my story.

Looking back on the chapters in my life, I recognize the transformative power of self-awareness and the continuous negotiation between the external world and my internal compass. The journey of self-discovery is ongoing, an ever-evolving exploration of the authentic self and a recognition of the divine imprint within.

In the epilogue of my story, I find solace in realizing that the shadows in my rain were not harbingers of darkness but dancers in the symphony of my existence. They contributed to the rhythm of my growth, the melody of my resilience, and the harmony of my self-discovery. The journey continues, guided by the unwavering truth that I am both the artist and the masterpiece, sculpting my destiny with each intentional brushstroke.

I must find the strength to leave my past behind, liberating myself from the shackles of yesterday. It's essential to realize that yesterday only exists within the confines of my mind. Embracing this truth, I enthusiastically welcome a fresh start and the dawn of a new beginning.

In acknowledging the rejections that have peppered my transit, I reframe them as valuable redirections. Rather than dwelling on past setbacks, I see them as guiding signposts directing me toward a more fulfilling path. I have become a product of the cumulative experiences that shape my narrative.

Resolute in my commitment to move forward, I refrain from harboring regrets or attempting to alter the past. Instead, I focus on the decisions and choices that will propel me toward my destined future. Reflecting on the person I am meant to become, I recognize that confident decisions from my past may not align with this vision.

However, I approach this realization with a sense of empowerment. Armed with self-awareness, I make decisions that harmonize with the trajectory leading me to my destiny. Each step is intentional, guided by the understanding that I am sculpting my path toward the envisioned future.

My journey has been one of self-discovery and purpose; I embrace the transformative power of choice. Every decision becomes a brushstroke on the canvas of my destiny, contributing to the masterpiece that is my life. Today, I stand in the present, armed with the wisdom of yesterday and the anticipation of a future crafted by the choices I make today.

In the rainbow of my existence, I recognize the intricate interplay of decisions, each thread weaving a unique pattern that contributes to the richness of my story. The journey of self-discovery is an ongoing process, and with every intentional step, I inch closer to the person I am destined to become.

Letting go of the notion of changing the past, I shift my focus to the present and the future. The sum of my experiences, both triumphs, and trials, has shaped the canvas upon which I now paint my aspirations. Each rejection, once seen as a roadblock, is now a stepping-stone guiding me toward new horizons.

Standing at the edge of endless possibilities, I am empowered by the knowledge that my past does not define me. Rather, it serves as the foundation for creating a life of purpose and intention. The choices I make today, enriched by the lessons of yesterday, drive me forward with clear determination and purpose.

The account of my life unfolds with each decision, and I approach these crossroads with a discerning eye. If confident choices from my past do not align with the vision of my true self, I confront them not with regret but with the resolve to make choices that resonate with my authentic identity.

This journey is not about erasing the chapters written but crafting a compelling narrative for the chapters yet to unfold. The power to shape my destiny lies in the choices I make in the present moment. I am the author of my story, and each decision is a keystroke that contributes to the unfolding annals of my life.

With a heart filled with gratitude for the lessons of the past, I step boldly into the unknown, embracing the adventure of self-discovery. The future I have imagined is not a distant mirage, but a tangible reality shaped by my choices today. This journey is mine to navigate, and I approach it with resilience, purpose, and an unwavering commitment to becoming the person I was born to be.

By weaving connections with the universal community, I aim to showcase the beauty of embracing one's true self. This narrative is not just a recounting of events but an affirmation of the authentic "who" that resides within me. The journey is a transformative odyssey, and my sincere hope is that as others engage with my story, they, too, find a catalyst for change within themselves.

I seek to inspire a collective affirmation of identity and purpose by embracing my authentic self. The journey extends an invitation to discard the shackles of doubt and embark on a voyage of self-discovery. The realization that yesterday is confined to the recesses of the mind empowers the embrace of a new beginning—a future imagined and now realized.

The rejections that once stung are reframed as redirections, guiding me toward the destiny I am meant to fulfill. While I cannot alter the past, I wield the power to shape my present and future through intentional decisions aligned with my true essence. It is a profound acknowledgment that I am the sum of my past, a culmination of experiences that have sculpted the intricate compound of my being.

In sharing my life's raw and unfiltered account. I aspire to dissolve doubts and illuminate a path toward self-discovery. The influence I hope to leave endures, leaving an unforgettable imprint on the lives of those who come across my story. May this journey become a beacon of inspiration, leading others to a deeper understanding of their narratives and the boundless potential that awaits them.

I endeavor to recount a personal story and offer a roadmap for transformation. As the chapters unfold, I invite readers to traverse the landscape of my experiences, understanding that each twist and turn has contributed to the person I am today. It is a narrative that goes beyond the temporal boundaries of past, present, and future, transcending the limitations of time.

This commentary is more than a personal chronicle; it is a testament to resilience, growth, and the unwavering pursuit of authenticity. I hope that as others delve into the mosaic of my life, they discover threads of their own stories and are inspired to embark on their unique pilgrimage of self-discovery.

As I share the essence of my experiences, I invite others to unravel the layers of their lives, discovering the beauty beneath them. It is a celebration of individuality and a recognition that within every journey, there exists the potential for profound transformation. May this narrative catalyze others to redefine their narratives and embrace the fullness of who they are meant to be?

My future unfolds with clarity, devoid of clouds, as I envision a serene, self-confident, and blissful existence. It is a prospect where Lady Luck finally bestows her favor upon me, contrasting the times when her smile seemed elusive. This realization has been a lifelong companion, although I find myself wrestling with it, especially in the realm of expectations from others.

In a moment of clarity, I acknowledge the peril of placing excessive expectations on external forces. The truth crystallizes—I am not entitled to anything from the world.

This recognition prompts a sobering self-reflection, steering me away from inevitable disappointment. Early lessons in life instilled the importance of self-reliance for success. I possess the intrinsic elements necessary for triumph, yet their activation hinges on the power of imagination.

Beyond mere self-reliance, the linchpin lies in unwavering belief. I understand the consequences of neglecting my instincts and entrusting my life purpose to others. Those instances served as poignant lessons, affirming the potency of listening to my inner compass. Through this, I've learned that true fulfillment begins with self-reliance, sustained by an unwavering belief in the boundless potential residing within.

This journey of self-discovery has emphasized the importance of trusting my instincts and activating my imagination. There were moments when I veered off course, surrendering the reins of my destiny to external influences. However, the wisdom gained from those experiences has fortified my resolve to stay true to myself.

The unfolding chapters of my life story are marked by a conscious decision to forge my path, relying on an internal compass that steers me toward authenticity. It is a journey where self-reliance is not just a strategy but a guiding principle, a philosophy that underscores the idea that my success is firmly within my grasp.

Believing in the capabilities embedded within me has become the cornerstone of my aspirations. It is an acknowledgment that my future is not subject to the whims of luck or the actions of others. Instead, it is a canvas I paint with the colors of my choices, the strokes of my efforts, and the artistry of my beliefs.

As I navigate the possibilities, I am determined to silence the doubts that may linger. The realization that my decisions shape my destiny is empowering and daunting. Yet, armed with the knowledge that I possess the key to unlock the doors of my potential, I stride confidently into the uncharted territory of my future.

In this journey of self-discovery, I am not merely a passive observer but an active participant, shaping my narrative with intentionality. With its rejections and redirections, the past has become the scaffolding upon which I construct a future aligned with my most authentic self. Every rejection transforms into a stepping-stone, redirecting me toward the path where my authenticity thrives.

My story, woven with the threads of resilience, self-reliance, and belief, seeks to inspire others to embark on their odyssey of self-discovery. It is an invitation to assess one's skills, embrace experiences, and derive value and significance from the unique combination of life. Through my history, I endeavor to illuminate the path to self-acceptance, genuine connections, and an unwavering affirmation of one's true identity.

The epiphany that my life will never be the same again fills me with hope and anticipation. Doubts dissipate, making way for a future illuminated by the radiance of self-awareness and purpose. As I share the profound revelations of my journey, I extend an invitation to others to embark on their quest for authenticity, for in doing so, they, too, can affirm the 'who' they were destined to be.

Commencing my narrative necessitates a genuine openness and willingness to delve into my values, infusing meaning into my journey. Acting as a receptive student, I look to the great teacher, the source upon which I rely, to guide me in establishing a non-judgmental and non-threatening tone. Being teachable is the key.

To share my story and values, I aspire to create an atmosphere where judgment is set aside, and openness prevails. I believe this will encourage others to reciprocate by sharing their stories.

As my narrative unfolds, I aim to lay bare the layers of my experiences, allowing my values to act as guiding threads through the fabric of my life. I recognize the transformative power of openness, not only in my willingness to share but also in my receptivity to the stories of others.

In this shared space of vulnerability and authenticity, the passage becomes a mutual exploration, fostering connections that transcend individual reports. The teacher-student dynamic blurs as each participant becomes a learner and a guide. Through this exchange, I hope we collectively unearth deeper understandings of ourselves and the shared human experience.

The ongoing exploration of values is not a solitary endeavor but a communal undertaking. The richness of our interactions lies in the diversity of perspectives and the shared humanity that binds us together. I commit to sustaining this dialogue, fostering an environment where our shared stories become bridges that connect us all.

Reflecting on the drapery of my life, woven with diverse experiences, profound events, and the lessons etched into the fabric of my being, I sense a transformative shift on the horizon. The notion of a lingering karmic debt, a specter that once loomed large, now dissipates as I stand on the beginning of a new chapter.

With unwavering certainty, I proclaim the emergence of hyper-beneficial angelic karma, poised to cast its benevolent influence upon my journey. Despite the current semblance of challenges and the daunting nature of my perceived obstacles, I embrace the belief that a paradigm shift awaits. The description of my life is destined for the infusion of good fortune and happiness.

Even when circumstances may suggest otherwise, and the weight of my struggles feels insurmountable, I stand ready to witness the dawn of positive change. It is never too late for the tides to turn, and the time has arrived for the convergence of favorable destiny and lasting joy in my life.

This impending transformation is not merely a shift in fortune but a cosmic alignment of the benevolent forces conspiring to usher in a new era. As I navigate the landscape of my existence, I am attuned to the subtle harmonies of the universe, signaling the culmination of my hyper-beneficial angelic karma.

In the face of apparent adversity and the shadows that may cloak my path, I stand resolute, ready to witness the manifestation of goodness and joy. The drapery of my life, once woven with threads of challenge, now anticipates the vibrant hues of fulfillment and serenity.

This moment marks the turning point where the intricacies of my journey cease to be dictated by past debts and instead become an ode to the symphony of positivity awaiting its crescendo. The cosmic dance of destiny, choreographed by benevolent forces, is poised to unveil a grand spectacle of prosperity and happiness.

With each step forward, I embrace the unfolding chapters of my life story, knowing that the karmic scales are tipping in my favor. The time has come for the universe to bestow its blessings upon me, and I stand ready to receive the abundant grace that awaits.

This doesn't diminish the importance of assistance we all require on our journeys, but as the saying goes, "You can lead a horse to the bank of the river, but you cannot make the horse drink." I firmly believe in my further transformation and progress in traditional, original Indigenous knowledge. This applies to my reality's education, research, policymaking, and private sectors.

Undertaking this endeavor won't be easy, especially for someone accustomed to being directed on how to think and what to do. I am aware that I've long been subject to the intellectual guidance and directions of others, whether from the cultural environment I grew up in, parental messages, educational systems, institutional religious orientations, or societal mentalities influenced by colonial perspectives from aid industries and international news media. Nevertheless, I am convinced that undertaking this task is essential for progress.

This realization marks a shift in my perspective. I am no longer content with being a passive recipient of guidance; instead, I am embracing the responsibility to shape my story.

It's a challenging endeavor, breaking free from the conventional molds that have shaped my thinking for so long. Yet, I am determined to reclaim the authority over my knowledge, ensuring it aligns with my unique experiences and cultural background.

This process of self-discovery and reclamation is a journey of empowerment. It involves unraveling the layers of external influences that have veiled my authentic self. As I embark on this path, I am prepared to confront discomfort and resistance from within and external sources. However, the promise of genuine autonomy and the ability to contribute authentically to various spheres of life motivates me.

In essence, this period of traveling is a testament to the resilience of my identity and the significance of embracing one's cultural roots. It's a personal quest to challenge existing paradigms and contribute to a more inclusive and diverse understanding of knowledge and success. I am ready to break free from the constraints of imposed ideologies and discover the wealth of wisdom embedded in my heritage.

I grasp the concept that, through the law of attraction, I possess the ability to draw towards me anything I desire from the universe. This metaphysical law operates based on the alignment of my abilities to access it. Engaging with mentors who have greatly influenced me was pivotal in my self-discovery. They revealed that within the human heart lies an

229

immense power—a force impartial and unemotional. This power doesn't discern my wants; it merely responds to my alignment. It functions as pure energy, reproducing whatever I introduce, akin to Newton's third law, stating that every action has an equal and opposite reaction. In Newton's terms, this law signifies that a pair of forces acts on the two objects involved in every interaction.

Understanding the law of attraction and Newton's third law led me to recognize that my thoughts, emotions, and intentions contribute to the energetic vibrations I send into the universe. If I align these energies positively, I can draw favorable circumstances and experiences into my life. This revelation marked a significant shift in my mindset and approach to life.

I discovered that my past decisions and actions had shaped my present reality. While I couldn't change the past, I realized the power I held in influencing my future through intentional choices. This awareness prompted me to be more mindful of my thoughts, emotions, and actions, creating a harmonious resonance with the energies around me.

As I delved deeper into self-discovery, I acknowledged the importance of taking responsibility for my life. Instead of playing the victim, I embraced the idea that I could shape my destiny through intentional living. This shift in perspective empowered me to navigate life's challenges with resilience and determination.

The journey of aligning myself with the metaphysical laws and the power within propelled me toward personal growth and fulfillment. It became clear that my connection with the universal energies and my ability to harness them played a crucial role in manifesting my desired life. This newfound understanding laid the foundation for a transformative voyage of self-discovery and intentional living.

Therefore, in alignment with the universal metaphysical law, impartial and unemotional to individual feelings and desires, it reflects these energies. This state of consciousness is often called the Christ consciousness or the universal mind. It enables us to recognize the supreme life force known as God and the fundamental law of nature called the mind.

In the vast landscape of life, the echoes of our thoughts and desires resonate with the metaphysical law. It is a mirror that reflects the energy we emit into the universe. This cosmic reciprocity emphasizes the need for conscious alignment with our aspirations, recognizing the impartial nature of the universal mind.

While the law of attraction emphasizes the power of positive thinking, it also underscores the importance of action. Newton's third law resonates not only in the physical realm but also in the metaphysical. Our intentional actions generate corresponding reactions from the universe.

In my pursuit of self-discovery, I have encountered mentors who guided me in understanding this cosmic dance. They illuminated the immense power within the human heart, emphasizing its neutrality to specific wants or fears. This power, akin to the Christ consciousness or universal mind, operates without judgment, responding solely to the energy we introduce.

I am often reminded that the Universe operates on the principles of impartiality and reflection. The energy I project is the energy I receive, a profound truth embedded in the metaphysical fabric of existence. Recognizing this truth, I embark on a journey of intentional alignment, seeking harmony with the universal mind and the divine energy that orchestrates the cosmic dance of life.

Deep Listening

In many situations, especially when a young individual faces challenges and seeks connection with an adult, active listening becomes crucial in determining whether the youth feels acknowledged or dismissed. Unfortunately, many adults neglect basic listening skills, leaving the youth feeling unheard, misunderstood, or disregarded.

Active listening is a fundamental aspect of effective communication, fostering understanding, empathy, and a sense of validation. The lack of this skill can contribute to misunderstandings and hinder personal growth. Reflecting on my journey, I recognize the pivotal role of genuine and attentive listening in my self-discovery.

In deep listening, the primary focus is on fully engaging with what others are communicating. It involves giving undivided attention to the speaker, not only hearing their words but also understanding the emotions, nuances, and unspoken messages beneath the surface. This practice goes beyond the superficial act of hearing and delves into the profound act of truly comprehending and empathizing with the speaker's perspective.

Deep listening requires an open mind, free from preconceived notions or judgments. It involves setting aside personal biases and agendas to create a space where the speaker feels genuinely heard and respected. This practice fosters a connection between individuals, promoting understanding, trust, and meaningful communication.

Deep listening is an intentional and transformative act that transcends the boundaries of ordinary conversation. It is a powerful tool for building bridges of understanding and cultivating more profound connections in personal and professional relationships.

233

In deep listening, the primary focus is on the ongoing conversation and the individual sharing their experiences with you. The skillful application of this technique ensures that the teenager confiding in you feels genuinely heard, acknowledged, and understood, fostering the strengthening of your relationship.

Engaging in deep listening also involves being mindful of our body language, such as maintaining appropriate eye contact, leaning in, and orienting oneself towards the teen, signaling genuine interest and curiosity rather than a dismissive stance. This intentional approach creates a space where open communication and connection can thrive.

In addition to the physical aspects of deep listening, the mental component plays a crucial role. It involves maintaining an open mind, free from preconceived judgments, and allowing the conversation to unfold without interruptions or premature assumptions. This mental receptivity creates an atmosphere where teenagers feel safe expressing themselves authentically.

Furthermore, deep listening goes beyond the immediate verbal content of the conversation. It involves tuning into the emotions, subtle nuances, and unspoken feelings underlying the words. This level of attunement helps establish a deeper connection, as it demonstrates genuine concern for the individual's holistic well-being.

I've recognized the significance of deep listening. By immersing myself in the experiences and emotions of others, I've cultivated stronger connections and fostered understanding. This skill has proven invaluable, especially when guiding the younger generation through challenges and uncertainties.

As deep listening becomes an integral part of communication, it enhances the quality of relationships and cultivates a sense of empathy and understanding. It transforms conversations into meaningful exchanges, fostering an environment where both parties feel valued and respected. Deep listening is a powerful tool for building bridges, fostering trust, and nurturing healthy connections with teenagers.

Mind and Body

The body serves as a vessel for the mind, acting as a conduit between the physical and the spiritual realms where decisions take shape before manifesting in the material world. A clear and pure mind contributes to a healthy body; conversely, the body's condition reflects the state of the mind. The human mind is a unique gift within the life ecosystem, providing the capacity to navigate and solve life's challenges.

A constant self-reminder underscores the reality that no one bears an obligation toward me, and the concern others extend is often tethered to the problems I can help resolve for them. This understanding emphasizes the reciprocal relationship between the clarity of one's mind and the condition of one's body, illustrating the interconnection of existence's spiritual, mental, and physical aspects.

I recognize this interplay between mind and body and maintain a clean, uncluttered mental space. The decisions and choices I make in the spiritual realm of my mind reverberate into the physical realm, shaping my actions and responses in the face of life's myriad challenges.

In the vast echo system of existence, the human mind stands out as a powerful tool for problem-solving. As I navigate through life, I am mindful that the value I bring to others is often linked to my ability to contribute solutions to their challenges. This awareness fuels my commitment to honing my problem-solving skills and providing assistance and support for those around me.

Understanding that the body is intricately connected to the mind, I recognize the importance of maintaining a healthy and harmonious balance. A clean mind fosters a clean body, contributing to overall well-being and resilience in facing life's uncertainties. This holistic approach underscores the significance of tending to mental and physical aspects to lead a fulfilled and purposeful life.

As I've come to comprehend, the brain is a soft mass composed of supportive tissues and nerves intricately connected to the spinal cord. Some of these nerves extend directly to the eyes, ears, and various head regions, while others establish connections throughout the body via the spinal cord. This network of nerves regulates personality, senses, and bodily functions ranging from breathing to walking. The brain, spinal cord, and nerves collectively form the central nervous system.

Situated at the base of the brain, the brain stem serves as a vital connector linking the cerebrum to the spinal cord. It comprises the mid-brain, the pons, and the medulla. This critical region exercises control over essential bodily functions, including but not limited to breathing, eye movements, blood pressure, heartbeat, and swallowing.

Moreover, the brain is partitioned into distinct regions responsible for specific cognitive functions. The cerebrum, the most significant part, governs intricate processes such as reasoning, problem-solving, and the interpretation of sensory information. It is further divided into lobes, including the frontal lobe, which is associated with decision-making and personality; the parietal lobe, responsible for sensory processing; the temporal lobe, managing auditory information

237

and memory; and the occipital lobe, which oversees visual processing.

The brain continually adapts and forms neural connections through neuroplasticity as a dynamic organ. This remarkable ability enables individuals to learn, remember, and modify behaviors in response to experiences.

Understanding the intricacies of the brain and its interconnected systems provides insights into the profound relationship between the mind and the body. The mind, operating within the spiritual realm, plays a pivotal role in shaping decisions before their manifestation in the physical world. Thus, fostering a clean mind contributes to a healthier body, emphasizing the profound connection between mental and physical well-being.

In navigating life, the awareness that nobody inherently owes anything and that one's value is often linked to the problems one can solve for others becomes a powerful reminder. This perspective fosters a proactive approach, prompting individuals to focus on contributing solutions and positively impacting those around them.

Delving into exploring how my brain functions through dedicated study, I've come to acknowledge that my brain comprises two hemispheres, each showcasing distinct personalities. This analogy parallels a computer operating with a processor, where the right brain hemisphere operates like a parallel processor, and the left hemisphere functions as a serial processor.

This intriguing duality in the operation of my brain hemispheres contributes to the complexity of my cognitive processes. The right hemisphere, often associated with creativity and intuition, works holistically, processing information simultaneously and recognizing patterns. On the other hand, the left hemisphere, known for its analytical and logical functions, processes information sequentially and excels in language and mathematical reasoning.

A bundle of nerves orchestrates the coordination between these two hemispheres called the corpus callosum. This communication bridge ensures that both hemispheres collaborate seamlessly, allowing me to harness the strengths of each for various cognitive tasks.

Understanding this internal synergy has given me valuable insights into my thinking processes, decision-making abilities, and overall cognitive functioning. As I explore the intricacies of my brain, I unveil the remarkable interplay between these hemispheres, shaping the unique way I perceive and interact with the world.

At a specific enchanting juncture in my past, I viewed the world through the lens of wonder and boundless potential. During this time, the notion of scarcity or constraints had not yet taken root in my mind, allowing me. Reflecting on this, I often pondered the transformation of that limitless childhood spirit.

It dawned on me that the seeds of abundance are sown in the fertile soil of imagination long before they sprout into tangible reality. The key lies in conditioning my conscious and subconscious minds for success, prosperity, and joy. Without this empowering mental foundation, I risk navigating a world of frustration and limitation. Conversely, by adopting more uplifting mental programs, my life has the potential to undergo an extraordinary transformation, unfolding blessings beyond my imagination.

In the insightful words of Julius Nyerere, the inaugural president of independent Tanzania, "True development cannot be imposed on individuals; rather, people must be granted the freedom to cultivate their growth."

This realization has propelled me on a journey of self-discovery and transformation. I've embarked on a quest to reprogram my mental framework, cultivating an environment conducive to success, prosperity, and joy. The process involves untangling the threads of limiting beliefs and replacing them with empowering thoughts.

Moreover, my exploration of the brain has taken me to the central nervous system—a complex network of tissues and nerves that governs fundamental bodily functions. The brain stem, nestled at the base of the brain, orchestrates vital processes such as breathing, eye movements, blood pressure, heartbeat, and swallowing. Understanding these intricate workings has empowered me to appreciate the symbiotic relationship between my mind and body.

In this journey of self-discovery, I've learned that the mind is a powerful force that shapes our perception of reality. It acts as a conduit between the spiritual and physical realms, influencing decisions before they manifest in the material world. This understanding has spurred me to maintain a clean mind, recognizing that my thoughts are vital in shaping my destiny.

As I refine my mental programs and cultivate a mindset of abundance, I am poised for a life blessed with success, prosperity, and joy. The quest has taught me that my life is a manifestation of the mental scripts I choose to run. With newfound clarity and purpose, I look forward to navigating the complexities of life with resilience, gratitude, and an unwavering belief in the boundless possibilities that lie ahead.

Emotional Health

I bear the weight of numerous sorrows and enduring emotional wounds that continue to haunt me to this day. These scars inflict profound mental anguish and emotional

241

suffering, casting a shadow over my passionate approach to life. The pain runs deep, often making me feel like I am losing control.

I recognize the need for emotional regulation and the imperative to control my feelings. In attempting to cultivate healthy relationships with those I cherish, I have found myself trapped by the expectations and actions of others. This struggle has become a recurring theme, impacting my journey towards meaningful connections and contentment.

I am determined to unravel the complexities of my emotional landscape. These sorrows, though burdensome, catalyze self-discovery and growth. It is a challenging journey, but I am committed to understanding the intricacies of my emotions and learning to wield them as tools for resilience rather than sources of distress.

In pursuing emotional mastery, I acknowledge the importance of setting boundaries and fostering healthy connections. It's a process of unlearning patterns that have entangled me in the past, replacing them with strategies that empower me to engage in relationships with clarity and strength.

I am on a quest to break free from the chains of emotional turmoil, forging a path towards serenity and self-control. As I confront the scars of my past, I am determined to emerge victorious, reclaiming agency over my emotional well-being and fostering relationships that enrich my life rather than hinder my progress.

I have resided in an environment that doesn't foster my well-being, hindering the cultivation of my inner virtues and harmony. Standing amidst a group of people, their laughter became a source of discomfort, highlighting the desire to be celebrated rather than merely tolerated. I aspire to break free from this negative energy cycle, preventing its transmission to future generations.

Reflecting on the impact of my surroundings, I've realized that it's not the objective reality that governs my behavior but rather my perception of it. Understanding that learned perceptions shape internal impulses, I am determined to transform my outlook and liberate myself from the constraints imposed by my environment.

In this quest for transformation, I am committed to reshaping my perception of the world around me. I acknowledge that the lens through which I view reality holds significant power over my behavior and emotions. Rather than succumbing to the influence of external factors, I am determined to take control of my internal narrative.

Recognizing the potential transference of pain and suffering from one generation to the next, I am motivated to break this cycle. I aspire to create an environment that nurtures the well-being of future generations, fostering positive energy and emotional health.

Navigating through the challenges of my past and present, I actively seek ways to cultivate a healthier mindset and emotional well-being. This involves developing a resilient emotional core and embracing a harmonious perspective on life. My journey towards self-discovery and transformation is a testament to my commitment to creating a positive legacy for myself and those who come after me.

In my youth, I was ensnared by the cruelty of others, leaving deep, lasting scars on my heart and mind. Though the weight of these haunting memories still lingers, I am grateful for both the great and humble blessings that have touched my path.

Along the path of life, I encountered trials—some anticipated, others unforeseen. Yet, within the crucible of these challenges, I discovered profound opportunities that paved the way for subsequent strokes of good fortune. The resilience that allowed me to emerge triumphantly from these trials also became a conduit for the influx of success.

Admittedly, while conquering the tests that presented themselves was an accomplishment in its own right, the true richness lay in the invaluable life lessons embedded within these experiences. Each trial served as a poignant instructor, imparting wisdom and molding the contours of my character in ways that extended far beyond mere circumstantial victories.

These life lessons, earned through the crucible of trials, became the cornerstones of my personal growth. They served as illuminating signposts, directing me toward a deeper understanding of myself and the world around me.

Amidst the adversities, I uncovered reservoirs of resilience and an untapped wellspring of inner strength. These qualities, forged in the crucible of challenges, equipped me with the fortitude to face the uncertainties ahead.

Reflecting on my journey, I acknowledge that the trials were not mere obstacles to overcome; they were profound tutors that shaped my perspective and fortified my resolve. The scars, once perceived as wounds, transformed into markers of endurance—a testament to the resilience that resides within.

In the grand picture of life, the threads of hardship intricately weave alongside those of triumph, creating a mosaic that is uniquely mine. Each trial and each lesson has contributed to the rich mix of my existence, revealing the depth of human resilience and the capacity for growth in the face of adversity.

Progressing on my growth path, I took bold steps forward, encountering many favorable circumstances that accelerated my journey, strengthening my resolve and character. When faced with trials or expected personal challenges, I choose not to see them as mere burdens but as new opportunities for growth and evolution.

In this perspective, every trial becomes a stepping-stone, a chance to refine my skills and navigate toward fulfilling my aspirations. I've learned that challenges, whether anticipated or unexpected, have potential for personal growth and development. By embracing each trial as an opportunity, I've discovered resilience and cultivated a mindset that propels me forward.

Moreover, these trials have become pivotal turning points, shaping not just my present but also steering the course of my future. Each challenge I overcome reinforces my foundation, equipping me with the strength to face future obstacles with a resilient spirit. As I move forward on this journey, I am increasingly attuned to uncovering the hidden lessons and opportunities within every hardship.

Ultimately, my evolving perspective has allowed me to turn setbacks into comebacks and view trials not as roadblocks but as gateways to progress. Life's challenges are no longer viewed with trepidation but embraced as the sculptors of my character, crafting a resilient and adaptable version of myself with each passing trial.

I had to establish a connection with my emotions, allowing them to undergo processing within the mind-body system, facilitating my healing and personal growth. Granting myself the permission and space to feel and express gratitude played a crucial role in this transformative journey. Having been influenced by external guidance from colonial powers, aid industries, and international media, I recognized the necessity of reclaiming my autonomy to make meaningful progress.

I gently turn inward, allowing myself to connect with the emotions that dwell within me. No longer resisting or pushing them aside, I give them space to surface, to be felt in their entirety. Each sensation, each stirring of emotion, flows through my mind and body like a quiet stream, seeking its course.

As I acknowledge these feelings, my body begins to process them—my breath deepens, my muscles release their tension, and the weight I've carried starts to lighten. I create room for healing in this sacred exchange between heart and mind. With each breath, I feel the transformative power of self-awareness, allowing my emotions to guide me toward personal growth. The pain, joy, and uncertainty are all part of this process, weaving together to form a blend of resilience and inner peace.

Through this practice of embracing and processing my emotions, I begin to heal, evolving into a stronger, more grounded version of myself. My feelings no longer bind me but are gateways to deeper understanding and wholeness.

In this process of self-discovery and healing, I began to unravel the layers of external influences that shaped my mindset. It became evident that progress required reclaiming control over my thoughts, emotions, and decisions. As I delved deeper into my emotional landscape, I realized the power of gratitude in reshaping my perspective.

Permitting myself to feel joy or sorrow allowed me to process emotions healthily. Gratitude was a guiding force, helping me find moments of positivity even in challenging situations. This internal shift became a catalyst for personal growth.

The journey involved confronting the impact of historical and societal influences that had long dictated the trajectory of my life. Breaking free from the intellectual chains imposed by colonial legacies and external narratives, I embraced the task of crafting my story. This newfound sense of agency opened doors to progress and self-determination.

Yet, what brings me joy is the realization that the enchanting sense of childhood wonder and abundance is still an integral part of who I am. Somewhere along life's adventure, however, I unwittingly adopted specific belief systems and mental programs that operated in the recesses of my subconscious. Ironically, I remained oblivious to their existence, yet they influenced my emotions, steering me toward a lifeless, joyous, and prosperous than I rightfully deserve.

It may not seem equitable that experiences from my distant past, stretching back to childhood, could cast such a negative shadow over my present life.

Nevertheless, this realization marks a turning point for me. I've understood that these deeply ingrained beliefs and subconscious patterns can be unraveled and transformed. Just as the echo in the valley responds to the sound that originated it, I recognize the importance of aligning my mental object with the rational intelligence of the universe.

Albert Einstein's insight that "imagination is the preview of life's coming attractions" resonates with me. I am equipped with unique skills, gifts, and abilities, each contributing to realizing my envisioned future. The Divine Intelligence has placed this imagination in my heart, and it is my responsibility to follow this mental object, allowing it to guide me toward fulfilling my purpose.

This shift in perspective and a commitment to self-discovery and emotional healing enable me to navigate life with a renewed sense of purpose and abundance. I grant myself the permission and space to feel, allowing emotions to be processed through the mind-body connection for healing and growth. As I break free from the intellectual guidance of external influences, I embark on a journey of self-guidance and empowerment.

The path ahead is illuminated by the awareness that the Universe operates with impartial rationality. Life's challenges are not arbitrary but invitations to evolve and move forward. With this understanding, I enter a future where my thoughts, decisions, and actions shape my desired reality. The echoes of the past may linger, but I am now attuned to the harmonious symphony of my potential, ready to create a life that reflects the boundless wonder and abundance of my true essence.

Reflecting on these thoughts now, I find strength in the words of Joseph Shabalala, the visionary founder of the South African choral group Legendary Ladysmith Black Mambazo, who proclaimed, "The task ahead of us can never be greater than the power within us." This resonates deeply with me – a reminder that our challenges are never insurmountable when we tap into our inner strength.

The journey ahead involves unlearning the habit of looking down on ourselves. It's a process of recognizing the inherent value in our reality and the knowledge we possess. The empowering realization is that I am not alone in this endeavor. I hold the power to bring about change.

Health and Human Relationships

Learning to connect with others is parallel to receiving eye treatment, fostering improved vision free from the disease of misunderstanding. We don't always see people for who they indeed are; instead, our perception is clouded by our distorted viewpoints.

Epidemiologists are gaining deeper insights into the effects of solitude on the body and how different individuals respond to it. Reflecting on the consequences of social isolation, I recall findings from a Wall Street Journal report and a study by the American Cancer Society. These sources revealed a striking thirty-two percent rise in the likelihood of death linked to social isolation. Dr. Douglas DeLong emphasized that both social isolation and loneliness pose significant health risks, surpassing a 25% increase, not only in mental health issues like anxiety and depression but also in various diseases such as heart disease, stroke, diabetes, and dementia. This underscores the urgency of addressing social isolation as a critical public health concern that has been largely overlooked.

This underscores the importance of connection, collaboration, and mutual support to achieve personal and collective growth. Recognizing the transformative power within, I embark on self-discovery and empowerment. It's a quest to shed the layers of limiting beliefs and mental programs that have unconsciously influenced my emotions, steering me away from a life of joy and prosperity.

I recognize social connections' profound influence on well-being and am dedicated to nurturing meaningful relationships. Moving forward, I aim to break away from self-sabotaging behaviors and embrace a mindset that honors personal and collective strength.

True vision goes beyond the present; it is the ability to see the future with clarity, yet much like how someone with macular degeneration experiences a blurred and distorted central vision, we, too, can fall victim to relational blindness. This distortion clouds our perception, making it difficult to see the real issues at hand, instead leading us to focus on the side effects and secondary consequences.

In this state, individuals may believe the world revolves around them, becoming blind to the needs and perspectives of others. Their attention drifts away, captivated by other concerns or material possessions that divide them and those they profess to care about. It's essential to undergo the "treatment" of genuine connection, shedding distorted perspectives and fostering clear vision in our relationships.

By cultivating genuine connections, we embark on a journey that aligns our relational vision with reality, transcending distorted viewpoints. Just as corrective lens aid in restoring clear sight, the act of connecting with others helps us overcome the blur caused by misperceptions.

Seeing people for who they are requires a willingness to understand their unique perspectives and experiences. This clarity in vision allows us to recognize immediate issues, fostering empathy and genuine concern for others. It's a shift from self-centeredness to an awareness of the intricate agglomeration of human emotions and needs.

In contrast, relational blindness, like macular degeneration, limits our ability to acknowledge and address the core issues. When we let material possessions or other distractions take precedence, we risk losing sight of the essential aspects of our relationships.

Therefore, the path to clarity involves acknowledging our distorted vision and seeking to correct it through meaningful connections. As we embrace this journey, we unlock the power to foster authentic, understanding relationships, transcending the illusions that hinder genuine connection.

The absence of interpersonal connections seems to have serious consequences, with social isolation emerging as a strong indicator of mortality risk in our society. Much like having cataracts impairs peripheral vision, the loss of human contact can lead to severe implications. Recognizing the developmental significance of both physical and social

253

interaction has progressed significantly over the past century, highlighting that social isolation can pose risks as substantial as smoking.

Engaging in meaningful connections with others is akin to providing a remedy for our eyes, improving our vision, and contributing to a life free of disease. Often, we may believe that our relationships offer a clear 20/20 vision, but this perception can be illusory. Distorted perspectives can prevent us from truly seeing people for who they are, leading to misunderstandings and overlooking immediate issues. In blurred vision, such as macular degeneration, individuals struggle to see things clearly in the center, focusing on peripheral aspects while missing the core realities.

Individuals with distorted vision may unintentionally make everything about themselves, becoming blind to the needs of others. Material possessions or other distractions may come between them and those they claim to care about. Acknowledging that clear vision involves seeing the immediate issues and recognizing our relationships' central and peripheral aspects is crucial.

The impact of social isolation is profound, suggesting that a lack of interpersonal connections can harm our overall well-being. Drawing a parallel to visual impairments, it's similar to having cataracts that hinder the recognition of peripheral realities. When we lose human contact, the implications can be even more severe. Research over the last century has underscored the developmental importance of physical and social interaction. Surprisingly, studies reveal that social isolation can be as detrimental to one's health as smoking.

Understanding these parallels emphasizes the critical nature of fostering and maintaining genuine connections with others. We must acknowledge the importance of interpersonal relationships and their need to become a cornerstone for a healthier and more fulfilling existence.

Delving into the recesses of my subconscious, I unveil the childhood wonder and abundance that still resides within me. It's a rediscovery of the unbridled curiosity and boundless possibilities that once defined my perspective. However, I acknowledge the influence of acquired belief systems that have quietly sabotaged my well-being.

The realization dawns that the negative impact of past experiences, dating back to childhood, doesn't have to dictate the course of my life. It's time to challenge and transform these reports, rewriting the script of my existence. The past does not bind me; I wield the power to shape my present and future.

Drawing inspiration from the wisdom of Joseph Shabalala, I affirm that the challenges ahead are not more significant than the power within. It's a collective journey, and

I am not alone. Embracing the value of our shared reality and knowledge, I step into the potential for positive change.

Physical Health Combined with Emotional Well-Being

The path through visual impairments has been a profound chapter in my life, a testament to the fragile dance between personal health and the forces beyond our control. I know well the struggles of fading peripheral vision, a truth etched into my being with a diagnosis of glaucoma. My journey began in the tender years of adolescence, marked by a moment that would change everything. Then, a tragic encounter unfolded—a young hunter, trespassing on our land, transformed an ordinary confrontation into an event that would forever shape the landscape of my existence.

In that fateful moment, he aimed his slingshot and released; the stone, finding its cruel mark—my left eye. The strike was swift, the damage profound, leaving a scar etched deep into the fabric of my vision. Though the initial pain seemed fleeting, time wove its own tale; the unseen repercussions revealed themselves slowly, with age as their accomplice. What began as an untreated wound turned to cataracts, and then to glaucoma, each step requiring the precision of a surgeon's touch. This journey has taught me the delicate, relentless connection between the body's fragility and the world's unforgiving nature, reminding me constantly of the vital need for vigilant care.

As I journeyed through the trials of cataracts and glaucoma, each surgical procedure stood as a silent witness to the indomitable resilience of the human spirit. Every incision, every careful touch of the surgeon's hand, became a hymn to endurance and the quiet power of hope. These moments were reminders that proactive care is not just a choice but a lifeline, a promise to honor the body's fragility while daring to fight for the light that remains.

My experience with glaucoma, in particular, heightened my awareness of the vital role interpersonal connections play in overall well-being. The isolation caused by deteriorating eyesight mirrored the broader societal impact of social isolation. Understanding the parallels between my struggles and the broader implications of loneliness on mortality risk deepened my commitment to fostering meaningful connections.

In the face of adversity, I have learned to appreciate the value of human relationships, recognizing that our vision extends beyond the physical realm. The journey through visual impairments has shaped my perspective on health and fueled my determination to bridge the gaps that isolation can create. As I continue to navigate life focusing on holistic well-being, I am reminded that genuine connections are essential for a fulfilling and vibrant existence.

My sojourn through visual impairments instilled a profound appreciation for the intricate connections between physical health, emotional well-being, and the external environment. As I grappled with the challenges of glaucoma and cataracts, the surgical interventions served as poignant reminders of the fragility of the human experience.

The encounter with glaucoma prompted introspection into the impact of isolation on health. The correlation between personal struggles with visual impairments and the broader consequences of social isolation on mortality risk became a focal point of my reflections. This realization fueled my commitment to advocate for the significance of genuine human connections in mitigating the adverse effects of isolation.

Beyond physical health, my journey underscored the interconnectedness of emotional resilience and social bonds. Understanding the complexities of visual impairment has cultivated a deep understanding of the profound impact of empathetic connections on one's overall well-being.

As I continue to navigate the intricate dosser of health and human relationships, my experiences serve as a guiding light. The expedition through visual impairments has shaped my narrative and instilled in me a passion for promoting holistic well-being and fostering meaningful connections in the lives of others.

The profound intersection of my health journey and the broader implications of social connections has become a driving force in my advocacy endeavors. Through my experiences, I have recognized the critical role of empathy, compassion, and community in nurturing physical and emotional health.

The story of my visual impairments extends beyond the medical realm into a broader exploration of resilience, adaptability, and the transformative power of human relationships. As I faced the challenges posed by my conditions, I discovered an innate capacity for inner strength and a heightened sensitivity to the significance of interpersonal bonds.

In sharing my story, I aim to illuminate the intricate interplay between physical health, mental well-being, and the communal fabric that weaves through our lives. The journey through visual impairments is a testament to the resilience of the human spirit and the collective strength found in genuine connections.

Moving forward, my commitment to advocating for the importance of holistic health and meaningful connections remains unwavering. I aspire to inspire others to embrace their challenges as catalysts for growth, fostering a collective consciousness that prioritizes individual and communal well-being.

In the quest to further unravel the layers of my narrative, I find myself diving into the essence of human existence—the intricate dance between vulnerability and strength, the symbiotic relationship between personal struggles and communal support.

The impact of my visual impairments on my life story is not confined to physical health; it extends its tendrils into the emotional and psychological dimensions, revealing the interconnectedness of our internal landscapes with the external jumble of relationships.

The complex terrain of adapting to visual challenges has added to the drapery of my experiences and has become a canvas upon which the brushstrokes of resilience and adaptability emerge. The scars left by the slingshot incident and subsequent health issues serve as a testament to the transformative power of embracing one's vulnerabilities and transmuting them into sources of strength.

My journey unfolds not as a solitary odyssey but as a shared exploration of the human condition. I find solace in knowing that my story, with all its twists and turns, resonates with the universal account of triumph over adversity. Through the lens of my struggles, I strive to foster a deeper understanding of the importance of empathy, compassion, and genuine connection in shaping our collective well-being.

In the chapters yet to be written, I embark on a mission to weave the threads of my experiences into a quilt that transcends individual reports. It is a mosaic that celebrates the beauty of imperfection, the resilience of the human spirit, and the profound impact of interconnected lives. Together, we continue to paint the canvas of existence, each stroke contributing to the masterpiece of shared humanity.

Receiving a glaucoma diagnosis signifies an ongoing drive involving lifelong treatment, frequent medical evaluations, and the potential for gradual vision impairment. Medical professionals emphasize that the harm caused by glaucoma is irreversible. Nonetheless, timely intervention and regular checkups can effectively decelerate or thwart vision loss, mainly when the disease is detected in its initial phases.

Treatment for glaucoma primarily revolves around reducing intraocular pressure in the eyes. Depending on the circumstances, available options may encompass prescription eye drops, oral medications, laser treatment, surgical procedures, or a combination of these therapeutic approaches.

Managing glaucoma is a multidimensional process, aiming not only to address the symptoms but also to maintain overall eye health. Prescription eye drops, a common approach, regulate intraocular pressure and impede the progression of the disease. Complementing this, oral medications may be prescribed to enhance the effectiveness of intraocular pressure control.

In some instances, laser treatment may be recommended. Laser therapy, such as trabeculoplasty or iridotomy, is designed to improve fluid drainage within the eyes, thereby reducing pressure. Surgical interventions, including trabeculectomy or drainage implantation, may be considered when other methods prove insufficient.

Early detection, regular eye checkups, and consistent adherence to prescribed treatments form the cornerstone of effective glaucoma management, which significantly contribute to maintaining visual acuity and minimizing the impact of glaucoma on one's quality of life. Individuals become advocates for their eye health, actively participating in discussions with healthcare providers, seeking second opinions when needed, and staying informed about the latest advancements in glaucoma research.

Moreover, alongside medical interventions, lifestyle modifications can play a vital role in managing glaucoma. A balanced diet rich in antioxidants, regular exercise, and maintaining a healthy weight contribute to overall eye health. Additionally, protecting the eyes from prolonged exposure to sunlight and maintaining optimal blood pressure levels are important factors in preserving vision.

Living with glaucoma can be emotionally challenging, and support from healthcare professionals, family, and friends is essential. Support groups and counseling services can offer valuable assistance in coping with the psychological impact of the condition. Understanding the importance of adhering to prescribed treatments and attending regular eye examinations is crucial for long-term management.

While glaucoma poses challenges, advancements in research and treatment options continue to offer hope for individuals affected by this condition. A proactive approach to eye care, coupled with ongoing medical advancements, empowers individuals to navigate the complexities of glaucoma and lead fulfilling lives.

Individuals find strength in the pursuit of knowledge and awareness. Understanding the disease, its progression, and available treatment options empowers patients to participate actively in their care. Regular communication with healthcare providers ensures that any changes in symptoms or concerns are promptly addressed, fostering a collaborative approach to managing the condition.

As part of the journey with glaucoma, individuals often discover the importance of resilience and a positive mindset. Embracing a proactive attitude toward one's health

263

involves addressing the condition's physical aspects and nurturing mental and emotional well-being. Engaging in activities that bring joy, maintaining social connections, and cultivating a sense of purpose contribute to a holistic approach to health.

The support of family, friends, and the broader community plays a pivotal role in the journey with glaucoma. Awareness campaigns, advocacy, and community education initiatives contribute to a more informed and compassionate society. By fostering understanding and empathy, individuals with glaucoma can navigate their challenges with a supportive network.

In pursuing improved treatments and potential cures, ongoing research initiatives drive progress in the field of ophthalmology. The collaboration between scientists, healthcare professionals, and advocacy groups fuels advancements that may lead to breakthroughs in glaucoma management. Individuals living with glaucoma and their supporters contribute to the collective voice advocating for increased research funding and awareness.

Ultimately, the exploration with glaucoma is one of resilience, education, and community support. By embracing a multidimensional approach to health and remaining hopeful about advancements in research and treatment, individuals affected by glaucoma continue to inspire and uplift others on similar paths.

As individuals embark on the journey with glaucoma, they often find solace and strength in the shared experiences of a community facing similar challenges. Support groups and online forums become valuable resources, allowing individuals to exchange insights, tips, and emotional support. Connecting with others who understand the nuances of living with glaucoma fosters a sense of camaraderie and diminishes feelings of isolation.

Moreover, the campaign involves adapting to lifestyle changes that may enhance overall well-being. Embracing a healthy lifestyle, incorporating regular exercise, and maintaining a balanced diet contribute to general health and potentially managing glaucoma-related factors. Additionally, managing stress and practicing relaxation techniques become integral components of a holistic approach to wellness.

Educational initiatives within communities play a crucial role in dispelling glaucoma myths and misconceptions. Increasing public awareness about the importance of regular eye examinations, especially for those at higher risk, contributes to early detection and intervention. Empowering communities with knowledge encourages proactive eye care and emphasizes the significance of vision health.

As the journey with glaucoma unfolds, the collective efforts of individuals, healthcare professionals, and advocacy groups contribute to a broader narrative of resilience, education, and community support. By fostering a culture of understanding, empathy, and collaboration, society can work towards creating an environment where those affected by glaucoma can thrive and inspire others on similar paths.

Upon receiving a diagnosis of glaucoma, the world takes on a different hue. The once precise edges and peripherals blur, creating a tunnel vision that limits our ability to grasp our surroundings fully. Similarly, this narrowed perspective may hinder our capacity to extend empathy and grace in our interactions with others, causing us to focus on perceived negativity and flaws rather than recognizing the broader context.

Glaucoma, both a physical and metaphorical condition, reminds us that distorted vision can influence how we see the world and perceive the actions and intentions of those around us. This distortion, akin to tunnel vision, prompts us to zoom in on the negatives, potentially leading to judgments and criticisms that may not align with a more comprehensive understanding.

There exists a notion that pain and suffering may be passed down through generations, influencing the well-being of subsequent offspring. Yet, it is crucial to recognize that our responses to the world are shaped not solely by external realities but by our internal perceptions. How we interpret behaviors is learned from our environment, and understanding this dynamic is fundamental to fostering empathy and breaking the cycle of transmitted suffering.

In essence, the distorted vision experienced in glaucoma serves as a metaphor for the subjective nature of perception. By acknowledging the impact of our internal lens on behavior and interactions, we open the door to a more compassionate understanding of ourselves and others. This awareness prompts us to seek clarity, not just in our vision but also in our interpretations, ultimately contributing to a more empathetic and interconnected society.

Moreover, the distorted lens of glaucoma prompts reflection on the broader implications of perception on our behavior and relationships. It serves as a metaphor for the potential transmission of suffering and biases from generation to generation. However, it is essential to distinguish between the external world and our internal interpretations. Objective realities do not solely dictate our responses to the world but are deeply influenced by our learned perceptions.

Recognizing the impact of our internal lens allows us to transcend the limitations of tunnel vision. Instead of fixating on the negatives, we can strive for a more comprehensive understanding of ourselves and others. This shift in perspective opens the door to empathy, compassion, and the breaking of cycles that perpetuate suffering.

In navigating the challenges of glaucoma, individuals often undergo lifelong treatments and regular checkups to mitigate the risk of progressive vision loss. While the physical effects of glaucoma may be irreversible, the metaphorical lessons it imparts about perception and empathy offer an opportunity for personal and societal growth.

In conclusion, the metaphor of glaucoma extends beyond the physical condition, inviting contemplation on how distorted vision influences our interactions and responses. By embracing a more nuanced and empathetic understanding, we can collectively work towards dismantling inherited patterns of suffering and fostering a world where clarity of vision extends beyond the literal to encompass the richness of shared humanity.

Genetic Memory

In a well-known experiment, scientists conducted a study involving a group of mice. They associated the scent of cherry blossoms with a mildly painful electric shock. Over time, when exposed to the aroma of cherry blossoms, the mice exhibited distress, anticipating the impending shock. Astonishingly, when the researchers tested the subsequent generations, even the sixth generation of mice, which had never experienced the electric shock, displayed anxiety in response to the scent of cherry blossoms. This phenomenon was attributed to the concept of "Genetic Memory" of Trauma.

The realization struck me deeply at that moment—I was inhabiting a body not only impacted by my individual stored trauma but also carrying the accumulated trauma of my ancestors. This revelation was entirely new to me, and as I reflected on my life and the experiences of my parents and grandparents, a sense of apprehension engulfed me. What burdens had I been carrying within my body for decades? This scientific revelation aligns with the age-old wisdom in ancient Eastern teachings, emphasizing that the unresolved traumas we carry in our bodies hinder us from manifesting the lives we desire, require, and deserve.

This understanding led me on a profound journey of self-discovery, prompting me to explore the depths of my ancestral history and the imprints it might have left on my being. I delved into the teachings of ancient wisdom traditions, seeking guidance on releasing these inherited burdens and creating a path toward healing.

As I embarked on this transformative voyage, I became increasingly aware of past, present, and future interconnectedness. The echoes of ancestral trauma, though seemingly distant, resonated within me, influencing my perceptions, reactions, and even the choices I made in my life. It became clear that breaking free from this cycle required a conscious effort to confront and release the imprints passed down through generations.

Drawing inspiration from the resilience of those who had come before me, I explored mindfulness, meditation, and self-reflection practices. These tools became instrumental in disentangling the web of generational trauma and forging a new path forward. It was a process of shedding layers, peeling back the emotional residues that had clung to my spirit.

Through this journey, I discovered the profound impact of acknowledging, confronting, and releasing inherited burdens. It wasn't just a personal catharsis but a profound shift in my consciousness that rippled through my relationships, perception of the world, and capacity to manifest a life of fulfillment.

The wisdom of scientific discovery and ancient teachings converged to affirm that our bodies carry more than our individual stories; they are vessels of collective memories. Armed with this knowledge, I found empowerment in the ability to rewrite the narrative, break the chains of generational trauma, and pave the way for a legacy of healing.

In sharing this revelation, I hope to inspire others to embark on their course of self-discovery, explore the layers of their existence, and liberate themselves from the unseen shackles of inherited trauma. In this liberation, we unlock the full potential of our being and create a legacy of resilience, wisdom, and profound transformation for the generations yet to come.

Understand this unequivocally: in our lives, we must assertively instill order into our surroundings. Life does not unfold passively; it demands our active decisions. Do not permit the evolution of a new world without your guidance and wisdom. Transformation does not necessitate magic; within us resides the inherent power for change. We can envision a better reality—a glimpse of future possibilities resides within us. The resurgent vitality within us reignites fading capabilities, urging us forward with the awareness that we live, move, and exist in a higher essence. Yet, many remain unaware of their narrow perspectives.

Embrace the understanding that our inherent power lies not in the external world but within ourselves. We must harness the strength to shape our environment through conscious decisions and deliberate actions to navigate life's twists and turns. Life's unfolding story should not be a spectator sport; instead, actively participate and mold your reality.

The notion of magic is unnecessary, for the transformative force resides within. We possess the

271

extraordinary ability to conceive a brighter, more profound existence. Our inner landscape is a preview, offering glimpses of potential future realities. This inherent resurrection power revitalizes our spirit, motivating us to persist on our quest, anchored in the profound realization that our existence is intricately woven into a higher cosmic tessellation.

Yet, it remains a common oversight for many to be oblivious to their limited perspectives. Recognizing and breaking free from this close-mindedness is the key to unlocking the full potential of our transformative capabilities. As we navigate the intricate dance of life, let us seize the power within and expand our horizons by embracing open-mindedness and continual growth.

In pursuing an enriched life, let us acknowledge that the world around us is not a passive stage where events unfold independently of our influence. Instead, we must be proactive architects of our destiny, contributing purposeful direction and imparting knowledge to the unfolding narrative. Life is not passive but demands our active involvement and conscious shaping.

There is no need to wait for external miracles to transform our world. The extraordinary power to instigate change resides within us. The ability to imagine a better future serves as a wellspring of creative potential. Within each of us lies the preview of the attractions that can shape our destiny.

This reservoir of resilience continually rejuvenates our fading capabilities, urging us to press forward with the awareness that our existence is anchored in a cosmic interconnectedness.

Yet, it is not uncommon for individuals to be oblivious to their narrow perspectives. Overcoming close-mindedness becomes paramount in unlocking the vast reservoirs of transformative potential. As we navigate the intricate dance of life, let us tap into our internal power and cultivate open-mindedness and perpetual growth, ensuring that our journey is marked by continuous expansion and self-discovery.

We often perceive ourselves as the focal points of our universes, inadvertently overlooking the broader, interconnected hanging of existence. Let's take a moment to reimagine this perspective. To influence and win over hearts and minds, it is essential to lead not only with the mind but also with the heart. The collective healing of our society is imperative as we stand at a crossroads where gradual decay threatens to consume us. Inch by inch, day by day, our collective fate hangs in the balance.

As we embark on a journey toward more meaningful connections, let's consciously reflect on the dynamics of our relationships. It is crucial to recognize how our fears, particularly the fear of inadequacy, compel us to construct emotional barriers. These shields, akin to suits of armor,

273

safeguard us from our vulnerabilities. However, I propose a different approach. Instead of clinging to these protective layers, let's courageously embrace our vulnerabilities and, in turn, foster empathy for the vulnerabilities of others. This shift promises a path to authentic connection and mutual understanding.

In this collective endeavor to redefine our relationships, let us be mindful of the transformative power embedded in vulnerability. Our fear of not measuring up often propels us to fortify ourselves against potential emotional wounds. However, as we shed the protective layers and allow ourselves to be authentically vulnerable, we create a space for genuine connections.

Imagine a world where empathy reigns supreme, where understanding flourishes in the fertile soil of shared vulnerabilities. This is the path we tread as we challenge the status quo and dismantle the emotional barriers that hinder genuine connection. It's a migration that demands courage and introspection, a commitment to unraveling the threads of our fears and embracing the beauty found in our authentic selves.

Let us acknowledge the interconnectedness of our narratives within the grand arras of humanity. Each thread contributes to the rich, diverse fabric of existence. In this collective exploration of vulnerability and empathy, we find the potential to heal ourselves and contribute to our world's healing. The power to imagine a better future lies within us, and through shared vulnerability, we can forge connections that transcend the boundaries of fear and isolation.

In our shared pursuit of a more compassionate and connected world, let us confront the tendency to perceive ourselves as solitary entities. Instead, envision a reality where we recognize our place within a broader, interconnected dosser. As we extend our hearts and minds, we bridge the gaps that separate us, fostering an environment where collective healing becomes possible.

Consider the profound impact of empathy. It is through understanding the fears and vulnerabilities that define us that we dismantle the emotional armor we've constructed. This unveiling allows us to embrace the shared human experience and forge bonds that transcend superficial differences.

In this ongoing exploration, let our interactions be guided by the principle that healing is a collective endeavor. Inch by inch, day by day, we contribute to the restoration of our shared humanity. The challenge is not only to recognize our fears but also to extend empathy to others navigating similar emotional landscapes.

The emotional suit of armor, woven from the threads of our insecurities, is shed in favor of an authentic vulnerability that paves the way for genuine connections. Together, we embark on a journey toward a more empathetic and inclusive world where hearts and minds converge to create a garment woven with understanding, acceptance, and love threads.

In building a world rooted in empathy and connection, it's crucial to acknowledge that our collective well-being hinges on acknowledging shared vulnerabilities. As we navigate the intricacies of human relationships, let us dismantle the barriers erected by the fear of inadequacy and other insecurities that often compel us to shield our true selves.

Imagine a reality where the driving force behind our interactions is not self-preservation through emotional defenses but rather a genuine curiosity about the experiences of others. We must lead with intellect and emotions to win hearts and minds, fostering an environment where authenticity flourishes.

As we move forward, it is imperative to reflect on the impact of fear—particularly the fear of not measuring up—in shaping our interactions. By confronting these fears, we open the door to a deeper understanding of ourselves and each other. Embracing vulnerability is a courageous act that binds us in our shared humanity.

In the grand pattern of existence, each thread represents an individual experience, a unique perspective, and a singular odyssey. By weaving these threads together, we create a fabric that celebrates diversity, resilience, and the collective strength that emerges when we embrace our vulnerabilities.

Let us challenge ourselves to cultivate relationships that transcend the superficial, acknowledging that our interconnectedness is the foundation upon which we can collectively heal and thrive. Through this shared commitment to empathy, understanding, and authenticity, we contribute to the ongoing story of a world characterized by compassion and unity.

Keep in mind that choosing empathy is a deliberate and exposed decision. To truly connect with you, I must tap into a part of myself that recognizes those emotions. This brings me back to the architect of the cosmic world, the origin of both the universe and the meticulous arrangement of existence.

I encourage us, as a collective, to instill order in every facet of our lives—both in our actions and words. Socialization has its place, as does conducting business and coming together in celebration. Those considering aligning with you should consider what you are willing to forego; this will foster a sense of order in your life.

Embracing order in our lives involves meticulously arranging our external affairs and carefully considering our internal landscape. As we navigate the intricate dance of relationships and connections, remember that each interaction is an opportunity for empathy.

In fostering empathy, we choose to connect not only with others but also with the profound depths of our own emotions. This conscious decision mirrors the cosmic order, where connections are made with a deep understanding of the underlying currents that shape our experiences.

Let us collectively recognize the significance of order in our lives. Whether engaging in social interactions, conducting business, or joining in celebrations, maintaining a sense of order contributes to the harmonious rhythm of existence. Those who seek to align with us will undoubtedly value our intentional choices and the order we bring into our lives.

Extending this principle to our spheres of influence becomes imperative as we strive for order. We are architects of our destinies, and the blueprints we create should reflect a harmonious design. Just as the universe thrives on order, so too should our cosmos.

Let empathy be the thread that weaves connections in the blueprint of relationships. Choosing vulnerability in our interactions allows us to forge bonds that transcend the superficial. It is a courageous choice to delve into the shared human experience, understanding that empathy bridges the gap between hearts.

Beyond the interpersonal realm, the order we cultivate within ourselves resonates with the cosmic order. Our thoughts, intentions, and actions ripple through the fabric of existence. By aligning our internal compass with the universal principles of order, we contribute to greater harmony beyond our immediate surroundings.

In embracing this holistic approach to order, we enhance our lives and become beacons of inspiration for others. As we continue this journey, let us be mindful architects, consciously shaping a world that reflects the beauty of empathetic connections and the cosmic order that governs our shared existence.

Coursing through your body, these hormones swiftly navigate toward the central nervous system, triggering a cascade of physiological responses. This includes an elevated heart rate, heightened blood pressure, dilated pupils, reduced saliva production, increased perspiration, and momentary oxygen deprivation. Consequently, disorientation ensues, accompanied by the separation of cognitive functioning and verbal skills—where the brain and the tongue seem momentarily disconnected.

This intricate physiological dance responds to the precipice of the fight-or-flight scenario. In that anxious moment, we stand at a crossroads, contemplating whether to stay and engage or succumb to the instinct to flee. Freezing is not a viable option, and running may not be practical, leaving us with the choice to remain and articulate our thoughts. At this critical juncture, our primary objective becomes self-preservation. Internally, we silently implore, "Please don't let me make a mistake," as we strive to navigate the situation unscathed.

Mindful Breathing

Throughout this ordeal, our breath becomes shallow or halted, our heart races like a jackrabbit, and our brain operates on the brink of exhaustion. Mastering the art of proper breathing serves as a potent ally in these moments of duress. It enables us to soothe the autonomic nervous system, providing a crucial tool to navigate the challenges unfolding in the dance between the mind and body.

Developing a mindful approach to breathing is a fundamental skill beyond mere survival. Learning to breathe correctly offers a pathway to harmonizing the autonomic nervous system, fostering a state of equilibrium. It becomes a potent tool for navigating the intricate interplay between mind and body, enhancing our immediate responses to stress and overall well-being.

As we delve into conscious breathing, we discover its transformative effects on our cognitive functions and emotional states. The rhythmic inhalation and exhalation patterns are calming, signaling the body that the perceived threat is subsiding. This, in turn, prompts the nervous system to shift from a heightened state of arousal to a more balanced and composed state.

Proper breathing becomes a bridge between the conscious and subconscious, capable of tempering the physiological responses triggered by stress. By cultivating a mindful connection with our breath, we empower ourselves to navigate the complexities of life with greater resilience, clarity, and a profound sense of self-awareness. The journey toward mastering the art of breath is a transformative odyssey that holds the potential to redefine our relationship with stress and unlock new dimensions of personal growth.

This journey into the art of mindful breathing unravels the layers of our internal landscape, revealing its profound impact on our mental and emotional realms. As we traverse this transformative path, we unearth the ability to manage stress and cultivate a deeper connection with ourselves.

Mindful breathing serves as a compass, guiding us through the intricate terrain of our thoughts and emotions. It

281

becomes a sanctuary, offering solace amid life's storms. Conscious inhalation and exhalation create a space to observe our thoughts without becoming entangled. It becomes a refuge, allowing us to detach from the mind's constant chatter and find stillness within.

In this sanctuary of breath, we encounter the essence of presence. Each inhalation becomes an anchor to the present moment, and with every exhale, we release the burdens of the past and the anxieties of the future. Through this rhythmic dance, we awaken to the power of now, a space where our true essence resides.

Moreover, mindful breathing extends its influence beyond the individual realm, radiating outward to shape the dynamics of our relationships. By fostering a state of inner calm, we enhance our capacity for empathy and understanding. We become attuned to the subtle nuances of communication, recognizing the unspoken language that binds us all.

As we continue to explore the transformative potential of breath, we find ourselves on a profound quest for self-discovery and resilience. The art of mindful breathing emerges not merely as a survival tool but as a gateway to a richer, more vibrant design of life—one where each breath is a brushstroke, painting a masterpiece of presence and profound connection.

One effective technique for proper breathing is Ujjayi breath, a form of diaphragmatic breathing that comes highly recommended. Ujjayi, also known as victorious breath or ocean breath, involves creating a soft, whispering sound during the breath. It is often likened to the gentle wind through trees or the rhythmic waves approaching the shore. This breathing method ensures that oxygen is initially drawn into the lower part of the belly before ascending through the chest.

Taking in increased oxygen plays a crucial role in generating internal body heat. This, in turn, naturally soothes the sympathetic portion of the autonomic nervous system—the aspect responsible for triggering feelings of panic. Ujjayi breath is a powerful tool to enhance relaxation and balance within the body, contributing to calm and well-being.

In addition to the calming effects on the sympathetic nervous system, Ujjayi breath offers a tangible anchor for mindfulness. The audible nature of the breath provides a focal point, drawing your attention away from external stressors and into the present moment. As you synchronize your breath with intention, the rhythmic sound becomes a guide, helping you navigate the currents of your inner experience.

Practicing Ujjayi breath regularly can also enhance lung capacity and respiratory efficiency. The deliberate expansion of the diaphragm facilitates a fuller exchange of oxygen and carbon dioxide, promoting respiratory health. This aspect of the practice contributes to an overall sense of vitality and well-being.

Implementing Ujjayi breath into your routine offers a multifaceted approach to wellness. As you engage in this diaphragmatic breathing, visualize the inhalation filling your lower belly, creating a soothing wave that rises through the chest. The deliberate focus on this rhythmic and intentional breath fosters increased oxygen intake and serves as a meditative practice.

The whispering quality of Ujjayi's breath creates a connection to nature, reminiscent of the wind's gentle rustle or the rhythmic ebb and flow of ocean waves. The symbolic resonance with these natural elements encourages a sense of harmony and interconnectedness, aligning your breath with the broader rhythms of the world.

Furthermore, the internal body heat generated through enhanced oxygen intake contributes to a subtle energizing effect. This can be particularly beneficial in calming the sympathetic nervous system and easing feelings of anxiety or panic that may arise in stressful situations.

As you continue incorporating Ujjayi breath into your daily routine, you'll likely find a profound shift in your overall well-being, experiencing increased relaxation, mental clarity, and a greater sense of inner balance.

Moreover, Ujjayi breath serves as a tool for emotional regulation. You create a foundation for managing emotional responses by cultivating a steady and controlled breath. This breathwork empowers you to navigate challenges with greater resilience, offering a moment of pause to respond thoughtfully rather than impulsively.

Incorporating Ujjayi breath into your daily routine becomes a holistic practice, fostering physical, mental, and emotional harmony. As you embark on this journey, the gentle whisper of your breath becomes a companion, guiding you toward a more centered and mindful existence.

Here's a step-by-step guide for those seeking to maintain composure and focus during presentations, especially when faced with anxiety. Begin by gradually drawing in your belly as you exhale through your nose, allowing your belly muscles to relax upon inhalation while keeping your chest still. Keep the pace unhurried, aiming for each breath to span three to five seconds.

Employ nasal breathing, as it warms and filters the air, inhaling with your belly out and exhaling with your belly in. This rhythmic breathing technique fosters relaxation and clarity of thought, activating the vagus nerve and triggering the relaxation response.

While initially demanding discipline to overturn ingrained habits, this breathing practice proves beneficial beyond presentations, particularly for those prone to anxiety. It's not just a relaxation tool; it's a comprehensive breathing practice applicable 24/7.

Consistently practicing this breathing technique, especially during moments of anxiety, proves invaluable for maintaining composure and focus. The deliberate inhalation, with the belly expanding and the chest remaining still, followed by a slow exhalation, with the belly contracting, establishes a calming rhythm. Nasal breathing further enhances this effect by warming and filtering the air.

Beyond its application in presentations, this breathing practice becomes a constant ally for individuals susceptible to anxiety. Its disciplined approach to changing ingrained habits ensures its reliability as a round-the-clock tool. As you incorporate this technique into your daily routine, activating the vagus nerve stimulates the relaxation response, empowering you to navigate various situations gracefully and clearly.

In addition to its immediate benefits during presentations, this intentional breathing technique holds long-term advantages for your overall well-being. As you commit to this disciplined approach, you cultivate a habit that transcends moments of anxiety. The vagus nerve activation becomes a constant ally, fostering a relaxation response that extends into your daily life.

Breathing with purpose, allowing your belly to rise and fall rhythmically, instills a sense of control and calmness. The slow, deliberate pace of inhalation and exhalation is a reliable anchor, helping you navigate challenges more easily. As you prioritize this intentional breathing, you empower yourself to face various situations with a centered and focused mindset.

8

Upon Returning Home

---

*T*he story of my life unfolds as a mosaic woven with rich experiences, a testament to who I am—a expedition marked by resilience, grit, courage, and an adventurous spirit fused with an infinite well of creativity. Among the many passions that set my soul alight, writing and journaling stand as unwavering pillars of self-expression and profound introspection.

In the quiet embrace of reflection, within the pages of my journal, I find both solace and sanctuary. These sacred spaces cradle my thoughts, dreams, and aspirations, where ink flows like a river, threading together the essence of my deepest emotions and whispered hopes.

Once, in a moment of clarity and determination, I penned, "Upon returning home, I will immerse myself in the activities I cherish." These words encapsulate my unwavering commitment to nurturing my passions and pursuing the activities that bring me joy and fulfillment.

Writing is more than just a hobby—it's a lifeline, a means of capturing moments in time and immortalizing them in words. Whether through prose, poetry, or storytelling, writing allows me to make sense of the world around me and explore the depths of my being.

On the other hand, journaling is a form of self-discovery—a journey inward to uncover the layers of my identity and unravel the mysteries of my soul. It's a practice of mindfulness and reflection, where I confront my fears, celebrate my victories, and chart the course of my dreams.

In the pursuit of my passions, I find purpose and meaning, breathing life into my existence and infusing each day with vibrancy and purpose. Whether lost in the pages of a novel, crafting a poem, or simply jotting down my thoughts, writing is my sanctuary, refuge, and greatest joy.

Delving into the pages of my journal, I am confronted with the poignant tale of transformation in the relationship between my father and me. Each entry serves as a testament to the evolving dynamics that have unfolded over time, meticulously chronicled in the ink-stained pages of my diary.

Emotions of anger, heartbreak, and occasional defeat punctuate my reflections, painting a vivid portrait of my tumultuous journey. The ache of separation from my father is palpable, a lingering presence that weighs heavily on my heart. Despite the physical distance that separates us, the bond between father and child remains unbreakable, tethering me to him even in his absence.

Within the pages of my journal, I grapple with a deep yearning—to return home, to reunite with my family, and, perhaps most significantly, to seek my father's elusive approval. His absence looms vast and heavy, a shadow that stretches across my life, wrapping me in a shroud of doubt and yearning that I strive, often in vain, to untangle.

Tracing the contours of our relationship through my journal pages, I am reminded of the complexities inherent in familial ties—the love, the conflict, the longing for connection. Each entry serves as a poignant reminder of my father's profound impact on my life and the enduring quest for reconciliation and understanding at the heart of our bond.

As I reflect on the contours of my report, I'm struck by the recurring motif of bittersweet echoes that reverberate through the corridors of my past. Each encounter, laden with its complexities, leaves behind a trail of betrayals, disappointments, and disheartening moments that have indelibly shaped the trajectory of my journey.

These bittersweet echoes are poignant reminders of the highs and lows punctuating the human experience. They are the threads that weave through the plan of my life, adding depth and nuance to the narrative of who I am and where I've been.

From moments of profound joy to depths of despair, each encounter leaves its mark, imprinting the lessons of resilience, grit, and introspection upon me. Through hindsight, I understand that proper growth and transformation emerge within the crucible of these bittersweet echoes.

Though tinged with melancholy, these echoes also carry the seeds of hope and renewal. They are a testament to the resilience of the human spirit, a reminder that even in the face of adversity, there is always the possibility of redemption and renewal.

Traversing the twists and turns of my journey, I carry with me the echoes of the past, knowing that they serve as guiding beacons, illuminating the path forward and reminding me of the inherent beauty and complexity of the human experience.

In my adolescent years, driven by a genuine desire to become a literary artist, I began writing my first storybook in high school. Fueled by a passion for storytelling and an insatiable thirst for creative expression, I poured my heart and soul into crafting each chapter, weaving together characters, plotlines, and settings with meticulous care and attention to detail.

Yet, as I delved deeper into the creative process, I felt a longing for guidance and validation from someone whose opinion I held in high regard. That someone was my father, an esteemed educator whose wisdom and knowledge I greatly admired. As a Traditionalist or Silent Generation member, he embodied values of discipline, hard work, and reverence for tradition.

Despite English not being his first language, my father took immense pride in his association with Cambridge, having been both a student and a scholar of Cambridge English. His deep-rooted reverence for the language and its academic pedigree instilled in me a profound respect for the power of words and the art of storytelling.

With trepidation and anticipation, I approached my father and handed him a chapter from my fledgling storybook, hoping for his guidance and approval. As he perused the pages discerningly, I awaited his feedback with bated breath, eager to hear his thoughts on my humble literary endeavor.

Little did I know that this moment would mark a turning point in my creative journey, shaping my relationship with my father and my identity as a burgeoning writer.

To my dismay, as my father swiftly perused the pages of my work, his reaction was not what I had hoped for. He promptly returned the chapter to me without much ado, his expression betraying no hint of approval or encouragement.

In that moment, the anticipation I had harbored for validation, mentorship, and perhaps even a word of praise evaporated.

Instead of constructive feedback or gentle guidance, I received a stark rejection that struck me at the core of my aspirations and left me with disbelief and disappointment. The abrupt dismissal of my creative efforts felt like a blow to the gut, leaving me at a loss for words and struggling to understand what had just transpired.

In the aftermath of this unexpected turn of events, I found myself fighting with a torrent of emotions—pain, frustration, and a profound sense of rejection. The dream of becoming a writer, which had once burned brightly within me, now flickered ominously, threatened by the cold winds of doubt and uncertainty.

I succumbed to the weight of that rejection for a time, retreating into a shell of self-doubt and disillusionment. The passion that had once fueled my creative endeavors now lay dormant, overshadowed by the lingering sting of my father's dismissal.

But even as I mourned the loss of my dream, I couldn't escape the gnawing sense of injustice that accompanied it. The realization that my creative voice had been silenced, not by lack of talent or effort, but by the arbitrary judgment of another, filled me with simmering anger—a righteous indignation at the injustice of it all.

Though initially directed at my father and his perceived lack of understanding, this anger soon found other outlets for expression. It seeped into moments of boredom when the absence of creative pursuits left me restless and unfulfilled. It colored interactions with my peers, heightening my sensitivity to perceived slights and injustices.

In retrospect, the rejection I faced at my father's hands was a pivotal moment in my journey as a writer and person. It forced me to confront the fragility of my dreams, the capriciousness of others' opinions, and the resilience of the human spirit in the face of adversity. And though it would take time—years, even—for me to fully reclaim my passion for writing, the seeds of resilience planted in those dark days would eventually bear fruit, guiding me back to the path of creativity and self-expression.

The rejection I experienced from my father cast a long shadow over my teenage years and persisted into adulthood, weighing heavily on my spirit like a burden too heavy to bear. What was once a vibrant dream of becoming a writer, filled with promise and potential, now seemed distant and unattainable, obscured by the lingering sting of that discouraging encounter.

I grappled with profound disappointment and disillusionment in the days and weeks following my father's dismissal of my creative efforts. The dream that had once fueled my aspirations and filled me with hope now felt like a distant memory, overshadowed by the crushing weight of rejection.

I no longer found solace in writing, once my greatest passion and source of joy. Instead, the mere thought of putting pen to paper filled me with dread and inadequacy. The words that had once flowed freely from my mind now seemed to elude me, lost in a fog of self-doubt and uncertainty.

Trying to comprehend the tumultuous waters of adolescence, the rejection from my father served as a constant reminder of my perceived shortcomings and limitations. It eroded my confidence and sapped my motivation, leaving me adrift in a sea of doubt and insecurity.

With each passing year, the dream of becoming a writer faded further into the background, buried beneath the weight of my father's disapproval and my self-imposed limitations. I resigned to the belief that perhaps writing was not meant for me, that I lacked the talent and ability to succeed in such a competitive field.

Yet, despite my best efforts to suppress it, the spark of creativity within me refused to be extinguished entirely.

Like a flickering flame in the darkness, it persisted in its gentle glow, a beacon of hope amidst the gloom of uncertainty.

In the depths of my despair, I clung to that flickering flame, nurturing it with small acts of defiance and determination. Though the road ahead seemed daunting and uncertain, I refused to let go of the dream that had once filled me with passion and purpose.

Little by little, I began reclaiming my voice, finding solace in writing again. Though the journey was fraught with setbacks and challenges, I persisted, fueled by a newfound resilience and determination.

Looking back on those difficult years, I realize that the rejection from my father, though painful and discouraging at the time, ultimately catalyzed growth and self-discovery. It taught me the importance of resilience in the face of adversity and instilled a newfound appreciation for the power of perseverance.

Despite the setback of my father's rejection, life carried on its course, propelling me through a myriad of experiences, both ordinary and extraordinary, as I journeyed into adulthood. Yet, amidst the ebb and flow of life's currents, the echoes of my thwarted writing ambitions remained ever-present, like a persistent whisper in the back of my mind, a constant reminder of the dashed enthusiasm of my youth.

As I matured and navigated the complexities of adult life, the dream of becoming a writer continued to flicker faintly within me, refusing to be extinguished entirely by the weight of past disappointments. Though I found fulfillment in other pursuits and responsibilities, some still longed to return to the creative endeavors that once brought me joy and satisfaction.

In the quiet moments of solitude, I often reflected on the path not taken, wondering what might have been had I pursued my passion for writing with incredible determination and resilience. The memory of that fateful encounter with my father lingered like a specter, haunting my thoughts and casting a shadow over my aspirations.

Yet, despite the doubt and uncertainty, there remained a glimmer of hope, a whisper of possibility that refused to be silenced. With each passing day, I found myself drawn back to the written word, compelled by an unspoken longing to reclaim the creative spark that had once burned so brightly within me.

Though the journey ahead was fraught with challenges and obstacles, I knew deep down that I could no longer ignore my heart's call. Though battered and bruised, the dream of becoming a writer still beat within me, a testament to the resilience of the human spirit and the power of perseverance.

And so, with renewed determination and steadfast resolve, I embarked on the journey toward realizing my long-held aspirations. Though the road ahead would be uncertain and fraught with setbacks, I knew that with each word written and each story told, I would be one step closer to reclaiming the passion and purpose that had once defined me.

It wasn't until much later, as I embarked on a journey of self-discovery and personal growth, that I found myself drawn back to the smoldering embers of my literary aspirations. With a newfound resilience from years of introspection and inner healing, I decided to resurrect my dream of becoming a writer.

The wounds inflicted by that early rejection from my father, once a source of deep pain and discouragement, now catalyzed transformation. Instead of allowing myself to be defined by the hurt and disappointment of the past, I chose to harness those experiences as a source of strength and determination.

In revisiting my long-dormant passion for writing, I realized that the journey toward realizing my aspirations would not be without its challenges. However, armed with a newfound sense of purpose and an unwavering belief in my abilities, I was ready to face whatever obstacles lay ahead.

The decision to pursue my dreams was not made lightly. It required courage, perseverance, and a willingness to confront the lingering doubts and insecurities that had plagued me for so long. Yet, with each step forward, I felt a renewed vitality and purpose coursing through my veins.

As I began to reacquaint myself with the creative process, I found solace and inspiration in writing. The words flowed from my pen with a newfound clarity and conviction, as if expressing myself on paper was a form of catharsis and renewal.

Though the road ahead was uncertain, I knew I was finally on the right path. Though still tender, the wounds of the past no longer held me back. Instead, they propelled me forward, urging me to embrace the fullness of my potential and reclaim the passion that had always burned brightly within me.

As I embarked on reclaiming my passion for writing, I discovered an unexpected source of solace in the simple act of self-expression. With pen in hand and blank pages before me, I delved deep into the recesses of my soul, excavating the myriads of emotions accumulated over the years.

Each word I carefully penned became a lifeline, a beacon of light illuminating the darkest corners of my mind. Through the art of storytelling, I found a safe space to confront my innermost fears and vulnerabilities, to give voice to the silent echoes of pain and longing that had long lingered within me.

299

With each sentence that flowed from my pen, I felt a weight lifting from my shoulders, as if putting my thoughts into words was a form of catharsis, a release from the burdens of the past. Writing became my sanctuary, a sacred refuge where I could pour out my heart without fear of judgment or reproach.

In the silence of my writing room, I discovered a sense of freedom and empowerment that I had long yearned for. The blank page became my canvas, and with each pen stroke, I painted a portrait of resilience and redemption, turning my pain into poetry and my sorrow into stories.

As I poured myself into my writing, I found that the wounds of the past began to heal slowly but surely. Self-expression became a form of therapy, a pathway towards self-discovery and self-acceptance. Through my words, I learned to embrace the fullness of my humanity, flaws, and all, and to find beauty in the brokenness.

Indeed, in reclaiming my passion for writing, I discovered a means of creative expression and a powerful tool for personal transformation. Each page I filled, I took another step towards healing, wholeness, and embracing the fullness of my being.

Embarking on this literary odyssey, I encountered a myriad of challenges and triumphs that tested my resolve and reshaped my understanding of myself and the world around me. While the journey was ostensibly about becoming a writer, it unfolded into a much deeper exploration of identity, resilience, and the transformative power of self-belief.

With each step forward, I confronted obstacles that threatened to derail my progress. There were moments of doubt and uncertainty when the weight of my past rejections threatened to suffocate my dreams. Yet, in the face of adversity, I discovered an inner strength that I never knew existed—a resilience born out of sheer determination and unwavering faith in myself.

The journey was not without its moments of triumph, however. Along the way, I experienced breakthroughs that filled me with pride and accomplishment. Whether it was finally completing that elusive first draft or receiving positive feedback from readers, each small victory reminded me of the power of perseverance and the potential within me.

Yet, beyond the tangible markers of success, the true essence of the journey lay in the profound transformation that occurred within me. Through writing, I unearthed hidden depths of my identity, tapping into emotions and experiences that had long laid dormant within me. With each word I penned, I discovered new facets of myself, shedding light on the complexities of my being and the richness of my lived experiences.

At its core, my literary odyssey became a journey of self-discovery—a voyage into the depths of my soul in search of truth, meaning, and purpose. It was a testament to the power of belief in oneself and the capacity for growth and change within each of us.

Reflecting on my path, I am grateful for the lessons learned, the challenges overcome, and the person I have become. My writing journey may have begun as a quest for creative fulfillment. Still, it ultimately became a journey of self-realization—a testament to our boundless potential, waiting to be unleashed.

That moment of rejection, though initially devastating, ultimately became the catalyst for profound personal growth and self-discovery. The turning point forced me to confront my deepest fears and insecurities. Still, it also ignited a fire within me—a fierce determination to pursue my dreams with unwavering resolve.

In the aftermath of that rejection, I found myself at a crossroads, with feelings of doubt and uncertainty about my abilities as a writer. Yet, as I sifted through the ashes of my shattered dreams, I discovered a hidden reservoir of strength and resilience deep within myself. It was a resilience born out of adversity—a refusal to be defined by failure and a steadfast belief in my potential.

With each passing day, I became more determined than ever to reclaim my passion for writing and forge ahead on my journey despite the obstacles in my path. The dream that had once seemed so out of reach now burned brightly within me, fueling my determination to succeed against all odds.

Charting a new course forward, I was guided by a newfound sense of purpose and clarity of vision. I refused to let setbacks or naysayers deter me from my path, knowing deep down that my words had the power to inspire, uplift, and transform lives.

In the following years, I poured my heart and soul into my writing, honing my craft with relentless dedication and unwavering perseverance. Slowly but surely, my efforts began to bear fruit. I found my voice as a writer, and with each word I penned, I felt a sense of liberation and empowerment unlike anything I had ever experienced.

Looking back on my journey, I am grateful for the adversity I faced and the lessons it taught me. Through the crucible of rejection and disappointment, I discovered the depth of my resilience and the boundless potential within me.

Today, as I stand on the brink of a new chapter in my life, I do so with a renewed sense of purpose and a steadfast belief in the power of my dreams. The dream that once lay buried beneath the weight of rejection has now blossomed into a beacon of hope and inspiration, guiding me forward into a future where my words will find their rightful place in the world.

Reflecting on my journey, I've reached a profound realization: my purpose extends far beyond the pain and challenges I've faced. Despite the setbacks and disappointments, my ambition remains steadfast and resilient, unwavering in the face of adversity.

I've emerged more robust and determined with each obstacle I've encountered. The setbacks have only fueled my determination to press forward, propelled by the belief that brighter days lie ahead.

Amid the darkness, I've glimpsed hope on the horizon—a beacon guiding me toward a future filled with promise and possibility. It's a future untainted by the shadows of the past, where my dreams can flourish, and my potential can be fully realized.

With this newfound clarity and resolve, I am ready to embark on the next chapter of my journey. Armed with resilience and fueled by hope, I step forward into the unknown, prepared to embrace whatever challenges and opportunities lie ahead, for I know that with each step I take, I am one step closer to fulfilling my purpose and realizing my dreams.

Meditation and Journaling

In my pursuit of well-being, I've discovered solace in two powerful practices: meditation and journaling. These rituals serve as anchors in the ebb and flow of life, offering me a sanctuary to explore the depths of my mind and heart.

Through meditation, I delve into the silence within, seeking clarity and peace amidst the chaos of daily life. With each breath, I quiet the noise of the external world and turn inward, finding refuge in the stillness of my being. In these moments of introspection, I connect with a more profound sense of self and tap into a wellspring of inner wisdom.

On the other hand, journaling allows me to externalize my internal landscape, transforming fleeting thoughts and emotions into tangible words on the page. With pen in hand, I embark on a journey of self-discovery, chronicling the intricacies of my inner world with honesty and authenticity. Through writing, I gain insight into my hopes, fears, dreams, and desires, weaving together the threads of my lived experience into a cohesive narrative.

In my journal, I capture the essence of my existence— the highs and lows, triumphs and tribulations, and moments of joy and sorrow shaping my journey. It serves as a repository for my reflections, a mirror that reflects the purpose of my life in all its complexity.

This report extends beyond the confines of my sphere to encompass the various facets of my existence. It spans the realms of home, where I find comfort and belonging in the embrace of family; school, where I cultivate knowledge and skills that shape my future; and the vibrant layout of my social activities, where I forge connections and create lasting memories with friends and loved ones.

Through meditation and journaling, I cultivate a deeper understanding of myself and my place in the world. These practices nurture my well-being and empower me to navigate challenges with grace and resilience. As I continue my journey, I am grateful for their solace and wisdom, guiding me toward a life of greater meaning, purpose, and fulfillment.

I've reached a point where my faith in my abilities eclipses any challenges that lie ahead. This newfound confidence serves as a compass, directing the course of my journey and illuminating the path toward my aspirations and potential. It encourages me to dream—to envision the life I desire and the accomplishments I aim to achieve.

Contemplating my career ambitions and personal goals, I allow myself to indulge in the act of dreaming. I let my imagination run wild, envisioning the heights I can reach and the impact I can make in my chosen field. I am fueled by purpose and determination with each trance, eager to turn my dreams into reality.

Part of this vision involves considering the financial aspect of my future. I set ambitious targets for the earnings I aim to accumulate in my bank account, recognizing that economic stability is a critical component of the life I envision for myself. These goals are tangible markers of success, driving me to work diligently and strategically toward their attainment.

Yet, amidst these lofty aspirations, I remain grounded in the present moment, mindful of the steps I must take to turn my dreams into tangible achievements. I approach each day with intention and focus, channeling my energy toward the pursuits that align with my long-term vision.

In embracing the power of dreaming, I embrace the full scope of my potential and the boundless possibilities that await me. With unwavering determination and a clear vision for the future, I confidently embark on this journey, knowing that my dreams hold the key to unlocking a life of fulfillment and purpose.

In my quest for self-discovery, I've stumbled upon a profound realization: my personal growth and development are solely my responsibility. No external force or individual can foster my evolution; it's an internal journey I must undertake alone. Understanding this truth has been pivotal in my healing process.

I've come to see myself as a vessel of energy, capable of immense transformation and growth. The power to propel my development resides within me, waiting to be harnessed and directed towards positive change. This recognition has shifted my perspective, empowering me to take ownership of my journey and actively engage in self-improvement.

Embracing this mindset has been liberating. Instead of waiting for external validation or support, I've taken the reins of my destiny, charting a course toward personal fulfillment and self-realization. I've learned to trust in my innate abilities and intuition, knowing that they are the driving forces behind my growth.

This journey of self-discovery has not been without its challenges. There have been moments of doubt, fear, and uncertainty. But with each obstacle, I've emerged more robust and resilient, fortified by the knowledge that I am the architect of my destiny.

As I continue this path of self-discovery, I do so with a sense of empowerment and purpose. I am no longer a passive bystander in my own life but an active participant, shaping my reality and embracing the infinite possibilities that lie ahead.

Realizing proper development is a self-driven endeavor sparked a profound shift within me. It became clear that waiting for external forces to catalyze change was futile;

instead, the impetus for growth must come from within. This understanding fundamentally altered my approach to personal development, igniting a newfound sense of agency and determination.

With this insight, I embraced the idea that I am the architect of my destiny. I no longer waited for circumstances to change or for others to provide guidance; instead, I took ownership of my journey and committed myself wholeheartedly to self-improvement. This shift in perspective empowered me to seek growth opportunities proactively and challenge myself to reach new heights.

Gone were the days of passively waiting for life to happen to me. Instead, I became active in my evolution, driven by a relentless pursuit of personal excellence. Every decision and action I took was guided by the belief that I held the power to shape my destiny.

This newfound commitment to personal growth has been both liberating and empowering. It has allowed me to break free from self-imposed limitations and tap into a reservoir of untapped potential within myself. Each step forward reminds me of the transformative power within, fueling my determination to continue growing, evolving, and becoming the best version of myself.

The intricacies of my past have caused me to see that my journey is a complex mosaic of experiences—some tinged with pain, while others gleam with joy. Each fragment adds depth and texture to the dynamic fusion of my life, imparting valuable lessons and insights along the way. Through the act of documenting my story, I not only revisit those moments but also weave together a narrative that transcends the confines of my past.

In the affirmative, I find the raw emotions and challenges that have shaped me into the person I am today. The moments of struggle have tested my resilience and forged my strength, while the moments of joy have filled my heart with gratitude and hope. Together, these experiences form a kaleidoscope of memories, each contributing to my existence's intricate pattern.

I am reminded of the power of storytelling to illuminate the human experience. Through my words, I seek to capture the essence of who I am and the journey that has brought me to this moment. In doing so, I embrace the transformative potential of storytelling to transcend the limitations of time and space, allowing me to connect with others on a deeper level and inspire reflection and introspection.

Ultimately, my narrative is a testament to the resilience of the human spirit and the endless possibilities that arise from embracing the full spectrum of life's experiences. As I continue to write my story, I do so with an open heart and a steadfast determination to uncover the beauty and meaning woven into every chapter.

The journey of self-care, anchored by meditation and journaling, has become my steadfast companion, illuminating the path through the intricate maze of memories and emotions. Once trapped by the weight of rejection and dismissal, I am buoyed by the promise of a brighter tomorrow. What were once wounds of rejection and pain have transformed into markers of resilience and grit, guiding me forward with newfound strength and determination.

In the stillness of meditation, I find sanctuary—a space where I can retreat from the world's noise and delve into the depths of my innermost thoughts and feelings. With each breath, I am reminded of my inherent worth and my boundless potential. In this sacred silence, I reclaim my power and rediscover the strength to confront life's challenges with grace and courage.

Likewise, journaling has become a sacred ritual—unraveling the tangled threads of my past and weaving them into a composite of self-understanding and growth. With pen in hand, I pour my thoughts and emotions onto the blank pages, allowing them to take shape and form. Through this process, I gain clarity and perspective, untangling the knots of confusion and finding solace in self-expression.

As I immerse myself in self-care, I am reminded that healing is not a linear journey but a deeply personal and transformative process. Each moment of introspection and self-reflection brings me closer to wholeness as I learn to embrace the light and shadow within myself. With each step forward, I am guided by the gentle whisper of my inner compass, leading me toward a future filled with hope, resilience, and boundless possibility.

In my quest to construct a narrative that encapsulates the essence of my being, I am driven to go beyond mere recounting of professional achievements and personal milestones. Instead, I am drawn to the intricacies of my social interactions and the relationships that color the landscape of my life, for it is within these connections—with family, friends, mentors, and even strangers—that the fabric of my existence unfolds.

Each interaction, whether fleeting or enduring, leaves an indelible mark on the framework of my story. From the laughter shared with friends over cups of coffee to the heartfelt conversations with loved ones beneath the glow of starlit skies, these moments shape the contours of my identity. They offer glimpses into the depths of my soul, revealing layers of vulnerability, resilience, and compassion.

Moreover, my social connections serve as mirrors, reflecting aspects of myself that I may not always recognize.

Through the eyes of those who know me best, I can gain insights into my strengths, weaknesses, and areas for growth. Their presence in my life is a source of support, encouragement, and accountability, guiding me through self-discovery and personal evolution.

But beyond the familiar faces of family and friends lie encounters with strangers—brief encounters that hold the potential to spark profound moments of connection and understanding. In the shared smiles exchanged with a passerby on the street or the meaningful conversations with fellow travelers on a journey, I find glimpses of humanity's collective spirit. These chance encounters remind me of all beings' interconnectedness and the beauty of embracing the diversity of human experience.

In weaving together the threads of my social connections, I aim to create a story that celebrates the richness of human relationships and their profound impact on shaping who I am. Through these connections—with loved ones and strangers alike—I can glimpse the vast montage of life and find my place within its intricate patterns.

Reflecting on my path thus far, I've arrived at a profound realization: my purpose, undeterred by the obstacles in my path, remains a steadfast beacon of hope guiding me forward. Despite the challenges that may arise, I am filled with a sense of empowerment, recognizing that the journey ahead is an expansive canvas awaiting the vibrant strokes of my ambition and determination.

With each step I take, I am reminded of my role as the architect of my destiny. I possess the creative power to envision my desired life—a life filled with fulfillment, growth, and meaning. This recognition fills me with a profound sense of agency, inspiring me to seize each opportunity and overcome every obstacle between me and my dreams.

In this journey of self-discovery and personal development, I am fueled by a deep sense of purpose and a relentless drive to carve out my path in the world. I believe no challenge is impossible, and no goal is too lofty. With courage as my compass and determination as my fuel, I navigate the complexities of life with clarity of vision and unwavering conviction.

Standing bordering on the future, I am filled with anticipation and excitement for the adventures. I embrace the unknown with open arms, knowing that within its boundless possibilities lies the opportunity to realize my fullest potential and to leave an indelible mark on the world.

With each passing day, I am reminded of the transformative power that resides within me—the power to shape my destiny, pursue my passions with unwavering dedication, and manifest my dreams into reality. And so, with a heart full of hope and a spirit brimming with possibility, I embark on the journey ahead, ready to embrace all the future holds.

The Journey of Isolation
Through Self-Discovery and Growth

The profound awakening I've experienced is the cornerstone of my healing journey. It signifies a definitive break from the shadows of doubt and resentment that once clouded my path, ushering in a new era characterized by self-love, resilience, and an unshakable belief in my boundless potential. No longer do I allow myself to be defined by the echoes of rejection; instead, my story has evolved into a dynamic account shaped by the authenticity of my experiences and the indomitable strength of my spirit.

With this newfound clarity and sense of purpose, I embrace each day as an opportunity for growth and self-discovery. I no longer dwell on past disappointments or allow them to dictate my future. Instead, I channel my energy into cultivating a deep self-acceptance and empowerment.

I've learned to nurture a positive relationship with myself through introspection and self-care practices like meditation and journaling, loving myself, and self-forgiveness. I've come to recognize my worth and appreciate the unique qualities that make me who I am. This journey of self-discovery has been transformative, leading me to embrace my flaws and imperfections as integral parts of my identity.

I can now embrace life's challenges, and I do so with a newfound sense of resilience and inner strength. I understand that setbacks are simply opportunities for growth and learning, and I face them with courage and determination. My journey is no longer defined by the obstacles I encounter but by my unwavering commitment to overcome them.

In embracing my authenticity and owning my story, I have found liberation. The expectations or judgments of others no longer bind me. Instead, I stand tall in my truth, confident that my potential knows no bounds. With each step forward, I move closer to realizing my fullest potential and living a life of purpose and fulfillment.

In my journey of self-discovery and healing, I consciously decided to embrace a state of loving presence and compassion. This marked a significant shift from the protective barrier I had erected around myself, allowing vulnerability to seep in. As I opened up to this vulnerability, I noticed subtle healing frequencies emanating from the universe around me.

At first, I hesitated, unsure how to interpret these energies that seemed to be reaching out to me. But as I tuned into them more deeply, I realized they were essential for my wholeness. Each frequency, with its unique vibration, held the potential to heal and restore balance within me.

With this realization, I embraced these energies wholeheartedly, allowing them to permeate every aspect of my being. As they integrated within me, I felt a profound sense of completeness. It was as if I had been reunited with pieces of myself that had long been forgotten or ignored.

This integration process became a powerful conduit for healing, not just for myself but for those around me. As I emanated this newfound vibration of healing, I noticed a subtle shift in the energy of my interactions with others. A deep sense of connection and empathy flowed effortlessly between us, fostering an environment of mutual support and understanding.

Through this journey, I learned that true healing begins from within. By embracing our vulnerabilities and opening ourselves up to the healing energies surrounding us, we can unlock the full potential of our inner selves and radiate healing energy out into the world. It's a journey of self-discovery, transformation, and liberation.

During my journey, I faced the difficult task of parting ways with old friends and creating distance from family members who didn't fully support or understand my true self. While this may have seemed daunting to some, for me, it was a necessary step on the path to aligning myself with the energy of the Universe.

Similarly, I disengaged from jobs that no longer served my growth or aligned with my true passions. It wasn't easy to let go of familiar routines and sources of stability, but I knew deep down that it was essential for my evolution and self-improvement.

Navigating through the challenges of letting go of old relationships and stepping into the unknown was a pivotal moment in my journey. It required courage and determination to move beyond the comfortable confines of the familiar and embrace the uncertainty of change.

But with each step I took away from the past, I felt myself growing more robust and aligned with my true purpose. The journey of isolation, though at times lonely and challenging, became a necessary chapter in my quest for self-discovery and enhancement.

Through this process, I learned the importance of letting go of anything that no longer served my highest good, even if it meant walking away from people and situations that were once familiar. It was a journey of liberation, allowing me to shed old layers of conditioning and embrace the fullness of my authentic self.

During self-isolation and deep introspection, I found myself diving into the depths of my being. The solitude offered me a sanctuary where I could confront the lingering echoes of past hurts and disappointments, allowing me to embark on a profound healing journey.

In this sacred space of solitude, I realized that healing is not a straightforward path. It's not about simply moving from point A to point B; instead, it's a dynamic and intricate dance with various energies, both light and shadow, that reside within me.

As I delved deeper into my inner landscape, I encountered aspects of myself that I had long ignored or suppressed. There were moments of joy and illumination where I felt the warm embrace of self-love and acceptance wash over me. Yet, there were also moments of darkness and discomfort, where I grappled with the pain and trauma that had been buried deep within.

But I understood that the light and the shadow are integral parts of the healing journey. In embracing and integrating these contrasting energies, true transformation occurs—each moment of discomfort and pain catalyzed growth, propelling me forward on my path toward wholeness.

Through this process of self-discovery and healing, I began to cultivate a more profound sense of compassion and understanding for myself. I learned to hold space for all aspects of my being, recognizing that each experience, whether joyful or painful, was an opportunity for growth and evolution.

Continuing the navigation of this healing journey, I do so with an open heart and a willingness to embrace the full spectrum of my human experience. I am grateful for the solitude that allowed me to embark on this transformative journey, and I look forward to the continued growth and expansion that lies ahead.

9

The Shadows in My Rain

As I journeyed through the intricate terrain of my inner world, I unearthed the transformative power of forgiveness. It wasn't merely about extending forgiveness to others for their transgressions, although that was certainly part of it. More profoundly, it was about extending forgiveness to myself.

For too long, I had carried the heavy burden of guilt and shame, allowing these emotions to weigh me down and impede my progress. But as I delved deeper into the process of self-exploration and healing, I began to realize that holding onto resentment and self-blame served no purpose other than to keep me trapped in the past.

With each act of self-forgiveness, I felt the weight of that burden gradually lift. It was a gradual process requiring patience, compassion, and understanding. But as I released myself from the shackles of self-condemnation, I experienced a newfound sense of liberation and lightness.

This process of forgiveness was instrumental in reshaping my relationship with my past. Instead of viewing it as a source of pain and regret, I began to see it as a series of valuable lessons and opportunities for growth. Each experience, no matter how challenging or painful, had played a crucial role in shaping me into the person I was becoming.

By embracing forgiveness, I opened myself up to a future unencumbered by the burdens of the past. I learned to navigate life with greater ease and grace, knowing that my mistakes or shortcomings no longer defined me. Instead, I was empowered to move forward with courage and resilience, embracing the infinite possibilities ahead.

Delving deeper into my journey of self-discovery and healing, I came to a profound realization: true self-love encompasses embracing our strengths and brilliance and accepting our flaws and imperfections. It's about recognizing that we are multifaceted beings, each with our unique blend of light and shadow.

As this understanding took root, I felt the healing frequencies reverberating. It was as though a harmonious symphony was playing within me, weaving together all the disparate parts of myself into a cohesive whole. I found a profound sense of peace and acceptance in this internal alignment.

This newfound sense of self-love began to radiate outward, transforming my external reality. I could approach relationships and challenges with a renewed perspective, unburdened by resentment or self-doubt. Instead of seeing my flaws as liabilities, I began to view them as opportunities for growth and self-improvement.

Each day, I felt myself becoming more grounded in my authentic self, more confident in my abilities, and more open to life's possibilities. It was a journey of profound transformation that taught me the true meaning of self-love and acceptance. As I continued to embrace all aspects of myself, both light and shadow, I discovered a newfound sense of freedom and wholeness that I had never known before.

In the assortment of my life, woven with threads of joy, pain, setbacks, and triumphs, I began to see the profound interconnectedness of healing and personal growth. Each experience, whether a setback that left me feeling defeated or a moment of pure joy that lifted my spirits, played a crucial role in shaping the person I was becoming.

Through this journey of self-discovery and healing, I came to understand that every challenge I faced held within me an opportunity for growth and transformation. Instead of viewing setbacks as roadblocks, I began to see them as stepping-stones on the path to becoming the best version of myself.

I also discovered that by embracing the full spectrum of my experiences—the good, the bad, and the in-between—I became a conduit for healing for myself and those around me. My journey of self-love and acceptance radiated outward, touching the lives of those I encountered.

Whether offering a listening ear to a friend in need, extending a helping hand to a stranger, or simply showing compassion to myself and others, I found that healing was not a solitary journey but a collective experience. As I continued to navigate the ups and downs of life with grace and resilience, I became a beacon of hope and inspiration for those around me, illuminating the path toward healing and personal growth for all who crossed my path.

Approaching the future, I am greeted by a vision of boundless possibilities stretching out before me. Once shrouded in uncertainty and doubt, the path ahead now glimmers with the radiant light of hope and opportunity. The journey of healing and self-discovery I once embarked upon alone has evolved into a collective experience—a symphony of growth and understanding shared with those around me.

No longer tethered to the shadows of my past or constrained by the expectations of others, I have stepped into my power as a co-creator of my reality. With each step forward, I am actively shaping a chronology that reflects the essence of who I truly am—authentic, resilient, and imbued with boundless potential.

Gone are the days of self-doubt and hesitation; I embrace a newfound sense of clarity and purpose in their place. I move forward confidently, guided by the inner knowing that I possess the strength and wisdom to navigate challenges.

Gazing at the horizon, I am filled with awe and wonder at the endless possibilities. The journey may be filled with twists and turns, but I face the future with an open heart and a steadfast determination to live an authentic life of authenticity, love, and limitless growth.

I also found myself drawn to wholeness and genuine healing on this journey. It was a quest born out of a recognition that various aspects of my life—physical, mental, financial, and relational—needed attention and restoration. Like so many others, I felt the pull towards healing, driven by a deep-seated desire to mend what felt broken.

The concept of healing resonated deeply with me, tapping into a narrative that seemed ingrained in the human experience—the belief that there are parts of ourselves or aspects of our lives that require fixing or improvement. It's a sentiment that permeates our culture and collective consciousness, fueling our pursuit of growth and transformation.

For me, this journey was not just about addressing surface-level wounds or temporary fixes; it was about delving into the depths of my being to uncover the root causes of my pain and discontent. It required a willingness to confront my fears, insecurities, and past traumas with courage and compassion.

In embracing this journey, I acknowledged that healing was not merely about patching superficial wounds or masking underlying issues. It was about embracing the process of self-discovery and growth, reclaiming lost parts of myself, and rediscovering my innate sense of wholeness and well-being.

Further into this exploration of healing, I realized that true transformation was not about erasing the scars of the past but integrating them into the fabric of my being. It was about accepting myself fully, flaws and all, and embracing the journey towards becoming the best version of myself.

In hindsight, I now see that the quest for healing is not just a destination but a continuous journey of self-discovery, growth, and self-compassion. As I continue to walk this path, I am filled with a sense of hope and possibility, knowing that each step forward brings me closer to the wholeness and authenticity I seek.

A profound realization also dawned upon me—a revelation that shifted the foundation of my understanding. I came to understand that I was already whole, complete in my essence, despite the turmoil and anxiety that often plagued me.

For so long, I had believed that my struggles and insecurities were evidence of a fundamental lack within myself, a void that needed to be filled. I searched tirelessly for external validation and solutions to fill this perceived emptiness, hoping they would bring me the wholeness I craved.

However, as I journeyed further into the depths of my being, I began to see things differently. I realized that the feelings of incompleteness and unrest did not indicate a deficiency within me but rather energies stored within, waiting to be acknowledged and released.

In the past, I had attempted to suppress these discomforting energies, burying them deep within the recesses of my subconscious to maintain a façade of strength and composure. But this suppression only perpetuated their existence, preventing their dissolution or integration into my being.

True wholeness, I discovered, could not be achieved through avoidance or denial. It required a willingness to confront the shadows lurking within, shine a light on the darkest corners of my psyche, and embrace all aspects of myself, even those I had long deemed unworthy or undesirable.

With this newfound understanding, I began approaching my healing journey with acceptance and compassion. I no longer sought to fix or change myself but to honor and integrate every part of myself—the light, shadow, joy, and pain.

In embracing my wholeness, I found liberation. I no longer needed to seek external validation or approval to feel complete. I was enough, just as I was, and that realization brought me a profound sense of peace and freedom.

Journeying further along the path of self-discovery and healing, I came to a significant realization—I needed to undergo a more profound transformation. It was time to shed the layers of conditioning and societal expectations that had clouded my true essence for so long and to embrace the authentic core of who I am.

With this awareness, I consciously chose to descend into the depths of my Soulful Self to connect with the raw, unfiltered essence of my being. It was a pivotal moment—a turning point where I surrendered to the process of inner rebirth, allowing myself to be transformed from the inside out.

Amid this internal wobble, I found a unique opportunity for growth and renewal. Rather than resisting the uncertainty and discomfort, I leaned into it, recognizing that it was precisely in these moments of vulnerability that I was most open to change.

During these times of upheaval and confusion, I discovered a heightened sense of receptivity within myself— a willingness to let go of old patterns and beliefs and embrace the possibility of something new emerging.

In the past, I had often clung to a sense of certainty and control, believing that I had a clear understanding of my path and purpose. But now, I understand that true transformation requires a willingness to let go of the familiar and step into the unknown.

In surrendering to the process of rebirth, I felt a sense of liberation wash over me. I was no longer bound by the limitations of my past or the expectations of others. Instead, I was free to explore the vast expanse of my potential to create a life aligned with my deepest desires and aspirations.

I discovered a newfound purpose and vitality in embracing my True Essence. I was no longer simply going through the motions of life; I was fully present and engaged in each moment, allowing myself to be guided by the wisdom of my Soulful Self.

Continuing to journey deeper into the depths of my being, I knew that the path ahead was filled with infinite possibilities. With each step I took, I was stepping into a brighter, more expansive version of myself—a version that was fully aligned with the truth of who I am.

Delving deeper into exploring my True Essence, I unearthed a rich and fertile ground for genuine healing and transformation. In the depths of my authentic self, I discovered the key to unlocking my true potential and experiencing a profound sense of fulfillment.

The process of integration was not always easy. It required me to confront and release old wounds, fears, and limiting beliefs that had held me back for far too long. But with each layer I peeled away, I felt myself becoming lighter, more accessible, and more aligned with my true purpose.

I began to see my perceived flaws not as weaknesses but as unique aspects of my being that added depth and richness to my experience. Instead of trying to hide or suppress these parts of myself, I learned to embrace them with love and compassion, recognizing that they were integral to my journey toward wholeness.

In embracing all aspects of my being—the light and the dark, the joy and the sorrow—I found a newfound sense of freedom and authenticity. I no longer needed to conform to societal expectations or hide behind a mask of perfection. Instead, I embraced my imperfections and celebrated my unique gifts and talents.

Each step I took on this journey toward wholeness made me more grounded, centered, and fully aligned with my true essence. As I continued integrating all aspects of my being, I knew I was moving closer to experiencing a life of profound joy, fulfillment, and purpose.

In the sanctuary of self-discovery and acceptance, I embarked on a profound journey to embrace every facet of my existence—the brilliance of light and the depth of shadow, the peaks of triumph, and the valleys of challenge. This process resembled an inner excavation, a courageous dive into the depths of my subconscious to unravel and comprehend the energies that had long lain dormant within me.

With each step inward, I confronted aspects of myself that had been buried beneath layers of conditioning and societal expectations. It was a journey of unveiling, peeling back the layers of false identities and masks to reveal the raw, unfiltered truth of who I truly am.

There were moments of discomfort and resistance as I unearthed memories, beliefs, and emotions that had been suppressed or ignored. Yet, amid this excavation, I found liberation and empowerment. I discovered I could reclaim my power and authenticity by facing my shadows and embracing my vulnerabilities.

Through introspection and reflection, I began understanding the origins of my fears, insecurities, and self-

331

limiting beliefs. I saw how past experiences and traumas had shaped my perception of myself and the world around me. In acknowledging these truths, I granted myself the permission to heal and grow.

Navigating the labyrinth of my subconscious, I encountered aspects of myself that I had long neglected or rejected—the parts that I deemed unworthy or undesirable. Yet, I extended compassion and acceptance with each encounter, recognizing that these aspects were integral to my wholeness.

The journey of inner excavation was not linear or predictable. There were moments of profound revelation and moments of deep resistance. Yet, through it all, I remained committed to the process, trusting that each excavation led me closer to the core of my being.

Emerging from my subconscious, I did so with a newfound sense of clarity, purpose, and self-love. I understood that the journey of inner excavation is ongoing, but with each step forward, I move closer to embodying my most authentic self.

I had encountered a myriad of energies lurking within the depths of my being. I allowed these energies to surface with courage and vulnerability, inviting them into the light of my awareness without judgment or resistance. This was a pivotal moment in my quest for wholeness—a moment where

I sat uncomfortably and listened intently to my inner self's messages.

In the past, I had often dismissed or overridden feelings of frustration, anxiety, or sadness, fearing their intensity or unsure of how to process them. However, I embraced a different approach in this sacred space of self-exploration. Instead of pushing these emotions aside, I welcomed them with open arms, recognizing them as valuable messengers from my subconscious.

With a compassionate curiosity, I delved deeper into the root causes of these emotions, seeking to understand the underlying beliefs, traumas, or patterns that had given rise to them. I allowed myself to unravel the layers of conditioning and societal expectations that had long obscured my true essence, trusting that beneath the surface lies a wellspring of wisdom and insight.

Sitting with these uncomfortable emotions, I discovered that they held profound lessons and opportunities for growth. No matter how painful or challenging, each feeling served as a guidepost on my journey toward wholeness, pointing me toward areas of my life that needed attention and healing.

Rather than viewing discomfort as something to be avoided or suppressed, I began to see it as a necessary catalyst for transformation. By embracing these emotions with love

333

and acceptance, I created space for healing and growth to unfold organically.

I found solace and liberation in this sacred space of self-compassion and introspection. The frustration and anxiety that once felt overwhelming now became signposts on my path, guiding me toward a deeper understanding of myself and my journey.

When navigating the complexities of my inner landscape, I cultivated a sense of trust in the process of self-discovery. I understood that true healing comes from facing our shadows with courage and compassion and that we can unlock the door to profound transformation and inner peace by honoring all aspects of ourselves.

I underwent a profound shift in perspective. Instead of seeing my emotions as hurdles to overcome, I began to perceive them as valuable messengers, each carrying gifts of insight and self-awareness. This shift in perception reframed my journey, allowing me to embrace my emotions with openness and curiosity.

I have also learned to trust in the wisdom of my emotions, recognizing them as signposts guiding me toward greater self-awareness and growth. Rather than viewing them as obstacles, I embraced them as allies, supporting me on the path to wholeness and authenticity.

I cultivated a more profound sense of self-love and acceptance by embracing my emotions with compassion and acceptance. I no longer sought to suppress or deny parts of myself but embraced the full spectrum of my humanity. In doing so, I discovered a profound sense of peace and wholeness that transcended any temporary discomfort or pain.

Ultimately, my journey was not about reaching a destination but embracing the journey itself—the messy, imperfect, and beautiful human experience of being alive. In that embrace, I found the courage to live authentically, to honor my truth, and to walk the path of healing with grace and resilience.

Vulnerability

Vulnerability was not a weakness but a wellspring of profound strength. This revelation shattered the illusions I had been taught to accept, reshaping my understanding of true courage. It was here, in the raw, unguarded spaces of my heart, that I discovered the essence of bravery—the power to stand exposed, yet unwavering.

For much of my life, I had been taught to equate vulnerability with weakness—to see it as a liability that should be avoided at all costs. But I began to see vulnerability in a new light. It wasn't about exposing my flaws or shortcomings but embracing my existence's raw, unfiltered truth.

Being vulnerable meant opening myself up to the full spectrum of human emotions—the joy, the sorrow, the fear, and the love. It meant allowing myself to be seen and heard, even when uncomfortable or frightening. It was an act of courage that required me to confront my deepest fears and insecurities head-on.

I discovered a newfound sense of authenticity and connection with my Soulful Self in embracing vulnerability. Allowing myself to be vulnerable opened the door to a deeper self-awareness and self-acceptance. I no longer needed to hide behind a façade of strength or perfection; instead, I embraced my imperfections and celebrated my humanity.

Through vulnerability, I forged more profound connections with others, sharing my truth and inviting them to do the same. I found healing and support through these authentic connections, realizing I was not alone in my struggles.

Ultimately, vulnerability became my most significant source of strength—the wellspring from which I drew courage, resilience, and authenticity. It reminded us that true power lies not in hiding our weaknesses but embracing them with open arms and allowing them to shape us into more compassionate, resilient, and wholehearted beings.

Through the ups and downs, I discovered that resilience wasn't about avoiding hardship or pain but about embracing it as an integral part of the human experience. Each stumble, and stumble became a stepping-stone on the path to self-discovery and empowerment. I learned to trust in my ability to navigate life's complexities with grace and courage, knowing that every challenge catalyzes growth.

Embracing this mindset, I found that the uncertainties of life became less daunting and more exhilarating. The dance of life became a source of joy and inspiration, a reminder that each moment held the potential for discovery and adventure. Amid it all, I was evolving—not into a fixed, final version of myself, but into a fluid and ever-changing expression of my true essence.

Journeying through self-discovery and acceptance, I unearthed a profound realization: at the heart of my being lay an innate wisdom, a guiding light that the clamor of societal norms and my insecurities had long overshadowed. With each step deeper into the recesses of my Soulful Self, this guiding force emerged more vividly, illuminating my path with clarity and purpose.

It was as though I had stumbled upon a hidden treasure within myself—a reservoir of knowledge and intuition that had always been there, patiently waiting to be rediscovered. This inner wisdom spoke in whispers, nudging me toward authenticity and self-awareness. It gently reminded me of my inherent worth and potential, urging me to trust in the unique journey unfolding before me.

Listening to the whispers of my inner wisdom, I began to see the world through new eyes. The challenges and uncertainties that once seemed overwhelming now appeared as opportunities for growth and transformation. I made decisions from a place of deep inner knowing, guided by a sense of alignment with my true purpose.

I discovered a newfound sense of empowerment and freedom in embracing my innate wisdom. No longer bound by external expectations or the need for validation from others, I embarked on a journey of self-expression and self-realization. Additionally, as I continued to honor the wisdom that dwelled within me, I found myself walking a path illuminated by the light of my truth.

With each layer of resistance I let go of, I felt a profound shift within me. I began to see myself in a new light—as someone worthy of love and acceptance, just as I am. As I embraced this newfound sense of self-worth, I noticed changes in various aspects of my life.

In the journey of self-discovery, my relationships experienced a profound transformation. Gone was the constant need for external validation, replaced by an inner compass that steered me toward connections based on mutual growth and understanding. The dance of vulnerability persisted, but it morphed into something beautiful—a dance of genuine connection, unencumbered by the chains of seeking approval.

Previously, I had often sought validation from others, allowing their opinions to dictate my sense of self-worth. This external validation was like a fleeting mirage, offering temporary relief but leaving me parched for more. However, as I delved deeper into my truth, I realized that proper validation comes from within.

With this newfound understanding, I began approaching relationships from a place of authenticity and self-assurance. I no longer sought validation or approval from others; instead, I focused on fostering connections built on mutual respect, trust, and shared values. These relationships were not based on the need for validation but rather on a genuine desire for growth and companionship.

As a result, my relationships became more prosperous and more fulfilling. I no longer needed to hide behind masks or play roles to fit in. Instead, I embraced my true self and allowed others to do the same. In doing so, I discovered a more profound sense of connection and intimacy that I had never experienced before.

The shackles of approval-seeking had been broken, freeing me to forge relationships rooted in authenticity and genuine connection. As I continue to navigate the intricate dance of relationships, I do so with a newfound sense of confidence and self-assurance, knowing that I am worthy of love and belonging just as I am.

In my journey of self-discovery, I underwent a profound shift in how I perceived financial challenges. Instead of seeing them as insurmountable barriers, I began to view them as opportunities for growth and exploration. I realized that my value as an individual was not solely defined by external measures such as wealth or possessions but rather by the richness of my experiences, the depth of my relationships, and the authenticity of my contributions to the world.

This shift in perspective allowed me to break free from the narrow confines of traditional notions of success and abundance. Instead of chasing after material wealth, I focused on cultivating a sense of abundance in all areas of my life. I began to appreciate the simple joys and pleasures money could not buy, such as spending quality time with loved ones, pursuing my passions, and making meaningful connections.

Moreover, I recognized the importance of aligning my financial goals with my values and priorities. Instead of pursuing wealth for its sake, I focused on using my resources to positively impact the world and create a life aligned with my deepest values and aspirations. My financial struggles became a fertile ground for personal growth and empowerment. Instead of viewing scarcity or lack as limitations, I saw them as invitations to cultivate abundance consciousness and resourcefulness. I learned to navigate financial challenges with resilience and creativity, knowing that every setback was an opportunity to expand my capacity for abundance and prosperity.

This shift in focus brought a greater sense of purpose and fulfillment to my financial journey.

Overall, my journey toward financial abundance was not just about accumulating wealth but about embracing a mindset of abundance in all areas of my life. I cultivated a more profound sense of fulfillment, meaning, and abundance by shifting my perspective and aligning my financial goals with my values.

Amid life's wobbles, I underwent a profound transformation in how I perceived and experienced uncertainty. What was once a destabilizing force became a rhythmic dance—a heartbeat synchronizing with the pulse of life itself. Rather than feeling lost in the chaos, I found my footing, grounded in the awareness of my Soulful Self.

Long concealed beneath layers of doubt and fear, this inner essence emerged as a guiding light in the darkness. It whispered insights and nudged me toward choices that resonated with my true nature. Instead of being swept away by the currents of uncertainty, I learned to trust in this inner wisdom, allowing it to lead me along the path of authenticity and alignment.

Each step forward made me feel a deeper connection to my Soulful Self. It was as if I had finally come home to myself, embracing all aspects of my being with open arms. No longer afraid of the unknown, I welcomed it as an opportunity for growth and expansion.

I discovered a profound sense of peace in this newfound presence and acceptance. The wobbles of life no longer shook me to my core; instead, they became gentle reminders of the inherent rhythm of existence. With each wobble, I learned to dance, gracefully navigating the ebbs and flows of life with a sense of grace and resilience.

Ultimately, the journey from instability to stability was not about finding solid ground beneath my feet but about embracing the fluidity of life itself. It was about learning to trust in the wisdom of my Soulful Self and surrendering to the natural rhythms of the universe; in doing so, life wobbles.

My journey was a energetic purpose of becoming—a continuous evolution where every step forward revealed a new facet of myself, every stumble offered invaluable lessons, and every moment presented a choice between staying true to myself or succumbing to societal pressures. It was a celebration of authenticity, a journey where I learned to embrace the messy, imperfect beauty of simply being.

In the past, I had been fixated on reaching a specific destination, believing that happiness and fulfillment awaited me at the end of some predetermined path. But as I traveled further along my journey of self-discovery, I realized that true liberation lay not in reaching a destination but fully immersing myself in the journey itself.

I learned to release the need for control and certainty and surrender to life's flow. In doing so, I found freedom in the uncertainty, joy in the unexpected twists and turns, and beauty in the serendipitous encounters. Each moment became an opportunity for growth and expansion, a chance to embrace the fullness of life with open arms.

I have also learned to trust my intuition's wisdom and my Soulful Self's guidance. I discovered that true fulfillment comes not from external achievements or accolades but from living authentically and aligning with my deepest values and desires.

I continue to journey forward with curiosity and wonder, embracing each new experience as an opportunity to learn, grow, and evolve. For me, the journey has become the destination—a never-ending celebration of becoming, unfolding with each step I take.

The story of my life continues to unfold—a rich drapery of self-discovery, resilience, and the ever-evolving dance toward wholeness. It's an account that extends far beyond the confines of a mere journal, intertwining itself with the fabric of existence itself—a testament to the profound impact of embracing one's true essence.

Sometimes, I find myself lulled into the illusion of understanding, feeling a sense of control over the unfolding events of my life. Yet, just as frequently, unexpected turns and challenges arise, shaking the foundations of my perceived composure. These moments are stark reminders of the fragility of my sense of stability and the limitations of my protective façade.

In embracing this realization at the level of my protective personality, I open myself to transformative possibilities. It's an admission that I don't have all the answers and that I'm not invulnerable to life's uncertainties and complexities. And within this vulnerability lies the potential for profound healing and growth.

By acknowledging my vulnerabilities and embracing the inherent imperfections of my human experience, I create space for authenticity and self-compassion to flourish. Through these moments of humility and honesty, I can connect with myself and others, forging deeper bonds and fostering genuine intimacy.

Each unexpected twist and turn in the narrative of my life serves as an invitation to lean into the discomfort, explore the depths of my being, and emerge stronger, wiser, and more whole. And so, I continue to navigate the ever-unfolding story of my life with courage, grace, and an unwavering commitment to authenticity.

In moments like these, the most powerful choice I can make is to greet the unfolding reality with a tender embrace of loving presence and compassion. This intentional act softens the protective barriers I erect to shield myself from specific experience frequencies. These frequencies, ranging from joy to sorrow and everything in between, carry the potential for healing and growth.

By opening myself to the full spectrum of these energies, I acknowledge that true wholeness encompasses my human experience—light, shadow, joy, and pain. It's a recognition that I need the richness of these diverse frequencies to weave together the checker of my existence and fully embody my authentic self.

In this state of gentle openness, the protective sheath that once surrounded me becomes permeable, allowing the healing frequencies to flow in and work their transformative magic. It's a surrender to the inherent wisdom of the universe, an invitation for healing to take root and flourish within the depths of my being.

As I continue to embrace the unfolding reality with loving presence and compassion, I trust in the innate intelligence of my body, mind, and spirit to guide me toward greater wholeness and alignment. Each moment becomes an opportunity for more profound healing and self-discovery as I journey toward profound integration and harmony within myself.

Delving deeper into the understanding that my protective persona isn't an impenetrable fortress, a new world of possibilities unfolds. I realize that I have the power to make different choices, ones that aren't rooted in resistance or denial but in acceptance and openness. Instead of bracing against life's unexpected twists and turns, I learn to dance with them, allowing the rhythm of existence to shape my responses.

In this dance, I recognize that the path to healing isn't just about embracing the comfortable and familiar; it's also about welcoming the uncomfortable and unfamiliar. These aspects of experience, often stored deep within my subconscious, demand my attention and integration. They hold within them the keys to profound transformation and growth if only I dare to confront them head-on.

It's a journey of radical acceptance and self-discovery, where every moment becomes an opportunity to lean into the discomfort and unearth hidden truths about myself. As I navigate this terrain with an open heart and mind, I trust that the healing process will unfold organically, leading me toward greater wholeness and authenticity.

With each step forward, I find myself shedding layers of conditioning and resistance, revealing the raw, unfiltered essence of my being. This process is both exhilarating and daunting as I confront aspects of myself that I had long suppressed or ignored. Yet, amid this discomfort, I discover a profound sense of liberation—freedom from embracing the totality of who I am, flaws and all.

Journeying further into my psyche, I realize that true healing requires me to confront my shadow self—the aspects of my personality that I have disowned or rejected. These shadow aspects hold valuable insights and lessons waiting to be acknowledged and integrated into my conscious awareness. By shining a light on these darker corners of my psyche, I can reclaim lost parts of myself and move toward a more balanced and integrated state of being.

I embrace the full spectrum of human experience by embracing the uncomfortable and unfamiliar. I recognize that growth often arises from moments of discomfort and challenge and that by leaning into these experiences, I can catalyze profound personal transformation. With each passing day, I move closer to a state of wholeness and authenticity, guided by the wisdom of my Soulful Self and the transformative power of loving presence.

In my quest for wholeness, I've realized that ignoring or suppressing uncomfortable emotions only prolongs healing. Instead, true healing necessitates a willingness to delve deep into the depths of my Soulful Self, where the raw truth of my being resides, untarnished by the masks I wear.

However, embracing this truth demands vulnerability—a willingness to confront the uncertainties and vulnerabilities of life head-on. In these moments of vulnerability, these wobbles, the potential for profound transformation becomes most apparent. It's as if the cracks in my protective armor allow the light of self-discovery and growth to seep in, illuminating the path to authenticity and wholeness.

I've learned to surrender to the rhythm of life rather than resist its unpredictable twists and turns. This surrender is not a sign of weakness but a gesture of trust—a trust in the innate wisdom of the universe and the guiding force of my Soulful Self.

Through this surrender, I've discovered an inner resilience—a strength that emerges not from controlling external circumstances but from embracing them with an open heart and mind. It's a resilience that allows me to weather life's storms with grace and poise, knowing that each challenge is an opportunity for growth and self-discovery.

Traversing this path of self-discovery and growth, I embrace the intricate dance between my protective and vulnerable selves. This dance is not a battle to be won but a harmonious interplay between two essential aspects of my being. It's a rhythm of integration and expansion, where each step forward brings me closer to profound healing and wholeness.

In this dance, I've learned to honor both sides of myself—the part that seeks safety and security and the part that yearns for authenticity and growth. I've discovered a newfound sense of balance and resilience by acknowledging and embracing these aspects of my being.

Every twist and turn in this dance is an opportunity for deeper self-understanding and self-compassion. Through moments of vulnerability, I've unearthed hidden strengths and capacities I never knew I possessed. In moments of protection, I've learned to offer myself gentle grace and understanding.

I continue navigating life's complexities with a heightened awareness of this delicate dance. It's a journey of exploration and evolution, where every step forward brings me closer to the essence of who I truly am—a being of infinite potential and boundless love.

Immersing myself in the embrace of various energies, I witness the beautiful process of integration unfolding within me. This integration brings forth a sense of wholeness, a feeling of completeness that permeates every fiber of my being. In this state of wholeness, healing flows effortlessly, like a gentle stream nourishing the landscape of my soul.

I've discovered that this healing energy isn't meant to be hoarded within the confines of my being. Instead, it yearns to be shared, to radiate outwards and touch the lives of those around me. As a result of my healing journey, I become a vessel for healing energies, channeling them into the world and positively impacting others.

But to truly harness the power of this healing energy, I must first believe in and honor the vast reservoir of wisdom that resides within me. This wisdom is not just a collection of knowledge and experiences; it's a sacred inheritance passed down through generations, a legacy of resilience and ancestral wisdom.

In recognizing the value and significance of my traditional, original, and indigenous knowledge, I pave the way for my transformation and advancement. This knowledge isn't just a relic of the past; it's a living, breathing force that guides me in my journey of self-discovery and self-realization.

By integrating this wisdom into every aspect of my life—education, research, decision-making, and personal convictions—I affirm its importance and relevance in today's world. I honor the wisdom of my ancestors and cultivate a deep sense of pride in my cultural heritage.

I continue to walk this path of self-discovery and healing; I do so with a profound appreciation for the rich patchwork of knowledge that shapes my identity. And with each step forward, I am reminded of the transformative power within me, waiting to be unleashed and shared with the world.

I find myself increasingly aware of the interconnectedness of all things. Every experience, every encounter, and every moment of introspection serves as a thread weaving together the synthesis of my existence.

I facilitate my healing and contribute to humanity's collective healing by embracing the energies within me. It's a symbiotic relationship—a continuous energy exchange that transcends individual boundaries and extends into the vast expanse of universal consciousness.

With each passing day, I deepen my understanding of the intricate web of life, recognizing my place within it and the impact of my actions on the greater whole. This awareness fuels my commitment to living in alignment with my highest truth and purpose, radiating love, compassion, and healing wherever I go.

Honoring the wisdom of my ancestors and embrace the fullness of my being, I step into my power as a conduit for transformation. I become a beacon of light, guiding others on their journeys of self-discovery and healing.

So, I continue to walk this path with courage and conviction, knowing that every step forward brings me closer to realizing my fullest potential. In the dance of life, I find solace, strength, and a profound sense of belonging—a knowing that I am exactly where I need to be, in perfect harmony with the universe.

Understanding this transition presents challenges, particularly for someone like myself who has been conditioned within a hybrid environment. For years, I've relied on external guidance to shape my beliefs and behaviors, especially within the structured frameworks of organized religion and sanitized societal norms.

Embarking on this journey of self-discovery and authenticity, I confront the need to recalibrate my internal compass. It's a process akin to rebooting a system—a deliberate effort to shed the layers of conditioning and rediscover the innate wisdom within me.

This journey demands courage and resilience as I peel back the layers of external influence and embrace my authentic knowledge. It requires me to question long-held beliefs and challenge the status quo, all in pursuit of a path that resonates with my true essence.

Navigating this unfamiliar terrain, I am reminded that growth often requires discomfort. Yet, in embracing the discomfort, I open myself to the possibility of profound transformation and alignment with my highest truth.

Though the road ahead may be uncertain, I am encouraged by the knowledge that I am forging a path uniquely my own. This path honors the wisdom of my ancestors and celebrates the richness of my heritage. And with each step forward, I move closer to embodying the fullest expression of myself.

Embarking on this journey of embracing my authentic knowledge and rebooting my system, I am undergoing a profound shift in perspective. My thoughts and actions have been shaped by the norms and expectations imposed by organized religion and societal standards for so long.

But now, I am challenging those norms that once dictated my beliefs and behaviors. I'm daring to step away from the constraints of conventional thinking and question the dogma that has long defined my worldview.

This process is both liberating and unsettling. It is liberating because it allows me to reclaim ownership of my thoughts and beliefs to chart a course that is true to my innermost convictions. It is unsettling because it requires me to confront the discomfort of uncertainty to navigate unfamiliar terrain without the comfort of familiar landmarks.

Yet, in embracing this shift, I am opening myself up to a world of possibility. I am discovering new perspectives

353

and ways of understanding the world and my place within it. I am reclaiming agency over my history, refusing to be bound by the limitations of external expectations.

This is a voyage of self-exploration and self-validation, giving me the strength to embrace who I truly am without hesitation. Even though the path ahead may be tough, I stride forward with bravery and certainty, fully aware that I am carving a trail that is exclusively mine.

Unlearning the Past

Reconnecting with my traditional, original, and indigenous knowledge, I realize that it's not just about acquiring new information but also about unlearning specific patterns and beliefs imposed upon me. This unlearning process is akin to shedding layers that have obscured my true essence over the years.

It requires courage to confront the discomfort of challenging deeply ingrained beliefs and stepping away from the familiar. It's like peeling back the layers of an onion, revealing deeper truths with each discarded layer.

But with each layer shed, I feel a sense of liberation, as if I'm reclaiming a part of myself that was long suppressed. I began to see the world through a different lens, more aligned with my ancestral wisdom and cultural heritage.

This process of unlearning is not easy. It requires humility and a willingness to admit I may have been wrong or misguided. However, it is also a source of empowerment for me, as it gives me the opportunity to regain control over my own story and create a journey that truly represents my genuine self.

In this journey of unlearning and reconnection, I am filled with a sense of purpose and possibility. I know that the road ahead may be challenging, but I am committed to honoring my roots and embracing the wisdom of my ancestors. And with each step forward, I feel myself drawing closer to the essence of who I truly am.

Delving deeper into the process of unlearning and reconnecting with my traditional, original, and Indigenous knowledge, I find strength in recognizing that my transformation is not just personal; it's also a step toward reclaiming a narrative that has been marginalized for far too long.

I realize that by embracing and integrating the wisdom of my heritage into contemporary contexts, such as education, research, decision-making, and personal beliefs, I am contributing to a broader movement of cultural revitalization and empowerment. This recognition fills me with a sense of purpose and responsibility. I understand that I am not only reclaiming my own identity and heritage but also standing in solidarity with countless others who have been marginalized and silenced by dominant narratives.

Incorporating traditional knowledge into modern frameworks is not without its challenges. It requires navigating complex power dynamics, confronting systemic barriers, and challenging deeply entrenched beliefs and practices. But I am determined to persevere, knowing that the journey toward cultural revitalization is both necessary and worthwhile.

Continuing on this path, I am guided by the belief that by honoring and preserving my ancestors' wisdom, I will enrich my life and contribute to my community's and future generations' collective well-being.

10

Reboot

Rebooting my system entails a profound shift in how I navigate the world. It means embracing my intuitive, indigenous knowledge as a guiding force. This journey requires creating a space where the energies of tradition and modernity can coexist harmoniously, forming a unique fabric that reflects the richness of my cultural heritage.

For too long, I have relied solely on external sources of guidance and validation, neglecting the deep wisdom within me. But now, I am reclaiming that inner knowing and allowing it to illuminate my path forward.

This process isn't about rejecting modernity or dismissing the advancements of contemporary society. Instead, it's about recognizing the value of traditional wisdom and integrating it with the insights of the present moment.

In doing so, I honor the generations of ancestors who have passed down their knowledge and experiences through oral traditions, rituals, and customs. Their teachings provide a timeless foundation for building my understanding of the world.

By harmonizing tradition and modernity within myself, I create a space to express my identity and values authentically. This integration empowers me to navigate the complexities of life with clarity, purpose, and a deep sense of connection to my cultural roots.

I realize that my healing journey is not solitary but interconnected with the healing of others. By embracing authenticity and self-discovery, I become a conduit for healing energies that resonate beyond my experience. This vibration of authenticity carries the power to inspire collective empowerment and cultural resurgence.

Delving deeper into my healing process, I uncover layers of ancestral wisdom and resilience passed down through generations. Rediscovering my cultural heritage enriches my journey and strengthens my community's collective identity.

Through my self-healing and cultural reclamation journey, I emit a frequency of authenticity and self-discovery that reverberates outward, touching the lives of those around me. This ripple effect creates a space for others to embark on their journeys of healing and self-discovery.

In embracing my true essence and honoring the wisdom of my ancestors, I contribute to a collective movement toward healing and empowerment. Each step I take towards wholeness becomes a beacon of hope and inspiration for others seeking to reconnect with their roots and reclaim their identities.

Continuing to navigate this transformative journey fills me with a sense of purpose and responsibility to catalyze positive change within myself and my community. Together, we can create a future that honors our past while embracing the potential for growth and transformation.

I've embarked on a profound recalibration of my mindset. This recalibration requires a deep commitment to recognizing and believing in the wealth of knowledge within me. It's about valuing the depth of wisdom inherited from my ancestors and acknowledging its significance in shaping who I am today.

To honor this ancestral knowledge, I am called to uncover and share it with others consciously. This involves delving into the depths of my cultural heritage, unearthing hidden gems of wisdom, and bringing them to light for all to see. It's a journey of self-empowerment and collective upliftment, where the richness of our traditions is celebrated and cherished.

I'm reminded of the significance of promoting acknowledgment and appreciation for indigenous knowledge. It is not only important to preserve our cultural legacy, but also to regain our proper position in human history. By sharing our knowledge with others, we can bridge the gap between past and present, fostering understanding and unity across diverse communities.

This journey of recalibration is not without its challenges, as it requires courage and determination to challenge existing paradigms and amplify voices that have long been marginalized. Yet, it's a journey worth undertaking, for in embracing and sharing our ancestral wisdom, we pave the way for a future rich in diversity, resilience, and cultural vibrancy.

Embarking on this journey of cultural and personal renewal is not without its hurdles, particularly for someone like me who has been conditioned by the directives of a hybrid educational environment and the influence of organized religion. However, I embrace these challenges as opportunities for growth and transformation, both personally and culturally.

Rebooting my system is not a one-time event but an ongoing process that demands continual self-reflection and a readiness to evolve. It requires me to unravel and dismantle the imposed constructs of thought and behavior that have shaped my worldview, making space for the reemergence of my authentic self. This process involves questioning deeply ingrained beliefs and ideologies, challenging the status quo, and embracing the uncertainty of stepping into uncharted territory.

I am also mindful that it will not always be smooth sailing. There will be moments of doubt, discomfort, and resistance. Yet, I approach these challenges with a sense of resilience and determination, knowing that they are essential catalysts for growth and transformation.

Ultimately, rebooting my system is about reclaiming my agency and sovereignty, freeing myself from the constraints of external influences, and forging a path aligned with my true essence and cultural heritage. It's a journey of liberation and empowerment that promises profound personal fulfillment and collective resurgence.

In my pursuit of reclaiming my authentic self and cultural heritage, I am acutely conscious of the societal expectations and norms I am transcending. This journey transcends mere personal growth; it's a deliberate effort to contribute to a broader narrative that honors and integrates the diverse knowledge systems that shape our world.

With each step along this transformative path, I am mindful that I am not just forging a path for myself but also paving the way for others to follow. It's a journey that requires resilience, courage, and a deep commitment to authenticity. Despite the challenges and uncertainties that lie ahead, I remain steadfast in my determination to restore indigenous wisdom in a contemporary context.

In this intricate dance between tradition and modernity, I am constantly reminded of the importance of honoring my roots while embracing the opportunities and possibilities of the present moment. It's a delicate balancing act that requires me to remain open-minded, adaptable, and receptive to the wisdom of both past and present.

With each passing day, I grow more attuned to the interconnectedness of all things and the profound impact my actions and choices have on the world around me. It's a humbling realization that fuels my sense of purpose and drives me forward on this transformative journey of self-discovery and cultural restoration.

I am committed to dismantling the barriers that have long obscured the brilliance of indigenous knowledge. It's about fostering a deeper understanding and appreciation for the wisdom passed down through generations and recognizing its relevance and value in today's world.

I need to address my prejudices and assumptions, examine the narratives that have built my vision, and adopt a more inclusive and comprehensive perspective.

It's a journey of unlearning as much as it is a journey of rediscovery—a process of shedding the layers of conditioning and socialization that have clouded my vision and obscured my true essence.

Yet, with each layer I peel away, I uncover a more bottomless reservoir of wisdom and insight—a reservoir that has patiently been waiting for me to tap into it. It's a humbling and empowering experience that reminds me of the resilience and strength inherent in my cultural heritage.

As I move forward on this path, I am guided by a deep sense of purpose and a profound reverence for the traditions and teachings of my ancestors. I am driven by a desire to honor their legacy to ensure that their wisdom lives on in the hearts and minds of future generations.

So, I continue to journey onward, embracing the challenges and uncertainties ahead with an open heart and steadfast resolve. With each step, I am moving closer to the truth of who I am and the richness of my cultural heritage.

During my formative years in the realm of spirituality, I discovered the profound practice of meditation. It was a time before the prevalence of modern technology, yet the concept bore a striking resemblance to the operating system of contemporary phones or computers. Interestingly, my introduction to rebooting the mind through meditation echoed a familiar practice in technology.

Computers were indispensable tools in my professional endeavors, mainly while working in hospitals and various medical facilities. They streamlined our tasks, managed patient records, and facilitated communication. However, like any complex system, they occasionally encountered sluggishness and minor glitches. In such instances, the first advice from IT support was often simple yet effective: reboot the computer—turn it off and then on again.

This seemingly mundane task held a profound lesson. It highlighted the importance of resetting, clearing accumulated clutter, and starting afresh. Similarly, meditation served as a tool for rebooting the mind in spirituality. It offered a way to quiet the constant chatter of thoughts, to release tension and stress, and to create space for clarity and insight to emerge.

Just as rebooting a computer can restore its functionality and efficiency, meditation allowed me to refresh my mental state, enhancing my focus, creativity, and overall well-being. It became a daily practice—a sacred ritual of self-care and introspection that grounded me amidst life's whirlwinds.

Through meditation, I discovered a profound sense of inner peace and resilience. It taught me the value of stillness in a world of noise and distraction. And like the gentle reboot of a computer, it reminded me of the power of simplicity—to pause, breathe, and reset.

In many ways, I yearn for a profound reboot in my life—a chance to rediscover how to love and appreciate it once more genuinely. I crave the time and space necessary for healing and recovery. Meditation is my version of closing all the applications running on my phone or computer and restarting the device afresh.

It's akin to a mental reset, enabling me to become more aware of the cognitive "apps" (thoughts and emotions) I have activated and to discern which ones genuinely deserve to be kept running. Just as rebooting a device clears unnecessary processes and clutter, meditation helps me clear my mind of distractions and negative thoughts.

Through meditation, I find sanctuary—a quiet refuge where I can untangle the complexities of my mind and reconnect with my inner self. It's a sacred space where I can release tension, let go of worries, and cultivate inner peace.

Like a gentle breeze sweeping through a cluttered room, meditation sweeps away the mental debris, leaving a sense of clarity and calm. It's a process of decluttering the

365

mind, making room for fresh perspectives and renewed energy.

In the stillness of meditation, I discover the power of presence—the ability to fully immerse myself in the present moment without being weighed down by regrets from the past or anxieties about the future. It's a reminder that true happiness and fulfillment can only be found in the here and now.

As I continue to cultivate my meditation practice, I feel more attuned to the rhythm of life—the ebb and flow of emotions, the subtle nuances of the present moment. It's a journey of self-discovery and self-acceptance, guided by the gentle rhythm of my breath and the whispers of my soul.

In essence, meditation is my sanctuary—a sacred oasis where I can find solace, clarity, and inner peace amidst the chaos of life. It's a gift I give myself each day—a chance to reboot, refresh, and reconnect with the most profound truths of my being.

Meditation is more than just a practice—it's a sanctuary, a refuge from the relentless noise of daily life where I can reconnect with the essence of who I am. Amid the chaos, it offers a precious pause, a moment of stillness to recalibrate my thoughts, emotions, and perspectives. It's a deliberate act of self-care, a gentle reminder to prioritize my well-being amidst the hustle and bustle of the outside world.

In the serene sanctuary of meditation, I embark on a journey through the depths of my inner world, guided by a deliberate reset. It's akin to navigating through the cluttered landscape of my mind, sorting through the various mental applications that vie for attention. As I surrender to the stillness, it feels like I'm initiating a shutdown of unnecessary processes, allowing the essential ones to reboot and realign.

Each breath becomes a gentle keystroke, signaling the beginning of this mental recalibration. With each exhale, I release the grip of tension and distraction, clearing space for clarity and focus. The external noise fades into the background, and I sink deeper into the quiet recesses of my consciousness.

In this sacred space of introspection, I confront the tangled web of thoughts and emotions that often cloud my perception. Like a skilled technician performing maintenance on a complex system, I methodically assess each mental application, discerning which ones serve my highest good and hinder my progress.

With each passing moment, the layers of mental clutter dissipate, revealing the pristine essence of my true self beneath. It's stripping away the illusions and distractions that obscure my inner light, allowing it to shine radiantly.

As I continue to navigate this inner landscape, I am filled with a profound sense of peace and empowerment. In the stillness of meditation, I discover the power to choose which thoughts to entertain and which to let go of. It's a liberating realization that I am not at the mercy of my mind but rather the master of it.

With each inhalation, I draw in fresh vitality and renewed clarity, infusing every cell of my being with a sense of purpose and presence. And with each exhalation, I release any lingering doubts or fears, surrendering to the boundless potential of the present moment.

As I settle into meditation, I enter a sacred space within myself, untethered from the demands and distractions of the external world. Here, I become a silent observer, witnessing the ebb and flow of my internal currents with compassionate detachment. Each breath becomes a bridge between the surface chatter of my mind and the more profound wisdom that resides within me.

In this tranquil haven, I discern the energies that nourish my soul, gently releasing those that no longer serve me. Like a gardener tending to a cherished plot of land, I cultivate a fertile inner landscape, nurturing seeds of peace, clarity, and compassion. I draw in the essence of serenity; with each exhalation, I release tension and negativity, allowing them to dissipate into the ether.

Meditation becomes a journey of self-discovery, a sacred exploration of the vast terrain of my inner world. Here, amidst the stillness, I confront the shadows lurking in my psyche's recesses with courage and compassion. I embrace the full spectrum of my human experience—the light and the dark, the joy and the sorrow—as integral parts of my journey toward wholeness.

I find solace, clarity, and renewal in the gentle rhythm of my breath. Each moment of stillness is a precious gift, an opportunity to connect with the deepest layers of my being. As I emerge from meditation, I carry a sense of peace and groundedness that infuses every aspect of my life.

With each inhale and exhale, I embark on a journey of release and renewal, consciously shedding the mental clutter that accumulates throughout the day. As I breathe deeply, I create a spaciousness, allowing a renewed sense of purpose and presence to emerge. This act of letting go goes beyond mere relaxation; it's a deliberate rebooting of my inner system—a recalibration of my thoughts, emotions, and energy.

In the calm sanctuary of meditation, I overcome the constraints of the technology metaphor, going deeply into my consciousness with amazing self-awareness and self-love. Here, in the silence, I retake control over what comes out of my thoughts, reclaiming the ability to pick which mental apps to run and which to turn off.

With each mindful breath, I navigate the labyrinth of my mind, discerning between the thoughts and emotions that uplift and empower me and those that weigh me down with their negativity and doubt. I cultivate a sense of agency, realizing that I can rewrite the script of my inner dialogue, replacing fear with courage, doubt with confidence, and chaos with calm.

In the sanctuary of meditation, I find refuge from the noise of the external world, immersing myself in the stillness within. Here, amidst the tranquility, I engage in the sacred act of letting go of worries, fears, and doubts and allowing myself to be enveloped in the embrace of the present moment. With each breath, I cultivate a sense of spaciousness within, creating room for clarity to emerge and resilience to flourish.

With each inhalation and exhalation, I find myself attuning to the rhythm of change, recognizing that life is a dance of impermanence. Nothing remains static; everything is in a perpetual state of flux. The reboot, whether in the digital realm or the contemplative space, serves as a poignant reminder of this fundamental truth.

Through this meditation, I cultivate a deeper connection with my true essence—a wellspring of wisdom, resilience, and infinite potential. I understand that my worth is not determined by external circumstances or the opinions of others but by the love and acceptance I hold for myself.

I'm discovering that the art of rebooting is far more than a temporary solution—it's a lifelong practice. It entails embracing mindfulness in every moment, acknowledging the thoughts and emotions that hinder my growth, and granting myself the compassion to initiate a reset. Meditation, therefore, evolves from merely a momentary reset to an ongoing wellspring of resilience and clarity in the perpetual narrative of my existence.

With each passing day, I'm honing the skill of observing my inner landscape with heightened awareness. I've come to recognize the patterns of thought and emotion that no longer align with my true essence. Rather than allowing them to linger and accumulate, I've learned to extend myself the grace to hit the refresh button—to release what no longer serves me and invite a renewed sense of presence and purpose.

I devoted myself to deepening my meditation practice. Through daily practice, I tapped into the vast reservoir of my subconscious mind, where thoughts, desires, mythical creatures, dreams, and nightmares reside.

This phase of my life has been a profound invitation to confront and explore my subconscious desires. Rather than resisting or battling against this powerful aspect of myself, I recognized the need to harness its immense power. After all, the subconscious mind holds a staggering 95% of the total energy within my psyche, far outweighing the influence of my conscious mind, which accounts for only 5%.

With this understanding, I embraced meditation as a tool to delve into the depths of my subconscious, to uncover hidden truths, and to integrate all aspects of myself into a harmonious whole. Instead of fearing the unknown within me, I approached it with curiosity and openness, knowing that by embracing and understanding my subconscious, I could unlock more significant levels of self-awareness and personal transformation.

During these sessions I confronted the pain and betrayal that had taken root within me. It was a challenging process, but with each breath, I let go of the anger and resentment that had consumed me.

In that sacred space of introspection, I realized that holding onto grudges only weighed me down, hindering my growth and happiness. I understood that forgiveness was not about condoning the actions of others but about releasing myself from the emotional burden they imposed.

With newfound clarity, I forgave my family members and friends who had betrayed my trust. It was a profound moment of liberation, as I felt the heavy chains of bitterness dissolve, replaced by a sense of peace and freedom.

In forgiving them, I reclaimed my power and control over my narrative. No longer held captive by past grievances,

I could embrace the present moment with renewed hope and optimism.

As I emerged from my meditation session, I felt lighter and more at peace than I had in a long time. The wounds of the past no longer defined me, and I could move forward with a heart full of love and compassion.

With the guidance of my guardian angels and the power of forgiveness, I found the strength to overcome adversity and reclaim my inner peace. As I continued on my journey towards wholeness, I knew that I was supported by divine love every step of the way.

The journey doesn't end with a single meditation session; it's a continuous process of self-discovery and growth. Each day presents new opportunities to reboot—to shed old layers of conditioning and embrace the fullness of my authentic self. Through this ongoing practice, I cultivate a deep sense of empowerment, knowing I can shape my narrative and chart a course toward fulfillment and inner peace.

In navigating the twists and turns of life's unfolding story, I find solace in the knowledge that meditation is always available to me—a timeless sanctuary where I can return to the center, recalibrate my intentions, and realign with my highest truth. Through this sacred practice, I cultivate resilience in the face of adversity and clarity amidst the chaos, anchoring myself in the boundless depths of my being.

I'm uncovering the profound beauty of embracing impermanence. It's a concept that mirrors the ever-shifting landscape of thoughts and emotions that arise during my contemplative practice. Just as the digital world requires periodic reboots to refresh and recalibrate, my inner world also benefits from moments of reset and renewal.

In meditation, I observe the transient nature of my thoughts and emotions as they arise and fade away like passing clouds in the sky. There's a certain liberation in embracing this impermanence, recognizing that clinging to fixed notions of identity or reality only leads to suffering. Instead, I learn to flow with the currents of change, gracefully adapting to each new moment as it unfolds.

The act of rebooting becomes a metaphor for this process of continual transformation. It's not a static event but a dynamic unfolding—a conscious acknowledgment of the ever-evolving nature of existence. Just as I refresh my digital devices to clear out accumulated clutter and optimize performance, so do I refresh my mind and spirit through meditation, clearing away mental debris and aligning with the natural flow of life.

In this ongoing exploration of impermanence, I discover a sense of freedom and spaciousness within myself.

I release the need to cling to fixed identities or expectations, embracing instead the fluidity of being. Each reboot becomes an opportunity for renewal, a chance to let go of the past and step into the freshness of the present moment.

As I continue this meditative journey, I deepen my understanding of impermanence, finding beauty in the ever-changing valance of life. With each reboot, I reaffirm my commitment to living in harmony with the natural rhythms of existence, embracing the flow of change with open arms and an open heart.

In the tranquil embrace of meditation, I am gently reminded of the profound power of presence. It's not merely a matter of shutting down unnecessary mental applications, but rather, it's about immersing myself fully in the present moment. Within the serene stillness, I find a vast canvas upon which I paint the strokes of awareness, observing the subtle nuances of my inner landscape without the burden of judgment.

This practice of mindfulness, akin to a constant reboot of the mind, equips me with invaluable tools for navigating the complexities of life with clarity and grace. As I re-engage with the world beyond the confines of my meditation space, I carry with me the wisdom gleaned from these moments of profound introspection. Each breath becomes a reset button, allowing me to adapt to the ever-changing circumstances with resilience and poise.

Through mindfulness, I can meet each moment with a sense of openness and curiosity, free from the constraints of past conditioning or future worries. The practice invites me to cultivate a deep understanding of presence, anchoring myself firmly in the richness of the here and now.

In this state of heightened awareness, I can respond to life's challenges with clarity and discernment rather than reacting impulsively out of habit or fear. The continuous reset mindfulness allows me to approach each situation with fresh eyes, untainted by preconceived notions or limiting beliefs.

With each breath, I surrender to the flow of life, embracing its ever-changing currents with an open heart and a receptive mind. The practice of mindfulness becomes my guiding light, illuminating the path ahead and infusing each moment with a sense of purpose and meaning. Through the power of presence, I discover a profound sense of peace and fulfillment rooted in the timeless essence of my true self.

Furthermore, the act of rebooting goes much beyond the scope of my personal experience. It goes beyond the confines of the ego and blends with a larger communal story, acknowledging that communities, cultures, and systems all require periods of recalibration and rejuvenation.

My journey intertwines with this larger tapestry of human existence, compelling me to contribute to the collective reboot by fostering compassion, understanding, and positive change in the world around me.

Thus, as I immerse myself in the stillness of meditation, I realize that my efforts to reset and realign my consciousness are intricately connected to the universal flow of energy and consciousness. It's a dance of energies—a harmonious reset that reverberates within the depths of my being and extends outward, creating ripples of healing and renewal in the interconnected web of existence.

In the stillness of meditation, I become attuned to the subtle rhythms of the universe, recognizing that my actions and intentions have the power to influence the collective consciousness. Each moment of mindfulness becomes a small yet significant contribution to the ongoing collective awakening and transformation process.

When breathing in and out, I synchronize my inner reset with the pulse of the cosmos, aligning myself with the greater flow of life. In this sacred space of interconnectedness, I find solace, strength, and inspiration to continue my personal and collective evolution journey. As I emerge from meditation, I carry a renewed sense of purpose and a deep commitment to contribute to the greater good, one mindful breath at a time.

Engaging in this introspective journey, I deeply explore my inner landscape, delving into the intricate realms of my mind, heart, and spirit. Much like troubleshooting software issues on a computer or phone, I meticulously examine the sources of any dysfunction that may be present, aiming to identify the root cause as a pivotal step toward addressing and potentially eliminating these challenges from my life.

In this analogy, I perceive my angels as a vigilant security system, steadfastly watching over me in the ethereal realm. When they detect the emergence of darker emotions, such as hatred or jealousy within me, it's akin to receiving a pop-up notification on my device. However, I must cultivate attentiveness and presence, too. If my mind is cluttered with distractions and noise, I risk overlooking these crucial notifications from my spiritual guardians.

Navigating the intricate corridors of my mind, I find myself enveloped in a shroud of thoughts, emotions, and memories. Each corner holds a story, each thread weaving together the fabric of my existence. In these moments of introspection, I am both the explorer and the cartographer, charting the terrain of my inner world with a curious heart and an open mind.

The journey sometimes feels like navigating through a dense forest, where the tangled undergrowth of fears and doubts obscures the path ahead. Yet, with each step forward, I discover hidden clearings bathed in the gentle light of self-awareness. Here, I pause to examine the roots of my challenges, tracing them back to their source like a diligent detective unraveling a mystery.

In this quest for understanding, I encounter the guardians of my spirit — my angels. They are the silent sentinels who stand watch over the citadel of my soul, ever vigilant against the encroachment of negativity and discord. When the shadows of anger or resentment loom, they gently whisper guidance, nudging me back into peace and compassion.

But their messages are subtle, like the rustle of leaves in the breeze, quickly drowned out by the cacophony of modern life. To heed their wisdom, I must cultivate a state of inner calm, where the world's noise fades into the background, and the voice of intuition rises above the din.

In these moments of stillness, I find clarity. Like a beacon in the night, the guidance of my angels illuminates the way forward, casting aside the shadows of doubt and uncertainty. With their support, I navigate the labyrinth of my mind with newfound confidence, trusting in the wisdom of my inner compass to lead me home.

Yet, even amidst the darkness, I find solace in knowing I am not alone. My ever-present and vigilant angels stand as beacons of light amid uncertainty, guiding me toward a deeper understanding of myself and the world around me.

In the sacred meditation space, I am reminded of my inherent connection to the divine, a truth that transcends the limitations of time and space. With each moment of stillness, I draw closer to the essence of my being, embracing the journey of self-discovery with open arms and a receptive heart.

With each moment of stillness, I become increasingly attuned to the subtle nuances of my mental landscape, discerning the patterns that govern my thoughts and behaviors. Through mindful observation, I identify the triggers of negative emotions—those subtle whispers that sow the seeds of discord within my psyche.

In the soft glow of awareness, I confront these triggers with courage and compassion, recognizing that they hold the key to my healing journey. With each breath, I embrace the discomfort that arises, acknowledging its presence without judgment or resistance.

While navigating the depths of my inner world, I cultivate a profound sense of acceptance, allowing myself to experience the spectrum of human emotions fully. In this space of radical self-compassion, I release the grip of pent-up emotions that have long held sway over my life.

With each exhale, I surrender to the healing power of letting go, relinquishing the burdens that no longer serve me. As leaves carried away on the gentle breeze, I release my attachment to anger, fear, and sorrow, allowing them to dissipate into the vast expanse of consciousness.

Emerging from meditation, I carry with me a newfound clarity and purpose, ready to navigate the complexities of life with grace and resilience. With each breath, I affirm my commitment to self-love and self-care, knowing that in honoring my well-being, I empower myself to create a life of joy, fulfillment, and abundance.

With each meditative reset, I bear witness to a subtle yet profound metamorphosis taking place within myself. It's as if I'm upgrading the software of my mind and spirit, shedding the layers of outdated beliefs and perceptions to make room for new insights and revelations. This process isn't about erasing the past or denying its existence; instead, it's about embracing the entirety of my journey—the highs and lows, the triumphs and tribulations—and integrating these experiences into the fabric of my present self.

I forge a profound connection with my spiritual essence. Here, amidst the stillness and silence, I delve into the core of my being, exploring the essence of who I truly am. This connection extends beyond mundane concerns, reaching into the infinite expanse of purpose and higher meaning. I

381

find solace and serenity in this sacred space, knowing that amidst the chaos of external circumstances, an eternal wellspring of peace exists within me.

This deep connection with my spiritual essence infuses my existence with a sense of purpose and clarity. As I navigate the complexities of life, I draw upon this inner reservoir of peace and wisdom to guide my actions and decisions. It serves as a steady anchor amidst the turbulent waters of change, grounding me in the truth of my being.

Through meditation, I gain insights into the interconnectedness of all things. I recognize that my journey is not solitary but woven intricately into the fabric of existence. With each moment of introspection, I delved deeper into the intricate web of connections that link me to the vast cosmos, reaffirming my significance within the expansive coverture of existence. These moments of contemplation serve as gentle reminders of the interwoven nature of all things, highlighting the profound interdependence that underpins the universe's fabric. As I reflect on my place within this intricate network, I am filled with a sense of awe and humility, recognizing the profound beauty and complexity of the cosmic dance in which I am privileged to partake.

In this sacred communion with my higher self, I find liberation from the constraints of ego and identity. I embrace the fluidity of existence, allowing myself to flow effortlessly with the rhythms of life. With each breath, I surrender to the divine orchestration of the universe, trusting in its infinite wisdom to guide me along my path.

Meditation has become a practice and a way of life— a sacred ritual through which I commune with the divine essence within and around me. In this timeless dance of consciousness, I discover the boundless potential of my soul to soar to ever-greater heights of love, compassion, and enlightenment.

In navigating my life's journey, the guidance I receive from my angels has become indispensable. It serves as a beacon, illuminating the path toward alignment with my true essence and purpose. Through meditation and introspection, I've honed my ability to discern between the ego-driven impulses of my protective personality and the subtle whispers of divine guidance.

This discernment acts as a compass, guiding me toward choices that resonate with my soul's deepest desires. It's a process of tuning in to the wisdom of my higher self, allowing me to make decisions that are in harmony with my authentic nature.

As I progress along this transformative path, I realize that my healing journey is intricately linked to the collective healing of humanity. The interconnectedness of our spirits becomes evident as I recognize that my personal growth contributes to the greater good. Every step toward aligning with my true self sends positive energy, impacting my life and those around me.

In embracing my authenticity, I become a conduit for healing energies to flow into the world. My journey is a testament to individual transformation's power in fostering collective change. With each moment of alignment, I play my part in bringing about a more harmonious and healed world.

In the grand scheme of existence, I find myself intricately woven into the fabric of life's unfolding journey. Each session of meditative reset serves as a thread, interlacing moments of deep introspection, profound healing, and transformative growth. With each breath, I actively participate in this intricate weaving, crafting a story that mirrors the ever-evolving landscape of my soul.

The practice of meditation acts as a gentle yet potent current, guiding me along the river of self-discovery. As I delve into the depths of my being, I navigate through the currents of my thoughts, emotions, and spiritual insights. With each moment of stillness, I become more attuned to the whispers of my inner wisdom, allowing them to guide me toward a deeper understanding of myself and my purpose.

Like a river flowing steadily toward the sea, meditation carries me forward on a journey of exploration and growth. It propels me towards the expansive ocean of wholeness and purpose, where I am invited to dive into the depths of my true essence. I find clarity, peace, and a profound connection to this vast expanse, more extraordinary tapestry of existence.

Formative Years

In the intricate dance of life, a poignant African proverb resonates deeply: "When the windstorm is blowing, it is wise to lay your head down until the storm is over to avoid dust particles blowing into your eyes." This wisdom reflects the innate human instinct to seek shelter and safety during turmoil and uncertainty. Similarly, in our formative years, we instinctively seek to blend in rather than stand out, driven by a primal urge to avoid conflict and seek acceptance within our social circles.

From a young age, we are subtly conditioned by our environment and societal norms to conform to certain expectations. The desire to fit in is ingrained in us as we observe the consequences of being different. We witness how those who deviate from the norm often face ridicule, ostracism, and even bullying. These experiences shape our behaviors and beliefs, leading us to adopt the mindset of conformity as a means of self-preservation.

The conditioning begins subtly, often reinforced through social interactions, media portrayals, and cultural influences. We learn to internalize societal expectations and norms, molding ourselves to fit within predefined boxes of acceptability. This process is reinforced by the fear of rejection and the desire for approval, driving us to suppress our unique qualities and conform to the prevailing standards of our peer groups.

The pressure to conform intensifies as we develop through adolescence and young adulthood. We are bombarded with messages that dictate how we should look, act, and think to be accepted and valued by others. The fear of being labeled as "different" or "weird" becomes a powerful motivator, compelling us to sacrifice our authenticity in favor of social approval.

In essence, the conditioning to conform is a complex interplay of societal expectations, peer pressure, and the innate human desire for acceptance and belonging. It starts subtly, seeping into our consciousness from a young age, and continues to shape our behavior and beliefs well into adulthood. However, recognizing and challenging this conditioning is the first step towards reclaiming our authenticity and embracing our individuality.

After years of being under the intellectual guidance and influence of various external sources—whether it's the educational system that shaped my thinking or the voices of foreign educators and international media—I find myself at a crossroads. I've grown weary of lingering at the doorstep of my destiny and that of my Indigenous community, grappling with the burden of a pervasive problem rooted in toxic, limiting beliefs.

Increasingly, my focus has shifted inward, prompting me to reassess my priorities and values. Rather than conforming to the expectations and standards set by others, I am drawn to carving out my path that bears the imprint of my unique identity. I'm tired of blending in; I want to stand out and be recognized for my identity.

In my interactions and presentations, I strive to inject my flair, a signature style that sets me apart from the crowd. I'm unafraid to embrace controversy and welcome the reactions of others to my unconventional approach. It's liberating to shed the constraints of conformity and express myself authentically, even if it means challenging the status quo and inviting scrutiny from those around me.

At the center of this endeavor is a yearning for self-discovery and self-expression, driven by an intense need to break free from the boundaries of conventional norms. I'm recovering my own power and story, refusing to be limited by conventional thinking. And though the path ahead may be fraught with uncertainty and resistance, I am determined to forge ahead, guided by the light of my truth.

I have developed a solid aversion to consistency, especially regarding anything that limits my self-expression and autonomy. It's become increasingly apparent to me that organized religion and Eurocentric education have played a significant role in stifling my sense of identity and self-determination. While these systems may have served the communities in which they originated, I find myself questioning why I am stripped of my indigenous knowledge and forced to conform to the expectations and standards of others.

From an early age, I was indoctrinated into belief systems and educational frameworks that didn't reflect my cultural heritage or values. Instead of nurturing my innate wisdom and traditions, I was compelled to adopt foreign ideologies and perspectives, often at the expense of my identity.

This imposition has left me feeling marginalized and disconnected from my roots, as if my Indigenous knowledge and beliefs are inferior or irrelevant in the broader context of society. It's a form of cultural erasure that denies me the opportunity to embrace and celebrate the richness of my heritage.

I resent being made to feel like a mere caricature of someone else's culture, forced to conform to their worldview rather than honoring my ancestral wisdom. It's a deeply ingrained pattern of colonization and assimilation that seeks to subjugate indigenous voices and perpetuate systems of power and control.

Breaking Boundaries: Reclaiming Identity, Empowering Self

Despite the challenges I face in reclaiming my cultural identity and autonomy, I am determined to break free from these oppressive structures. I refuse to be confined by the narrow confines of Eurocentric norms and expectations. Instead, I am committed to rediscovering and revitalizing the knowledge and traditions intrinsic to my heritage, forging a path of self-discovery and empowerment rooted in authenticity and self-determination.

In my quest for excellence, I always seek innovative and groundbreaking ways of accomplishing tasks. When I find something I am passionate about, I am relentless in my pursuit of success, willing to face challenges head-on and overcome obstacles. Dependability is a hallmark of my character; I prefer to take ownership of tasks rather than delegate them to others.

I thrive on being the one to lead the way, initiating projects, and taking on responsibilities.

Being in the spotlight, at the forefront of action, is where I feel most comfortable. I enjoy being in a leadership position and taking charge of important tasks. With a strong sense of initiative and a drive for success, I possess all the necessary skills to excel in my endeavors.

However, I am also aware of the importance of maintaining balance. While I may be assertive and driven, I recognize the value of allowing others the space to express their ideas and abilities. Collaboration and teamwork are essential to success, and I strive to create an environment where everyone can contribute their best.

Ultimately, my greatest desire is autonomy— to chart my course and pursue my beliefs and convictions. As long as I can maintain this sense of independence and self-direction, I can achieve my goals and fulfill my potential in whatever field I choose.

There are moments when I feel a longing to inject more playfulness into my life, to embark on adventures, and to rediscover the joy and wonder that defined my childhood. It's as if my inner child is clamoring to break free, urging me to embrace the lightness and spontaneity of being truly present in the moment. I sense that now is the time to step into the spotlight and approach life with the carefree enthusiasm of the divine child within me.

In embracing this playful spirit, I am reminded that no matter what challenges or trials I may have faced recently, there is always room for joy and prosperity. It's a time of renewal when I can confidently move forward, knowing that success and abundance are on the horizon. With this mindset, I am ready to welcome whatever adventures await me, knowing that each experience will only add to the richness of my journey.

I allow myself to be guided by this sense of playful optimism. There, I find that my perspective on life begins to shift. The mundane tasks and responsibilities that once felt burdensome now take on a new light as I approach them with curiosity and wonder. Each day becomes an opportunity to explore, learn, and experience the world with fresh eyes.

In reconnecting with my inner child, I rediscovered a sense of spontaneity and creativity buried beneath the weight of adult responsibilities. I enjoy simple pleasures, whether taking a stroll in nature, indulging in creative pursuits, or sharing laughter with loved ones. It's a reminder that life is meant to be lived fully, embracing both the ups and downs with an open heart.

In doing so, I find that doors open, opportunities present themselves, and abundance flows effortlessly into my life. It's as if the universe responds to my newfound joy and possibility, guiding me toward experiences that align with my highest good.

With each step I take on this journey of rediscovery, I feel more aligned with my true self, more connected to the magic of life, and more grateful for the abundance surrounding me. As I continue to dance through life with the carefree spirit of a divine child, I know that the best is yet to come.

In my journey through career and vocation, I've encountered situations where my experience alone hasn't fully prepared me. Success, I've come to realize, is often a blend of hard work and luck. People usually attribute their success to timing or being in the right place at the right time. But beneath these varied expressions lies a common truth: readiness for opportunity.

I ponder, "Am I truly prepared for my moment to arrive? Am I willing to push beyond my comfort zone, embrace challenges, and pursue my dreams with unwavering determination?" These questions linger in my mind, urging me to confront my fears and insecurities.

If I am indeed ready, then the time is now to embark on this journey. I must harness the outgoing, friendly, and pleasant energy that flows through me, recognizing it as divine guidance guiding me toward my destiny. With humility and gratitude for the blessings bestowed upon me, I am infused with vitality, drive, and the courage to pursue my deepest desires.

I recognize the importance of expressing my adventurous, positive, and friendly nature through my work and life's mission. By staying true to myself and aligning with my life's purpose, I trust that the universe will reward me abundantly. It's a journey of self-discovery, growth, and fulfillment, and I am ready to embrace it wholeheartedly.

This readiness isn't just about being prepared for any opportunity that may come my way but also about actively shaping my destiny. It's about embracing the unknown with optimism and resilience, trusting in the universe's guidance as I navigate the twists and turns of my path.

Embarking on this journey, I'm fueled by a sense of purpose and a deep connection to my inner self. I understand that challenges may arise, but I am determined to face them head-on, drawing strength from the wellspring of courage within me.

I am reminded that success isn't just about achieving external milestones; it's also about staying true to my values and passions. By aligning my actions with my authentic self, I know I'm fulfilling my potential and contributing positively to the world.

With each step forward, I am guided by the universe's wisdom, trusting that every experience, whether smooth or challenging, is a valuable opportunity for growth and self-discovery. And so, I embrace this journey with open arms, ready to embrace the adventure.

11

Who Am I?

"Somewhere, something incredible is waiting to be known."
— *Blaise Pascal*

There's a paradox in aspiring to claim integrity while feeling disconnected from oneself. True integrity is about being in harmony with oneself, yet within me exist two personas: the authentic self I was meant to be and the persona I've adopted in my search for identity. Though they may seem identical to my senses, they are distinct, and I've found myself associating more with the latter persona as I journeyed in search of my true essence.

In moments of introspection, I've felt compelled to reach out to the one entity that genuinely comprehends my authentic self—the source from which I originated. In expressing my deepest aspirations to this source, I've realized that mere words cannot fully convey the depths of my desires. Only the silent language of my soul, the innermost stirrings of my being, can articulate the essence of who I truly am to the entity from which I emerged.

In this recognition, I discover comfort in knowing that my origin understands the depths of my inner self. As I convey my aspirations, I know that my essence transcends mere words. The silent dialogue of my soul and the unspoken melodies of my thoughts resonate with the receptive ears of my origin. In this connection, I pursue fulfillment and unity, embracing the assurance that the true nature of my being is both acknowledged and embraced.

In this sacred interchange, I release the constraints of language and embrace the profound connection that transcends mere words. It's a mutual recognition that ventures beyond the superficial, delving into the very core of my being. My origin, the one who intimately knows me, becomes the recipient of my unfiltered aspirations and the silent stirrings of my heart. This acknowledgment empowers me to navigate the intricacies of self-expression, finding resonance in the silent dialogue between my soul and the divine. As I traverse this path of acknowledgment, I am guided by the certainty that my origin perceives the purest essence of myself, transcending the limitations of spoken language.

In the profound moment of fully embracing my vulnerability and surrendering entirely to the essence of my being, I felt the dissolution of negative energy, making way for the emergence of positive forces within my mind and body. A serene balance enveloped my sense of self and purpose, emanating a newfound tranquility that surpassed my previous expectations and perceptions of the future. This transformative journey even reshaped my anticipation of what awaited me. Amidst this process of metamorphosis, I uncovered a deep connection to my life, perhaps for the first time, envisioning myself immersed in the destiny I was destined to fulfill. However, it's essential to acknowledge that this revelation was not untouched by the transformative touch of pain.

The Alchemy of Pain:
A Journey of Transformation and Resilience

I experienced a deep transformation as a result of enduring intense suffering. The distress prompted a more profound comprehension of the complexities of life's metaphorical window covering. The threads of pain, intricately intertwined into the fabric of my life, became vital components of the masterpiece that is my path. During times of openness and surrender, I experienced a change in my viewpoint.

Embracing the pain, I discovered reservoirs of resilience and strength previously unknown. The contours of my identity seemed to merge with the universal forces guiding my path. As I navigated life's ebbs and flows, the once-pervasive negative energies gave way to a wellspring of positive vitality.

This transformation wasn't without its obstacles; instead, it was a recognition that growth often springs forth from the fertile soil of discomfort. Once perceived as an adversary, the pain transformed into a companion on my journey of evolution, guiding me toward a prosperous future with purpose and connection.

In the depths of profound surrender, I found a resonance with the essence of my being and a seamless alignment with the universe. The life I envisioned ceased to be a distant dream; instead, it became a tangible reality, each step infused with the transformative essence of my journey.

Traveling through the complex web of my life, the bond with my inner self grew stronger. My experiences intertwined with time began to create a coherent story. What used to be a challenging experience of change is now proof of my strength and flexibility.

The journey of discovering myself unfolded as a sequence of revelations, where each layer of vulnerability exposed the true essence buried within. In the midst of suffering, I discovered the magic of self-improvement, turning my hardships into valuable lessons.

The positive energy that blossomed from this transformative journey illuminated my path and extended its reach, touching the lives of those around me. I felt a tangible interconnectedness with all beings, sensing a universal harmony resonating with the purpose that guided me forward.

I became a co-creator of my destiny by embracing my vulnerability and surrendering to the cosmic currents. The pain, once a source of anguish, catalyzed a more profound comprehension of life's intricate balance between joy and sorrow, growth and stagnation.

Tantamount to my envisioned life, I carry the profound lessons engraved in the fabric of my being. The metamorphosis continues an ongoing journey of self-discovery and purposeful existence, where the crucible of pain is the forge for a life abundant in meaning and connection.

Who am I? I am rooted in self-awareness, bearing a name that echoes my essence and harboring aspirations for a brighter tomorrow. Confronting conflicts and standing against injustice are inherent in my character, guided by deep compassion and generosity. Individuals like me are pivotal in illuminating the world with kindness and empathy.

In the vast expanse of existence, I believe someone remembered and cherished my presence somewhere in the tapestry of time. I trust that my name is whispered in someone's prayers as night fades into dawn, for a kindred soul extends its sheltering embrace, offering solace and support for both of us.

In the intricate window shade of my life, I intertwine threads of resilience and determination, transforming challenges into stepping-stones for growth and self-discovery. Amidst the storms that arise, I remain steadfast, anchored by my core values and lofty aspirations. Even amidst adversity, the echoes of my laughter resonate, a testament to my indomitable spirit.

As a seeker of knowledge, I traverse the expansive landscapes of wisdom, exploring beyond the visible horizon. My mind is a vast canvas adorned with the vibrant colors of curiosity and the intricate brushstrokes of intellectual exploration. Each book I delve into, and every conversation I partake in contributes to the ongoing masterpiece of my evolving understanding of the world.

As I traverse the intricate fabric of relationships, I tread mindfully, guided by the compass of empathy. Each interaction is an opportunity to offer support, lend a listening ear, and ignite inspiration in those who journey alongside me.

In quiet contemplation, I attune myself to the emotions that course through my being. From the joyful crescendos to the somber refrains of introspection, I embrace the full spectrum of my humanity. In this embrace, I discover the wellspring of authenticity that nourishes my soul.

Driven by the pursuit of purpose, I chart a course guided by a North Star that illuminates the path ahead. I dream of envisioning a world where kindness reigns supreme, and each individual's unique light shines brightly. Every action I take leaves imprints of compassion etched into the fabric of time for all eternity.

In life's elaborate tapestry, I am just one thread intricately connected to the overall pattern. Every choice and statement adds a thread to the evolving story of my journey. While I continue to shape my destiny, I recognize that my unique story is woven together with many others.

Who do I find within? An ever-unfolding spirit, a weaver of personal chronicles, and a collaborator in humanity's collective saga.

I've often pondered the possibility of newborn babies having memories. As Plato suggests, could they possess untold stories of distant places and events predating their birth? If only they could speak, perhaps they could reveal chillingly accurate details and bizarrely specific tales.

On my birthday, as I drew my first breath on this earth, it was as if a snapshot of the skies was taken—a personalized map of stars guiding the trajectory of my life in a predictable pattern. This realization offers me a unique opportunity to refine and adjust the structures of my life without causing unnecessary upheaval.

While I haven't always felt eager to take on new challenges, I've learned over the years that I can stretch beyond my previous limits. Each New Year, I resolve not to hold back, determined to embrace whatever opportunities come my way.

Now, in the prime of my life, I grasp more profoundly the interconnectedness of all living beings. I've also cultivated my spiritual side and committed to generosity and charity.

I once came across a quote by Steve Jobs that left a lasting impression on me: "You can't connect the dots in the future; you can only connect them looking backward. You must trust that the dots will somehow connect in your future." Reflecting on my own life, I realize that this sentiment holds.

As I trace the dots of my past, it becomes evident that I've made choices of which I'm not proud. Some moments fill me with shame. However, before anyone rushes to judgment, it's essential to acknowledge the many dots that connect to moments of pride and accomplishment.

I hail from humble beginnings, raised by modest parents and surrounded by siblings. My parents were educators—my father was in high school, and my mother was in elementary school. Our family had a routine: my mother would finish her teaching day early to prepare lunch for us. Since elementary schools dismissed earlier than others, we'd arrive home to find a warm meal. These moments, though meant to be lunch, often felt like dinners. They're cherished memories filled with happiness and warmth.

Those afternoons spent around the table, sharing stories and laughter, are etched in my mind as some of the fondest memories of my childhood. Despite our modest circumstances, there was always an abundance of love and togetherness in our home.

They grew up in such an environment that instilled in me a strong sense of values and work ethic. My parents taught me the importance of perseverance and kindness through their dedication to education and family. They may not have had much material wealth, but they gave us a wealth of love and support that money cannot buy.

I constantly draw upon the lessons and values instilled in me during those formative years. While there may be moments of regret and shame for past mistakes, there are also moments of pride and gratitude for the positive impact I've made, thanks to the foundation laid by my upbringing.

In connecting the dots of my past, I am reminded of the interconnectedness of all experiences—the highs and lows, the triumphs and challenges—that have shaped me into the person I am today. As I continue to move forward, I do so with a sense of faith and optimism that the dots will indeed connect in ways that lead to a fulfilling and purposeful future.

Life wasn't always this way. My family lived a lifestyle reminiscent of a military family. We were constantly on the move, akin to nomads, because of my father's role as one of the pioneering educators who volunteered to travel from the South to the North to help establish schools and train teachers. He was always willing to lend a hand wherever a new school needed him.

As a foundational teacher in these new schools, he typically stayed for around three years before being transferred to the next assignment. Once the school ran smoothly, it was time to pack up and relocate again. Unfortunately, this also meant uprooting the entire family each time a new opportunity arose.

This transient lifestyle meant our family became accustomed to constant change and adaptation. Moving from place to place meant leaving behind familiar faces and routines and providing us with unique opportunities for growth and exploration.

Despite the challenges of uprooting our lives every few years, my parents instilled a sense of resilience and adaptability. They emphasized the importance of embracing new experiences and learning from every situation we encountered.

Living as part of this nomadic educational mission also fostered a deep sense of community and camaraderie among us. We formed strong bonds with other families in similar situations, finding solace and support in our shared experiences.

I vividly recall the annual festivity organized by the emir of the northern Nigerian community where we live. It was a special dinner held exclusively for non-indigenous expatriate children, a gesture of hospitality and cultural exchange that left a lasting impression on me.

The event took place in the grand courtyard of the emir's palace, a majestic setting that added to the allure of the occasion. There was a palpable sense of excitement as we gathered around a long rectangular table adorned with traditional decorations. The table was set with simple yet delightful treats: cabin biscuits (cookies) and generous servings of margarine, sodas, and peanuts.

For us children, it was a rare and cherished opportunity to indulge in these delicacies, especially in the regal ambiance of the palace courtyard. The festive atmosphere was contagious, as laughter and chatter filled the air, blending seamlessly with traditional music playing in the background.

As I eagerly reached for a biscuit and dipped it into the margarine, I couldn't help but notice the jagged edge of the cup. In my haste to savor the delicious treat, I accidentally grazed my right finger, leaving a visible mark beside my thumb. Though minor, it serves as a tangible reminder of that memorable evening spent in the emir's palace.

Looking back, it's not just the taste of the biscuits or the palace's grandeur that I remember most. It's the warmth of the hospitality extended to us, the sense of inclusion and acceptance in a community that was not our own. In that moment, we were not just guests; we were embraced as part of the fabric of the community, united by the spirit of camaraderie and shared experiences.

While it wasn't always easy, I can see how this nomadic lifestyle shaped me into the person I am today. It taught me to be open-minded, adaptable, and resilient in the face of change. Though the journey was often challenging, the memories and lessons learned are invaluable.

By graduating from high school, I had attended eight different schools and three more during my graduate studies. While some of these moves were due to my parents' nomadic lifestyle, others were driven by my choices. Though each relocation came with valid reasons, the impact on my life was undeniable.

Resolving unfinished business became my priority, whether tying up loose ends or reconciling relationships left behind. These experiences shaped my understanding of the transient nature of life and the importance of seizing every opportunity for growth and connection.

Navigating through numerous transitions and upheavals, I learned to prioritize closure and resolution in every aspect of my life. Whether it was wrapping up loose ends from a previous chapter or seeking reconciliation with estranged connections, I embraced the opportunity to confront and address unfinished business.

These experiences taught me resilience, adaptability, and the importance of embracing change and uncertainty. While the transient nature of my upbringing may have initially hindered my ability to form deep connections, it ultimately instilled in me a sense of independence and self-reliance.

Reflecting on my journey, I recognize the profound impact that my nomadic upbringing has had on shaping my identity and worldview. It has taught me to approach life with an open mind and a willingness to embrace the unknown, knowing that every transition brings the potential for growth and transformation.

Figuring out the path to finding my way forward, my belief in a brighter future never wavered. Despite the challenges I faced, I remained steadfast in my faith. However, I realized the distinction between overcoming those struggles and holding onto them unnecessarily. I understood that I ultimately had the pen to my own story.

With this realization in mind, I propelled myself forward, fueled by a determination to harness newfound energies and forge a path toward something extraordinary. While the challenges persisted even after this decision, I saw an opportunity to rewrite my story and embark on a fresh chapter of life. And so, with unwavering resolve, I seized the chance to craft a new story and embrace a new way of living.

Despite the lingering challenges that persisted, I refused to be deterred. With each obstacle encountered, I saw it as an opportunity for growth and transformation. Armed with this mindset, I embraced the journey ahead with a renewed sense of purpose and determination.

Working with these newfound energies, I began to lay the foundation for something remarkable in my life. It wasn't about escaping the challenges or pretending they didn't exist;

instead, it was about facing them head-on and using them as catalysts for positive change.

Venturing into this new chapter, I embraced the unknown with open arms, knowing that every step forward was closer to realizing my dreams. And so, with optimism and resilience guiding my path, I embarked on the journey of rewriting my story and creating a life filled with purpose, passion, and possibility.

The catalyst for my resolve to seize control of my destiny stemmed from a profound frustration with constantly being relegated to the sidelines in my narrative. It was a feeling of discontentment that had been simmering beneath the surface for far too long, urging me to break free from the shackles of passivity and assert my presence at the forefront of my story.

I vividly recall countless instances where I found myself overshadowed by others, my aspirations and ambitions taking a backseat to the needs and desires of those around me. Whether in my relationships, career, or creative pursuits, I felt like a spectator, watching life unfold before me without actively participating.

However, with each passing day, my discontent grew stronger, fueling a burning desire to reclaim my agency and assert myself as the protagonist of my narrative. I realized that I held the power to shape my destiny, and it was up to me to seize that power and chart a course that aligned with my deepest aspirations and values.

It was a pivotal moment of self-realization, a turning point where I made a conscious decision no longer to accept a supporting role in my own life. Instead, I resolved to step into the spotlight with confidence and determination, ready to embrace the challenges and opportunities ahead.

From that moment onward, I embarked on a journey of self-discovery and empowerment, breaking free from the constraints of self-doubt and fear that had held me back for so long. I began to assert myself in all areas of my life, setting ambitious goals and pursuing them with unwavering determination.

It wasn't always easy, and there were undoubtedly obstacles along the way. But with each obstacle I faced, I grew more robust and resilient, fortified by the knowledge that I was the master of my destiny.

Today, as I reflect on the journey that led me to this point, I am filled with profound gratitude for the courage and determination that propelled me forward. I may have once played second fiddle in my own story, but now I stand firmly in the spotlight, ready to embrace whatever the future may hold with open arms.

During this pivotal moment, I began to sense a divine illumination beckoning me forward, offering its compelling energy to guide me along my soul's journey. Much like the sun in our solar system, around which all other planets orbit, I realized that the stars of my destiny were also aligning around me. I embraced the perspective that I am the orchestrator of my destiny, calling the shots in my own story.

With this newfound sense of empowerment, I harnessed the masculine energy of Divine Intelligence to propel myself forward and transform my dreams into reality. Whenever doubt or fear threatened to hold me back, I reminded myself how far I had come.

Today, I am more determined than ever to seize every opportunity and make the most of the power within me. With unwavering resolve, I am charting my course, confident in my ability to shape my destiny and fulfill my highest potential.

Every trial and tribulation I've faced has served a purpose, preparing me for the next phase of my journey. These challenges pushed me to tap into reservoirs of strength I never knew existed, fostering a resilience that enabled me to bounce back stronger from adversity. Each obstacle forced me to grow, shaping me into who I am today.

I've come to understand that resilience isn't just about weathering storms; it's about bouncing back even stronger from threats or vulnerabilities. Through this process, I engaged in essential shadow work, delving into the depths of my psyche to confront my fears and insecurities. These

411

introspective journeys primed me for the beautiful new path that lies ahead.

In the grand orchestration of life, I've come to recognize that nothing happens by chance. Divine Intelligence has meticulously orchestrated every experience, every setback, and every triumph. My soul chose this precise moment to embark on a profound course correction in my life journey.

During moments of introspection, I pondered what I truly desired, even if the answers were darker than anticipated. Yet, I embraced honesty and authenticity, understanding, accepting, and showing compassion to myself in the process.

Basking in the radiance of divine light illuminating my path, confidence becomes my beacon, guiding me toward manifesting my soul-resonating dreams. However, I remain humble and mindful not to let my ego cloud my judgment. My goals are imbued with a more profound purpose, anchoring me in a place of abundance and fulfillment.

Now is not the time to hold back or shrink from challenges; it's the time to seize every opportunity with unwavering determination. I am ready to embrace the journey ahead, knowing that I have the strength, resilience, and wisdom to navigate whatever lies on the path to my soul's fulfillment.

This newfound understanding and clarity encourage me to pursue my dreams with unwavering conviction. I refuse to be held back by doubt or fear, knowing I can achieve greatness.

Moving forward, I am mindful of remaining humble and grounded. I understand that true success lies not in accolades or achievements but in the depth of my character and the integrity of my actions.

Each step I take is guided by the deeper purpose behind my goals, aligning me with my soul's calling and attracting abundance into my life. I trust in the journey and embrace the challenges that come my way, for I know they are simply opportunities for growth and transformation.

Now is the time to fully embrace my potential and live authentically, honoring the path that I have chosen for myself. With the divine light shining brightly within me, I am ready to step into my power and create the life of my dreams.

The saying "discover first and then recover later" has gained deep meaning for me as I journeyed through months of self-discovery. The more I delved into understanding myself, the more I realized the role of achievement in building self-confidence. Each past success became a stepping-stone, boosting my belief in my abilities and setting high standards for myself.

These moments of triumph bolstered my confidence and fueled my aspirations for the future. Each accomplishment gave me a greater understanding of my capabilities and a renewed sense of purpose.

Reflecting on this journey, I am reminded of the importance of self-belief in navigating life's challenges. By recognizing my past achievements, I am better equipped to face adversity with resilience and determination.

Moving forward, I am committed to continuing this journey of self-discovery, armed with the knowledge that my past successes serve as a foundation for future growth and achievement.

Despite identifying as an adult child of an alcoholic long ago, it wasn't until my journey led me to psychotherapy and later psychodrama that I truly grasped the extent of the trauma I had endured. My early life experiences had woven intricate patterns into the fabric of my being, shaping the scripts by which I navigated through life. I marveled at how these experiences manifested in various contexts and relationships, influencing my actions and interactions with others.

Through introspective self-work, I gained a profound understanding of how my experiences of trauma had elicited intense emotional reactions within me. I realized the profound impact of these experiences on shaping my worldview and influencing how I engaged with the world around me.

This journey of self-discovery has been both illuminating and challenging. It has forced me to confront painful truths about my past and how it continues to shape my present reality. However, it has also allowed me to heal and grow in ways I never thought possible.

Through psychotherapy and psychodrama, I have delved deep into the recesses of my mind, uncovering layers of trauma and unresolved emotions. Each session has been a step closer to unraveling the complex web of my life experiences and understanding how they have influenced my thoughts, behaviors, and relationships.

One of the most profound realizations from this journey is the recognition of the strong emotional reactions that specific triggers evoke within me. These reactions, rooted in past trauma, have often colored my perceptions and interactions with the world around me. By shining a light on these deeply ingrained patterns, I have been able to work towards healing and breaking free from their grip.

Continuing on this journey, I am filled with a sense of hope and empowerment. I know that confronting my past and embracing my vulnerabilities paves the way for a brighter and more fulfilling future. With each step forward, I am reclaiming my agency and rewriting the tale of my life.

Now, with a newfound understanding of the decisions made in my formative years, I am equipped to forge a path forward with clarity and intention. This insight has empowered me to approach communication and relationships with authenticity and sincerity, free from the need for manipulation or games.

I've realized that my thoughts are the driving force behind my feelings and behaviors rather than external circumstances or events. By cultivating inner peace and prosperity, I've transformed my external reality to reflect the harmony within.

This transformation hasn't come without effort. I've dedicated myself to the ongoing work of self-improvement, focusing on nurturing my internal identity. As a result, I now wield control over my destiny, starting with the realm of my mind and internal world.

I recognize that many of my traumatic experiences stem from my relationship with my father during my formative years at home. Understanding this root cause allows me to confront and heal from these wounds, paving the way for greater self-awareness and personal growth.

By acknowledging the impact of my early experiences with my father, I have taken a crucial step towards healing and self-discovery. These reflections have illuminated the deep-seated patterns and beliefs that have influenced my relationships and interactions.

Through introspection and inner work, I am gradually untangling the emotional knots that have bound me to the past. Each moment of self-awareness brings me closer to liberation from the grip of old wounds and allows me to embrace a future filled with possibility and growth.

I am committed to nurturing a compassionate and authentic relationship with myself. By honoring my truth and embracing vulnerability, I am creating a foundation of resilience and empowerment to build a life of fulfillment and joy.

Though the road ahead may be challenging, I approach it with courage and determination, knowing that I am the architect of my destiny. With each step forward, I reclaim more of my power and move closer to living a life aligned with my highest potential.

My father, an educator and a strict disciplinarian at home and in the professional sphere of school, held himself and others to exceedingly high standards. At times, I found these standards overly idealistic and unattainable, mainly when I was on the receiving end of his unwavering belief system. Surprisingly, despite any shortcomings I perceived in myself, my father, like most fathers, only saw a future filled with promise and potential for me. However, there were moments in my early years when I felt a sense of unease, as if there were peculiarities surrounding me that I couldn't quite grasp.

My father firmly believed in distributive justice and refused to overlook any transgressions against societal norms or the ethical code he deemed necessary for successful living. Consequently, whenever I faltered or made poor decisions, he ensured that I faced the consequences of my actions. While I resented this approach and often sought solace from within, I now recognize the invaluable lessons it imparted.

I know the potential within me to construct something extraordinary, akin to an empire. However, I understand the importance of directing or redirecting, as necessary, my energy and concentration purposefully. With a soul characterized by strength and nobility, I hold firm confidence in channeling my inner power and envisioning grand aspirations. My being resonates with the vitality required to manifest something genuinely remarkable.

Growing up, I was immersed in a culture where authority figures were revered and rarely questioned. It feels like eons ago, a time when common knowledge was far from widespread, and those in positions of power often dictated truth. This mindset persisted into my upbringing, perpetuating deep-seated subconscious patterns that hindered my ability to manifest abundance.

These deeply rooted beliefs have left a lasting mark on my karma, causing me to remain stuck in a pattern of limited resources and difficulties. Now I realize I can change this story and escape these restrictive behaviors. With a fresh realization, I am prepared to accept my inherent abilities and create the successful future I am worthy of.

I am taking the first step toward liberation by acknowledging the influence of my upbringing and the subconscious patterns that have shaped my beliefs. I recognize that true wealth lies in material possessions and the abundance of opportunities and possibilities surrounding me.

I am committed to releasing myself from the shackles of lack and scarcity. With each moment of introspection and self-awareness, I am rewriting my wealth imprint and aligning myself with the infinite abundance of the universe.

With a newfound sense of empowerment and purpose, I am ready to channel my inner strength and build the empire I envision. I embrace the journey ahead with optimism and determination, knowing that I have the power to create the life of my dreams.

The reality is that each of us harbors a shadowy side within ourselves. Some shadows are inherited from our parents, learned during childhood, or carried over from past lives. They may be ancient, hidden deep within our souls, obscured by societal conditioning and expectations.

Often, we are unaware of these shadows, buried beneath layers of programming and societal norms. Alternatively, we may ignore them, hoping they will disappear if we ignore them long enough, akin to the boogie man lurking under the bed.

However, these shadows persist, wreaking havoc in our lives, quietly limiting our potential and blocking the flow of abundance. Until we confront and acknowledge these shadows, we cannot truly embrace our full potential and experience the abundance life offers.

Yet, facing our shadows head-on opens the door to profound transformation and growth. It requires courage to peer into the depths of our souls and confront the aspects of ourselves we may prefer to keep hidden. However, in doing so, we reclaim our power and liberate ourselves from the constraints of fear and limitation.

Embracing our shadows is not about succumbing to darkness but integrating all facets of our being. It is a journey of self-discovery and self-acceptance, where we acknowledge our imperfections and embrace our humanity.

As we shine a light on our shadows, we begin to dissolve the barriers that have held us back, allowing abundance to flow freely into our lives. With each step forward, we move closer to living authentically and experiencing the richness of life.

I experimented with positive thinking, visualization, and goal setting to overcome my inner blocks. However, I soon realized these obstacles would persist until I addressed their root causes. My dark side proved to be stubborn and resilient.

But, as you may have guessed, I wouldn't be sharing this story if I hadn't discovered a solution. There is purpose in my pain, and I'm eager to share the pivotal moment when everything changed for me.

It was a day unlike any other when my life was suddenly flooded with light instead of darkness, hope instead of despair, and purpose instead of aimlessness. I forged deep connections and no longer felt isolated and alone.

What's even more remarkable is the profound impact on my physical well-being. I sleep soundly, wake up with boundless energy, and feel rejuvenated, as if I've regained the vitality of my youth.

But perhaps the most astonishing change is the newfound ease with which I manifest wealth—something I had only dared to dream of before.

This transformation wasn't instantaneous or effortless. It required dedication, introspection, and a willingness to confront my deepest fears and insecurities. Through therapy, meditation, and soul-searching, I peeled back the layers of my psyche, gradually releasing the grip of my inner shadows.

As I confronted and healed my inner wounds, I began to experience profound shifts in my outer reality.

421

Relationships blossomed, opportunities presented themselves, and abundance flowed into my life with unprecedented ease.

Now, I stand on the portal of a new chapter, filled with boundless potential and limitless possibilities. Armed with the knowledge that I can shape my destiny, I step forward with confidence and determination, eager to embrace all life offers.

In my formative years, I was immersed in a culture where authority figures were often perceived as infallible, leading to a prevalent acceptance of abuse. This phenomenon was evident within religious institutions and secular environments, where minimal mechanisms were used to address and prevent misconduct. Consequently, I became entangled in a web of emotions characterized by low self-esteem, shame, and fear, all of which were deeply rooted in the traumas I experienced.

For instance, within my religious community, there was a pervasive belief that questioning or challenging the actions of leaders was tantamount to blasphemy. This unchecked authority often enabled instances of emotional and psychological abuse to go unchecked, leaving lasting scars on those affected. Similarly, in secular settings such as educational institutions or workplaces, power imbalances and a lack of accountability contributed to an environment where abuse would flourish unchecked.

These experiences left me grappling with a sense of inadequacy and vulnerability as I struggled to reconcile the image of authority with the realities of abuse. It took considerable introspection and healing to recognize that the fault lay not with me but with the systems that allowed such abuses to occur unchecked. Through therapy, support networks, and personal growth, I have begun to reclaim my sense of self-worth and resilience, shedding the shackles of shame and fear that once held me captive.

Like countless others, I devised coping mechanisms to safeguard myself from enduring additional harm. During my formative years, these strategies offered a semblance of protection, enabling me to navigate challenging circumstances with resilience. However, as I transitioned into adulthood, I began to recognize that the coping mechanisms I had relied upon were no longer serving me effectively. Rather than empowering me to thrive, they inadvertently became barriers, perpetuating a cycle of limitation and despair.

For example, one coping mechanism I developed was to withdraw emotionally from difficult situations, convincing myself that detachment was synonymous with strength. While this approach temporarily relieved immediate stressors, it hindered my ability to form meaningful connections and authenticate with others. Instead of fostering genuine resilience, it bred a sense of isolation and loneliness that left me feeling emotionally depleted.

Similarly, another coping mechanism I adopted was to suppress my emotions and bury painful memories deep within myself, believing that acknowledging them would only exacerbate my suffering. However, I soon realized that this strategy only served to intensify my inner turmoil as unresolved emotions continued to fester beneath the surface, poisoning my mental and emotional well-being.

In hindsight, I understand that these coping mechanisms were born out of necessity during a time of vulnerability and adversity. Yet, in adulthood, I recognized the need to reassess and reframe these outdated strategies. Through therapy, self-reflection, and a commitment to personal growth, I have begun to cultivate healthier coping mechanisms rooted in self-awareness, self-compassion, and emotional resilience. By embracing vulnerability and embracing my emotions rather than suppressing them, I have found greater freedom and authenticity in navigating life's challenges.

I realized that temporary circumstances influenced my decisions, anchoring me to my past traumas. This profound insight served as a wake-up call, urging me to reevaluate my mindset and break free from the constraints of my history. It dawned on me that I had been allowing past experiences to dictate my present and future, limiting my growth and potential.

For instance, I had been avoiding taking risks or pursuing new opportunities out of fear of repeating past failures or experiencing further pain. This fear had paralyzed me, preventing me from fully embracing life and all its possibilities. However, upon recognizing the transient nature of my circumstances, I understood that my past did not have to define my future.

In light of this revelation, I embarked on a journey of self-discovery and personal growth, determined to release myself from the grip of past traumas. Through therapy, self-reflection, and intentional mindset shifts, I began to dismantle the mental barriers that had been holding me back. I learned to challenge negative thought patterns and reframe my experiences in a more empowering light.

By acknowledging that my past experiences were just that—experiences—I freed myself from the burden of allowing them to dictate my present and future. Instead of viewing setbacks as permanent roadblocks, I started to see them as temporary detours on the path to personal evolution. This shift in perspective empowered me to embrace change and pursue my aspirations with renewed vigor and optimism.

Armed with this newfound awareness, I embarked on a profound journey of self-discovery and healing. Recognizing the need for professional guidance, I actively sought out therapy sessions to delve into the depths of my past and unravel the layers of trauma that had accumulated over the years. Through these therapeutic sessions, I confronted painful memories, explored the roots of my coping mechanisms, and unearthed the underlying beliefs that had been shaping my worldview.

Additionally, I dedicated myself to regular self-reflection practices, carving out time in my daily routine to journal, meditate, and engage in introspection. These moments of solitude allowed me to clarify my emotions, identify recurring behavior patterns, and cultivate a deeper understanding of myself.

Moreover, I made a conscious effort to surround myself with supportive individuals who fostered an environment of empathy, understanding, and validation. Their unwavering encouragement and acceptance gave me the safe space to share my experiences, express my emotions, and receive the validation I had long yearned for.

For example, I confided in trusted friends who listened without judgment, offering comfort and reassurance. Their willingness to stand by my side through the highs and lows of my healing journey was a testament to the power of genuine connection and solidarity.

These therapeutic interventions and supportive relationships formed the foundation of my healing journey, empowering me to confront my past traumas, cultivate self-compassion, and embark on a path of profound transformation and personal growth.

As I immersed myself further in this transformative process, I embarked on unraveling the deeply ingrained limiting beliefs and patterns that had hindered my growth and happiness for years. Through introspection and self-awareness, I confronted the negative narratives I had internalized about myself and my worth.

For instance, I recognized that I had long believed my worthiness was contingent upon external validation or achievement. This belief led me to seek approval and validation from others, often at the expense of my well-being. However, through therapy and self-reflection, I began to challenge this belief, realizing that external factors did not determine my inherent worthiness but were an intrinsic aspect of my being.

Moreover, I learned to cultivate self-compassion—a practice that involved treating myself with kindness, understanding, and acceptance, especially in moments of struggle or failure. Instead of harshly criticizing myself for past mistakes or perceived shortcomings, I learned to offer myself the same empathy and compassion I would extend to a needy friend.

For example, when I made a mistake at work or experienced a setback in my personal life, I consciously refrained from self-criticism. Instead, I chose to offer myself words of encouragement and support. This shift in mindset allowed me to navigate challenges with greater resilience and self-assurance.

Through these practices of self-compassion and self-reflection, I began dismantling the barriers of self-doubt and insecurity that had once held me back. I embraced the truth of my inherent worthiness, recognizing that I deserved love, respect, and acceptance simply by being human. This newfound sense of self-compassion and self-worth became the foundation upon which I built a life of authenticity, fulfillment, and empowerment.

Gradually, I started to make different choices, ones that were aligned with my true desires and aspirations. I refused to let my past define me any longer, recognizing that I held the power to shape my destiny.

Through perseverance and determination, I gradually reclaimed my agency and sovereignty. I opened myself up to new possibilities and embraced the boundless potential that lay before me.

Now, as I stand on the edge of a new chapter in my life, I am filled with optimism and empowerment. I know that the journey ahead may have its challenges, but I face them with courage and resilience, secure in the knowledge that I am the architect of my future.

Stop the presses! A recent revelation has rocked my world: I have an undeniable craving for the approval and admiration of others, yet I frequently subject myself to harsh self-criticism. While acknowledging certain flaws in my character, I've developed coping mechanisms to offset them.

For instance, I may go to great lengths in social situations to ensure others perceive me favorably. I meticulously craft my words and actions, striving to be perceived as likable and competent. However, behind the façade of confidence lies a nagging sense of insecurity, driving me to seek validation from external sources.

Moreover, I often find myself dissecting my behavior critically, scrutinizing every word spoken and every decision made. While this self-awareness can be beneficial in certain respects, it can also lead to feelings of inadequacy and self-doubt.

To compensate for these perceived weaknesses, I may engage in behaviors to bolster my self-esteem or shield myself from criticism. For example, I might avoid taking risks or seeking new opportunities that could expose my vulnerabilities. Instead, I may cling to familiarity and routine, seeking refuge in the comfort of the known.

Additionally, I may adopt a perfectionistic mindset, setting impossibly high standards and berating myself when I fall short. This relentless pursuit of perfection can be exhausting and counterproductive, preventing me from fully embracing my authentic self and pursuing my passions confidently.

Despite these challenges, I am slowly learning to embrace my imperfections and cultivate self-compassion by acknowledging that it's okay to make mistakes and that my worthiness is not contingent upon the approval of others; I am gradually breaking free from the cycle of self-criticism and striving for authenticity.

Through mindfulness, self-reflection, and therapy, I am learning to quiet the voice of my inner critic and cultivate a more compassionate and accepting attitude towards myself. By treating myself with the same kindness and understanding I extend to others, I find greater peace and fulfillment in my journey of self-discovery and personal growth.

Despite outward appearances of discipline and self-control, I've realized that within me lies a reservoir of untapped potential, yearning to be free. Beneath the façade of composure, I struggle with internal battles of worry and insecurity, which have often hindered my ability to embrace my capabilities and pursue my passions fully.

For example, in my professional life, I may project an image of confidence and competence, meeting deadlines and achieving goals with apparent ease. However, beneath the surface, I may harbor doubts about my abilities or fear of failure, leading to moments of self-doubt and anxiety.

Similarly, I may strive to maintain an aura of strength and stability in my relationships, offering support and guidance to others in need. Yet, internally, I may wrestle with feelings of inadequacy or fear of rejection, causing me to second-guess my worthiness or avoid vulnerability.

These internal struggles have often held me back from fully embracing my potential and pursuing my aspirations with confidence and conviction. Instead of stepping boldly into new opportunities or challenges, I have sometimes hesitated, allowing self-doubt and insecurity to dictate my actions.

However, with this newfound awareness, I am committed to confronting these inner demons and unlocking the full extent of my potential. I am learning to challenge negative thought patterns and cultivate a more resilient and empowered mindset through self-reflection, therapy, and personal growth practices.

For instance, when faced with worry or self-doubt, I now practice self-compassion and mindfulness, acknowledging my feelings without judgment and reminding myself of my inherent worthiness and capabilities. Additionally, I seek support from trusted friends, mentors, or therapists who guide and encourage me as I navigate these internal struggles.

By embracing vulnerability and facing my fears head-on, I am gradually breaking free from insecurity and stepping into my power with newfound confidence and resilience. Though the journey may be challenging, I am committed to unleashing the full extent of my potential and living a life guided by authenticity, courage, and self-assurance.

At times, I find myself plagued by doubts regarding the decisions I've made or the actions I've taken. This uncertainty often leads me to seek control over others' responses as I try to validate my choices and actions.

This inner conflict has led me on a journey of self-discovery and introspection. I've begun to explore the roots of my need for approval and the underlying insecurities that drive my behavior.

Through therapy and self-reflection, I've gained insight into how my past experiences and upbringing have shaped my perception of myself and others. I've learned to challenge the negative self-talk and self-doubt that have held me back and to embrace a more compassionate and accepting attitude towards myself.

As I continue to work on building my self-esteem and confidence, I am gradually letting go of the need to seek validation from others. Instead, I am learning to trust in my judgment and to find fulfillment from within.

It's a journey filled with ups and downs, but I am committed to overcoming these inner obstacles and living authentically. I know that true self-acceptance lies not in the approval of others but in the unconditional love and acceptance of myself.

Fear

The fear of failure has become a significant barrier to my effective communication. This fear often leads me to over-explain or apologize excessively as I desperately seek to avoid potential misunderstandings or adverse reactions. In doing so, I unwittingly assume responsibility for how others perceive me, burdening myself with the weight of their opinions.

This struggle has been akin to shedding old skin, much like a snake molting in ecdysis. I've realized that to integrate and grow into my entire self truly; I must shed the protective layers of my childhood and adolescence.

For years, I've been trapped in the confines of perfectionism, constantly striving to meet the impossible standards set by my inner child and inner critic. However, I've recently had a breakthrough: I've realized that true self-acceptance and empowerment stem from within. Rather than seeking validation from external sources, I'm embarking on self-discovery and liberation.

In the past, I allowed my sense of worth to be determined by the approval of others, constantly seeking validation and affirmation from those around me. Whether in my personal relationships or professional endeavors, I felt the need always to be correct, to meet everyone else's expectations, and to avoid making mistakes at all costs.

However, I've understood that this constant striving for external validation only imprisoned me further, stifling my authenticity and hindering my personal growth. It's like I've been living in a self-imposed cage, afraid to step out and embrace my true identity for fear of judgment or rejection.

But now, I'm breaking free from these shackles. I'm learning to trust myself, to honor my intuition, and to embrace my imperfections as part of what makes me uniquely human. Instead of allowing my inner critic to dictate my actions, I'm cultivating self-compassion and self-awareness, recognizing that I am worthy of love and acceptance just as I am.

This shift in mindset has been transformative. I'm no longer seeking validation from others or striving always to be correct. Instead, I'm turning inward, drawing strength and confidence from introspection and self-awareness. I'm learning to silence the voices of doubt and insecurity that once held me back and to embrace the courage to be authentically myself.

For example, in my professional life, I'm no longer afraid to speak up and share my ideas, even if they go against the grain or challenge the status quo. I'm confident in my abilities and willing to take risks, knowing that failure is not a reflection of my worth but an opportunity for growth and learning.

Similarly, in my relationships, I'm setting boundaries and prioritizing my well-being rather than constantly seeking approval and validation from others. I'm learning to trust my instincts and honor my needs and desires, even if it means disappointing or upsetting those around me.

Overall, this journey of self-liberation and empowerment is still a work in progress. Still, I'm committed to embracing the courage to be authentically myself, unburdened by the opinions of others. As I continue to trust in my worth and embrace my true identity, I know I'll find greater peace, fulfillment, and authenticity in every aspect of my life.

This journey of self-discovery has been both challenging and rewarding. As I confront my fear of failure and relinquish the need for external validation, I reclaim my autonomy and embrace my true identity.

With each step forward, I am shedding the layers of self-doubt and insecurity that have held me back for so long. It's a process of liberation as I let go of old patterns and beliefs that no longer serve me and forge a new path based on authenticity and self-acceptance.

I cultivate a more profound sense of self-confidence and resilience through introspection and inner work. I am learning to trust my abilities and instincts and communicate with clarity and conviction, free from fear and self-doubt.

As I continue to grow and evolve, I am excited to see where this journey will take me. With each hurdle overcome and each layer shed, I am moving closer to living a life of purpose and fulfillment, guided by the light of my inner wisdom.

I am naturally inclined towards change and variety, and I often feel restless when confined by restrictions and limitations. As an independent thinker, I value evidence and proof over unquestioningly accepting others' statements. I am cautious about revealing too much of myself to others, recognizing the importance of maintaining discretion.

My personality is multifaceted, sometimes exhibiting extroverted, generous qualities, while at other times, I withdraw into introversion and reserve. I am comfortable navigating between these different states, adapting as needed to various social situations.

Others may view Some of my aspirations as unrealistic, but I am undeterred by their skepticism. I embrace my dreams with determination and resilience, refusing to let the opinions of others hinder my pursuit of what truly inspires me.

Despite the skepticism I encounter, I remain steadfast in pursuing my aspirations, confident in my ability to overcome challenges and achieve my goals. While others may view my dreams as lofty or unattainable, I see them as opportunities for growth and personal fulfillment.

My willingness to embrace change and pursue my passions sets me apart, driving me to explore new horizons and push the boundaries of what is possible. I understand that the path to success may be fraught with obstacles, but I am prepared to face them head-on with courage and determination.

In my journey towards self-realization, I continue to evolve and grow, learning from successes and setbacks. I refuse to be confined by the expectations of others or limited by their perceptions of what is achievable.

Instead, I chart my course, guided by my inner convictions and driven by a relentless desire to live life to the fullest. With each step forward, I embrace the opportunity to defy expectations and prove that even the most audacious dreams can become a reality.

Amidst the turmoil of my life, I found myself feeling like a refugee within my own body—a stranger in unfamiliar territory, fleeing from the pain, trauma, and dysfunction that plagued me. Lost in the labyrinth of my emotions and intellect, I struggled to navigate the tumultuous waters of my inner world, resorting to irrational decisions as my coping mechanism.

I became adept at intellectualizing my emotions, erecting walls of logic to shield myself from the rawness of my pain and trauma. However, this intellectual detachment only deepened the chasm between my emotional and rational selves, leaving me adrift in a sea of confusion and disconnection.

In my quest for affection, intimacy, and purpose, I sought solace in relationships that offered fleeting moments of comfort but lacked the foundation of commitment and honesty. These relationships, borne out of my dysfunction, inflicted pain not only upon myself but also upon those around me. It became painfully clear that hurt people, in turn, hurt others—a painful cycle of dysfunction and suffering that reverberated outward like a magnetic ripple, leaving a trail of destruction in its wake.

The consequences of my dysfunction reverberated deeply, leaving a trail of hurt and turmoil in the lives of those I cared about most. Despite my genuine intentions, my behavior frequently led to pain and heartbreak, perpetuating a cycle of disappointment and distress.

For instance, in my relationships with family and friends, my inability to communicate effectively or manage my emotions often resulted in misunderstandings and conflict. I would react impulsively or withdraw altogether, inadvertently causing tension and discord in my professional life, my dysfunction manifested as procrastination, indecision, and an inability to meet deadlines or fulfill responsibilities. This not only impacted my own success and career advancement but also affected the productivity and morale of my colleagues.

Overall, my dysfunction had far-reaching implications, affecting not only my well-being but also the happiness and stability of those around me. Recognizing the impact of my actions was a pivotal moment in my journey toward healing and growth, motivating me to seek help and make positive changes for the benefit of myself and others.

Reflecting on the wreckage left in the wake of my dysfunction, I am confronted with the harsh reality of my shortcomings and the impact they have had on others. It is a sobering realization that fills me with regret and remorse.

Yet, amidst the wreckage, there is a glimmer of hope. Through introspection and self-awareness, I have begun to confront the root causes of my dysfunction and take steps toward healing and redemption.

I recognize that true healing requires honesty and accountability—acknowledging the harm I have caused and taking responsibility for my actions. It is a journey of self-discovery and growth that requires courage and humility.

Moving forward, I am committed to breaking free from the chains of dysfunction and forging a new path guided by compassion, integrity, and a genuine desire to cultivate healthy, fulfilling relationships.

Though the road ahead may be fraught with challenges, I am determined to embrace the journey with an open heart and willing to confront my past to create a brighter future for myself and those I care about.

Listening to the stories of pain and suffering others shared was overwhelming and captivating. It stirred up a whirlwind of emotions within me, often triggering a secondary trauma that reignited my unresolved pain. The memories remained raw and unbearable, as I had yet to confront and process my wounds, leaving me on a long and arduous journey toward healing.

Pain is a powerful force that shapes and defines a person's life. It exposes vulnerabilities and leaves one feeling exposed and defenseless. In my attempts to shield myself from further harm, I made decisions that only served to perpetuate my suffering. I sought to assert my strength and independence, viewing vulnerability as a weakness to be avoided at all costs.

However, through reflection and introspection, I've come to realize the importance of addressing the root cause of my pain. True healing and wholeness can only begin once we confront the underlying issues contributing to our suffering. It requires courage to confront our pain head-on, but it is the first step toward reclaiming our lives and finding peace within ourselves.

Recognizing the necessity of addressing these deep-seated issues, I have embarked on a journey of self-discovery and healing. It is a journey fraught with challenges and obstacles but holds the promise of transformation and renewal.

Through therapy, self-reflection, and the support of loved ones, I am slowly unraveling the layers of pain and trauma that have held me captive for so long. I am learning to embrace vulnerability as a source of strength rather than weakness, allowing myself to be seen and heard in all my authenticity.

Confronting my inner demons and the root causes of my suffering, I am beginning to experience glimpses of healing and wholeness. It is a gradual process, marked by moments of breakthrough and setbacks, but I am committed to seeing it through to the end.

Ultimately, I know that true healing is not just about alleviating pain symptoms but addressing the underlying wounds and transforming them into sources of resilience and growth. It is a journey of self-discovery and self-compassion, guided by the belief that I am worthy of love, acceptance, and healing.

The truth is that our bodies are repositories of both major and minor traumas. These physical, emotional, or spiritual traumas create blockages within us, hindering the flow of our innate bioenergy and preventing us from manifesting the life we truly desire, require, and deserve.

I've realized many famous "manifestation" techniques fail to account for the intricate interplay between the body, brain, and spirit. They overlook the essential harmony required for true transformation and fulfillment.

With my understanding of holistic wellness, it becomes evident that genuine manifestation arises from aligning all aspects of our being—physical, emotional, and spiritual. We can only unlock our full potential and create the life we envision through this holistic approach.

By acknowledging the interconnectedness of our body, mind, and spirit, I have begun to explore holistic practices that honor this unity. Through techniques such as mindfulness, energy healing, and somatic therapy, I am working to release the stored traumas within me and restore balance to my being.

It is a journey of self-discovery and empowerment as I reclaim ownership of my body and spirit. No longer content to live under the weight of past traumas, I am committed to breaking free from the blockages that have held me back and embracing the boundless potential within me.

This path of healing and growth fills me with a renewed sense of hope and possibility. I am learning to trust in the wisdom of my body and the resilience of my spirit, knowing that true manifestation comes from within, from a place of alignment and authenticity.

The biblical tale of the Samaritan woman at the well resonates deeply with me on many levels. Like her, I have experienced feelings of isolation, loneliness, and low self-esteem. I have struggled with fear, shame, and guilt, carrying the weight of my wounds to familiar places in the wilderness of my soul.

Like the woman at the well in the biblical story, I, too, have erected barriers around myself, guarding my vulnerabilities from the scrutiny of others. Outwardly, I projected an image of contentment and vigor, masking the inner turmoil that lay hidden within. My emotional odyssey resembled that of a nomad, wandering through transient relationships and temporary connections.

For instance, I maintained a cheerful demeanor in my interactions with friends and acquaintances, masking any signs of inner distress or turmoil. I sought solace in superficial connections, avoiding meaningful conversations that might expose the depth of my emotional struggles.

In romantic relationships, I grappled with the challenge of dismantling the barriers I had erected around my heart. Driven by a deep-seated fear of rejection and judgment, I found it difficult to relinquish my defenses and expose my true self to others. Like sturdy fortress walls, I fortified my emotions, unwilling to grant anyone access to the vulnerable depths of my being. This reluctance to open up stemmed from past experiences of hurt and disappointment, which instilled a sense of caution and self-preservation. As a result, I navigated romantic encounters with trepidation, hesitant to lower my guard and embrace the intimacy that comes with authenticity and vulnerability.

The cycle of emotional detachment and surface-level interactions left me stranded in a landscape of loneliness and disconnection, yearning for genuine intimacy yet unable to transcend the barriers I had erected. Like the woman at the well, I found myself at a pivotal juncture, craving a transformative encounter that would shatter the walls encasing my heart. Only through an authentic exchange—one steeped in honesty, vulnerability, and unconditional acceptance—did I gradually dismantle the fortifications that had confined me to a state of emotional isolation.

In my earnest endeavor to protect myself from the piercing sting of past hurts, I unknowingly inflicted wounds upon those within my sphere. Opting for shallow connections became my refuge, a strategy born from the dread of reliving the anguish of previous heartaches. Little did I realize, in fortifying these emotional barricades, that I was blind to the ripple effect of harm reverberating through the lives of those around me.

For instance, I often maintained a certain distance in my friendships, hesitant to invest deeply for fear of eventual disappointment. While this guarded stance served as a shield against potential pain, it inadvertently gave my friends a sense of disregard. They felt sidelined, as if their emotional needs were relegated to a secondary position behind my self-preserving instincts.

Similarly, in romantic relationships, my fear of vulnerability led me to keep my partners at arm's length, unwilling to commit or expose my true feelings fully. This behavior left them unfulfilled and unloved as if they were mere placeholders in my life rather than cherished companions.

Ultimately, my pattern of self-protection inadvertently caused harm to those I cared about, leaving a trail of broken connections and wounded hearts in its wake. It was a painful realization, prompting me to confront my actions' destructive impact and strive for deeper, more meaningful relationships built on trust and authenticity.

Looking back on my journey, I realize that authenticity and meaning are elusive concepts that require deep introspection and vulnerability to grasp fully. In the past, I often hid behind a mask of strength, afraid to confront my vulnerabilities and uncertainties.

However, reflecting on my experiences, I understand the importance of embracing my emotions and experiences fully. I've realized that genuine authenticity lies not in presenting a polished image to the world but in embracing the messy, imperfect aspects of myself with compassion and acceptance.

This journey of self-discovery has led me to confront uncomfortable truths and navigate through challenging emotions. It's been peeling back the layers of societal expectations and personal insecurities to uncover my true identity.

Through this process, I've learned to appreciate the beauty in vulnerability and the power of genuine connection. By allowing myself to be seen and understood authentically, I've forged deeper, more meaningful relationships with others based on mutual understanding and acceptance.

Moving forward, I'm committed to continuing this journey of self-discovery and introspection. I know that it won't always be easy. Still, I'm confident that by embracing my vulnerabilities and the complexities of my emotions, I'll find the clarity, healing, and genuine connection I seek.

Reflecting on my experiences, I am confronted with profound introspection and self-awareness. I realize that my tendency to shield myself from vulnerability has led to a cycle of superficiality and emotional detachment in my relationships.

Yet, amidst the pain and uncertainty, I find solace in the story of the Samaritan woman at the well. Her encounter with Jesus is a potent reminder that redemption and healing are possible, even in the darkest moments of despair.

Like the Samaritan woman, I am learning to confront my fears and insecurities to embrace vulnerability as a path to authenticity and connection. I am beginning to see that true fulfillment lies not in hiding from my pain but in embracing it with courage and compassion.

I hope to find the strength to break free from the patterns of isolation and self-protection that have held me back. With each step forward, I reclaim my power and forge a path toward wholeness and healing.

As I journey towards greater self-awareness and self-acceptance, I accept the reality of my identity and path. Like the woman at the well depicted in the gospels, I recognize that actual reality is found in that which remains unchanged.

Looking back on past relationships, I realize many lacked depth and sincerity. I was desperate for connection and intimacy, yet I failed to recognize the underlying fears and insecurities driving my actions. I longed for affection and closeness but hesitated to fully commit to experiencing these emotions. In my quest for fulfillment, I searched in all the wrong places.

Now, with a clearer understanding of my desires and vulnerabilities, I am learning to approach relationships with greater authenticity and discernment. I understand that true fulfillment comes from within, and I am no longer willing to settle for shallow connections that offer temporary comfort but lack lasting substance.

I am committed to cultivating meaningful relationships built on mutual respect, trust, and genuine connection. I recognize that true intimacy requires vulnerability and courage, and I am ready to embark on this journey with an open heart and a renewed sense of purpose.

With this newfound clarity, I am learning to navigate the complexities of relationships with greater wisdom and discernment. No longer driven by desperation or fear, I am empowered to seek connections that align with my values and aspirations.

I understand that genuine intimacy requires a willingness to be vulnerable and authentic, to open oneself up to the possibility of both joy and pain. I am no longer afraid to confront my insecurities or to express my needs and desires openly and honestly.

I am discovering a sense of liberation and self-empowerment in embracing my authenticity. The expectations or judgments of others no longer define me but my inner truth and integrity.

I am committed to cultivating relationships that nourish and uplift me and honor the depth and complexity of who I am. I am excited to see where this path leads me and confident in creating a life filled with love, connection, and fulfillment.

Like the woman at the well in the gospel of John, I recognize my tendency to mask my inner turmoil with distractions such as work, superficial relationships, and empty words. Behind these facades, I harbored feelings of inferiority, insecurity, and a deep-seated fear of abandonment.

For far too long, my life was overshadowed by fear and anger—the fear of failure and the fear of enduring more pain. I carried a simmering anger towards myself and those I believed had caused me harm or allowed it to happen. Yet, amidst this turmoil, I have found a glimmer of growth.

My journey towards healing has led me to confront my vulnerability and embrace it as a part of my humanity. I have learned to make space for others to walk alongside me through moments of failure, pain, isolation, and anger. In doing so, I have discovered that vulnerability is not a weakness but a pathway to connection and resilience.

I have opened myself up to genuine connection and growth by embracing vulnerability. I no longer hide behind walls of fear and anger; instead, I invite others to share my journey and support me through life's challenges.

This newfound willingness to be vulnerable has transformed my relationships, allowing for deeper understanding and empathy. I have realized that true strength lies in acknowledging and expressing our vulnerabilities rather than burying them beneath a façade of toughness.

I am committed to remaining open and authentic, even in the face of uncertainty and discomfort. Growth often requires stepping outside our comfort zones and embracing the unknown.

I have found a sense of liberation and empowerment in embracing vulnerability as a source of strength. The constraints of fear and anger no longer bind me, but instead, I am free to live authentically and wholeheartedly.

I've come to a place where I'm willing to trust and rely on others despite facing hurt, judgment, or rejection. I've realized the importance of trusting others instead of trying to control them. But what motivates me to take this risk again and again? Simply put, I've discovered that I already possess everything I need within myself to feel whole and content.

I've tapped into my inherent energetic power to manifest my desires. As a result, I no longer need to seek external validation or affirmation to feel good about myself. I've transcended feelings of insecurity and dependence on others, recognizing that true fulfillment comes from within.

This shift in perspective has brought me a newfound sense of freedom and empowerment. I no longer feel tethered to the opinions or judgments of others. Instead, I trust in my abilities and intuition to guide me along my path.

I've unlocked a deep wellspring of self-confidence and inner peace by releasing the need for external validation. Insecurities or fears of inadequacy no longer shackle me. Instead, I embrace my inherent worthiness and recognize my boundless potential.

As I continue to walk this journey of self-discovery and growth, I do so with grace and resilience. I navigate life's challenges with a newfound sense of confidence, knowing that the unwavering strength of my spirit supports me.

In trusting myself and surrendering to the flow of life, I move with greater ease and purpose. Each step forward is imbued with clarity and intentionality as I confidently embrace the unfolding of my journey.

My journey hasn't always been smooth sailing, starting from my childhood. While I hesitate to dwell on the hardships of my early years because childhood memories are an integral part of the dreams we cherish within us, I soon realized that life wasn't simply a fairy tale. The harsh realities of life set in much sooner than expected.

Interestingly, I've understood that these challenges weren't solely the result of fate or cosmic alignment. Like any subject matter, life has its share of ups and downs. Instead of labeling them "bad," I view them as "challenges."

I've learned that there are multiple perspectives through which to view reality. While some people adopt a simplistic "black and white" outlook, categorizing events as good or bad, I've seen that life operates on a spectrum. It's not as binary as a computer system; every experience we encounter is a stepping-stone on our journey of growth and evolution.

While daunting, these challenges have served as opportunities for growth and self-discovery. They've propelled me forward, shaping me into who I am today. Rather than allowing myself to be defined by adversity, I've embraced it as a catalyst for transformation.

By adopting a more nuanced perspective, I've learned to appreciate the complexity of life. Each experience, whether joyful or challenging, contributes to the richness of our journey. We understand ourselves and the world more deeply by navigating these varied landscapes.

Reflecting on my past, I recognize the resilience and strength that have carried me through even the darkest times. Every challenge has strengthened my resolve and expanded my capacity for empathy and understanding.

Moving forward, I approach life with a sense of optimism and curiosity, knowing that each twist and turn has the potential to lead me closer to my true purpose. With each step, I embrace the unknown, confident in my ability to overcome whatever obstacles may come my way.

I acknowledge and value my talents and abilities; I understand that I am meant to excel in my unique area of giftedness rather than seeking to dominate or control others. This realization has bolstered my ego integrity and boosted my self-esteem.

I must nurture my confidence and self-esteem in cultivating and maintaining my competence. In my professional endeavors and personal growth, healthy self-esteem and confidence are essential to navigating my interactions with others and leading authentically.

This journey of self-awareness and growth has taught me the importance of striking a balance between asserting my abilities and respecting the autonomy and talents of others. By focusing on honing my skills and talents, I empower myself to contribute meaningfully to the world around me without feeling the need to overshadow or control others.

Furthermore, as I continue to develop my confidence and self-esteem, I am better equipped to handle the challenges and opportunities that come my way. A strong sense of self-worth allows me to approach professional and personal endeavors with resilience and grace, fostering positive outcomes and healthy relationships.

In essence, embracing my giftedness while honoring the gifts of others is not only a path to personal fulfillment but a means to foster collaboration, growth, and mutual respect in all aspects of my life.

When I speak of confidence, I refer to a deep-seated belief in my worth and abilities. It's about recognizing and embracing my strengths with conviction. Achieving this level of personal growth is incredibly empowering. However, it's important to acknowledge fear's role in hindering my effectiveness. My worries have corroded me from within, like termites silently undermining a house's foundation.

I've understood that some of these fears stem from my upbringing. The belief that "I will never amount to anything" echoes the doubts instilled by my father, while the reluctance to seek help stems from my mother's example. Yet, despite their shortcomings, I still love and respect them, just as I did as a child.

Early on, I realized the importance of prioritizing my mental, emotional, and spiritual well-being if I genuinely want to thrive. This recognition has guided me on a journey of self-care and personal development, allowing me to cultivate resilience and embrace life's challenges with courage and resilience.

By addressing these fears and nurturing my mental, emotional, and spiritual health, I've learned to navigate life's complexities with greater clarity and confidence. It's been a journey of self-discovery and healing, marked by moments of triumph and introspection.

Despite my challenges, I've realized that my past does not define me. Instead, it serves as a foundation for building a brighter future. With each step forward, I grow more robust and resilient, empowered by the knowledge that I possess the inner strength to overcome any obstacle.

Moving forward, I am committed to continuing this journey of self-improvement and growth. I embrace the opportunity to cultivate a more profound self-awareness and inner peace, knowing I can positively impact the world by nurturing my well-being.

I've come to understand that love isn't simply a product of fleeting emotions or hormonal impulses; it's a skill that can be cultivated and honed over time. Erich Fromm aptly described it as "an act of will." Without mastering the art of love, one risks not only feeling disconnected but also experiencing repeated failures, leading to feelings of depression.

Recognizing the importance of effective communication in fostering trust and deepening connections, I was determined to learn and refine these skills. I realized that the more I can express myself and honestly be heard and understood, the less I struggle with feelings of depression. In essence, I've found that faith is strengthened through listening to the wisdom of Divine Intelligence, and it is through effective communication that this wisdom is conveyed and received.

This understanding has led me to pursue the development of my communication abilities actively. By learning to express myself authentically and listen attentively to others, I've found a sense of connection and fulfillment that transcends surface interactions. In the process, I've discovered that true intimacy and meaningful relationships are built on a foundation of open and honest communication.

Continuing to cultivate these skills, I'm guided by the belief that genuine connection and understanding are essential components of a fulfilling life. By nurturing these qualities within myself and fostering them in my relationships, I can experience a more profound sense of harmony and purpose. Through intentional communication, I embrace the transformative power of love and connection in shaping my journey toward wholeness and fulfillment.

Honing in my communication skills, I've noticed a profound shift in my sense of vulnerability. Rather than feeling exposed or at risk, I've found empowerment in expressing myself authentically. Each time I share openly, I create an opportunity for others to reciprocate, fostering a more profound sense of connection and understanding.

In this self-disclosure process, I've encouraged others to open up to me and unearthed new aspects of myself. With each revelation, I understand the purpose the Divine Intelligence has set for me. This clarity brings a newfound sense of freedom, allowing me to pursue my passions with unwavering dedication and purpose. Through the power of authentic communication, I can align myself more closely with my divine calling and embrace the journey of self-discovery with open arms.

Continuing to explore the depths of my being through communication, I find myself on a journey of profound self-discovery. Each interaction becomes a gateway to understanding myself more deeply and connecting with others on a level that transcends surface interactions.

In this process, I've realized that love isn't merely a fleeting emotion but a skill that can be cultivated and nurtured. By honing my ability to communicate openly and honestly, I create fertile ground for love to flourish. This love isn't just romantic; it's a deep-seated appreciation and understanding of others rooted in empathy and compassion.

I remember Erich Fromm's words: love is an act of will. It requires effort, intentionality, and a commitment to understanding and supporting those around me. Through communication and self-disclosure, I strengthen my relationships and deepen my understanding of myself and my place in the world.

With each conversation, I feel a sense of liberation and empowerment, knowing that I am actively shaping my reality and aligning myself with the purpose laid out by the Divine Intelligence. As I continue to communicate authentically and embrace vulnerability, I open myself up to new experiences, insights, and connections, enriching my life in ways I never thought possible.

Throughout the years, I've gained insight into the typical reactions to the extraordinary events that have shaped my life's narrative. It's become evident to me that my choices have been instrumental in shaping my journey thus far.

Engaging in various therapeutic approaches has equipped me with valuable skills for navigating my emotions, thoughts, and actions, fostering resilience, and aiding in my quest for healing and completeness.

I am now equipped to make more informed decisions, leading to growth and fulfillment. My journey unfolds gradually, with each breath, heartbeat, and step guiding me toward recovery and wholeness.

I've realized that my journey is a continuous process of self-discovery and growth. Each experience, whether positive or challenging, contributes to my evolution. Through introspection and therapy, I've learned to navigate life's ups and downs with resilience and grace.

Exploring my inner landscape, I discover new facets of myself and gain insights into my motivations and aspirations. This self-awareness empowers me to make intentional choices that align with my values and goals, steering me toward a life of authenticity and purpose.

With each passing moment, I embrace the opportunity to embrace my true self and live fully in the present. I remain committed to my journey of self-improvement, knowing that every step I take brings me closer to realizing my full potential and living a life of meaning and fulfillment.

As I journeyed through self-discovery, I confronted the pervasive fear of failure that has shaped much of my life. I found myself inclined to defend and deceive rather than confront and be vulnerable to shame. Recognizing this pattern was like lifting a veil, revealing a long-standing familial tendency toward secrecy.

Acknowledging this truth was both humbling and liberating. I understood that to live with integrity, I needed to embrace acceptance and take ownership of my actions. This realization brought tears to my eyes as I confronted emotions that seemed ancient in their depth.

My connection with the ivine has profoundly transformed, filling me with confidence and inner strength. I now carry myself with assurance and respect both my boundaries and those of others. Like the woman at the well, who boldly proclaimed her newfound confidence to the townsfolk, I also feel excitement about my journey of self-discovery.

Gone are the days of feeling like a stranger in my own body; instead, I stand as a liberated individual, embracing the many gifts bestowed upon me by the Divine. With gratitude for these blessings, I embark on a journey of self-awareness, self-revelation, and self-actualization. This is my hero's journey, my triumph over adversity. I am who I am and embrace my identity with pride and gratitude.

Moving forward, I hold steadfast to the belief that every challenge I've faced has been a stepping-stone toward personal growth and empowerment. Through introspection and acceptance, I've shed the cloak of shame and insecurity, emerging as a beacon of strength and resilience.

Just as the woman at the well-found courage in her vulnerability, I embraced my authenticity and newfound self-worth. With each step, I affirm my existence and celebrate the journey that has led me to this moment.

Moving forward, I carry the lessons learned, the wisdom gained, and the unwavering belief that I can manifest my deepest desires. With a heart filled with gratitude and determination, I embrace the path ahead, confident in my ability to navigate life's twists and turns with grace and purpose.

12

The Unveiling of My True Purpose

The more precise and concise my communication with the Universe, the swifter my manifestations materialize. As I concluded my introspection, I found solace in understanding my situation better, equipped with a clear roadmap for navigating what lies ahead. Yet, this journey of self-discovery is time-sensitive, compelling me to maintain a steadfast connection with my consciousness until its culmination. Having traversed numerous trials, I am adamant about uncovering the authentic truths that define my existence.

Recent celestial alignments have injected tension into my life, unsettling me with their unexpected revelations. Despite my shock, I recognize these events as catalysts for uncovering vital truths that demand acknowledgment. The disparity between my expectations and reality has rattled me, leaving me blindsided and grappling with the need to confront what has transpired. However, an invisible force seemed to impede my progress, fostering feelings of anxiety and uncertainty.

In moments of introspection, I sensed a loss of control, as if my life were being guided by an unseen hand nudging me down an unwanted path. Unbeknownst to me, potent cosmic energies were clandestinely at work, exerting their influence and thwarting my endeavors.

My current circumstances are a stark reminder of the untapped potential within me. I envision a life abundant with joy, love, and inner peace, yet these aspirations seem increasingly elusive. My disconnect from the Universe has caused me to overlook numerous opportunities, allowing them to slip through my grasp unnoticed. Rather than attributing my challenges solely to external factors, I recognize the importance of taking accountability for my actions.

Like many, I once believed that I was at the mercy of fate, resigned to a fate of perpetual struggle and disappointment. However, I've realized that this defeatist mindset only hinders my growth and potential. It's time to dispel the notion of "bad luck" and reclaim control over my destiny.

I refuse to let my dreams continue to drift out of reach. Instead, I'm committed to demonstrating how proactive preparation and a shift in mindset can pave the way for future success and fulfillment. It's time to bid farewell to constant worry and embrace a future brimming with possibility and abundance.

In my subconscious energy is where the essence of my purpose lies concealed. Questions have lingered within me for some time, and it's time to uncover the answers. I've realized that there's a radiant light within me yearning to shine brightly, yet too often, I find myself dimming it by wearing masks to appease others at the expense of my needs.

It's essential to highlight the unique amalgamation of qualities that shape my character by examining the core traits that define my psychological profile. While each trait may appear ordinary, when viewed collectively, they paint a picture that elucidates much of the meaning behind my existence.

My sense of beauty, love for life, simplicity, intelligence, grounded nature, ambition, tenacity, loyalty, and warmth all contribute to the complex web of my being. Additionally, I've been fortunate in many aspects of life, with fate seemingly smiling upon me naturally. However, the potential for greatness lies dormant within me, waiting to be fully realized if only I can learn to harness it to its fullest extent.

The depth of my genuine love becomes apparent as I move beyond mere emotional desires and delve into a more profound understanding of my cognitive processes. Reflecting on my experiences in love, I acknowledge its significant role in shaping my life, prompting me to engage with enthusiasm, wisdom, and gratitude. It's crucial to recognize that mature, committed love transcends personal emotional needs, evolving into a commitment to meeting relational and communal needs.

Love, by its very nature, is dynamic, continually beckoning us to ascend to higher realms of relationship. This journey towards authenticity demands ongoing self-transcendence and a willingness to undergo multiple conversion processes. As I strive for happiness, I eagerly anticipate reciprocity from my significant other. I yearn to witness desire and passion reflected in their eyes, cherishing the exclusivity of our connection.

However, I tread cautiously, mindful not to let possessiveness overshadow the purity of our love. Destructive jealousy can potentially undermine the foundation we've built, threatening the very essence of our bond. Instead, I aspire for our actions to reflect our affection, manifesting in gestures that prioritize the well-being of each other.

Here's some invaluable advice that's guided me along my journey: I've learned to safeguard my intimacy, allowing

465

only those I trust deeply into my inner circle. When facing challenges, I refrain from discussing my struggles with anyone I don't wholly confide in. I prioritize my peace of mind in matters of the heart, asserting my autonomy over my affairs.

My social life thrives on its merit, brimming with personality and magnetism, free from external authority. I hold unwavering faith in myself, my ideas, and my ventures, allowing me to forge ahead with confidence even in adversity. Through resilience and determination, I've navigated through precarious situations unscathed.

While I've harbored various beliefs about myself, others, and the world around me, I've realized that not all of these beliefs are rational or beneficial. Overcoming self-limiting beliefs is no easy feat; they've likely been ingrained within me for quite some time. However, as I embark on the pilgrimage self-awareness and pursue my dreams, I've discovered that these limitations and challenges have served as catalysts for personal growth, propelling me toward becoming the best version of myself.

As I've matured, I've become more discerning and cautious, trusting my instincts to avoid past pitfalls. While some may perceive me as skeptical or judgmental, I see myself as grounded and pragmatic, unimpressed by superficiality. My success is rooted in my resilience and determination, fueled by a strong work ethic instilled in me from a young age.

Despite facing setbacks and failures, I can persevere and forge ahead. The challenges of the past 13 years have only fortified my resolve, sharpening my ability to confront new obstacles head-on. I thrive in the face of adversity, constantly seeking opportunities for growth and advancement.

Approaching retirement age, I remain vigilant against complacency, striving to maintain a sense of purpose and drive. I am a natural leader, unafraid to seize opportunities and chart my path forward. While optimistic about the future, I understand the importance of planning and preparation.

Though uncertainties may lie ahead, I approach the future confidently and optimistically, knowing that the best is yet to come. With a clear vision and determination, I am poised to achieve great success and fulfill my potential.

I aspire to achieve success and am resolute in executing my plan. My purpose is the foundation of my strategy, guiding me toward meaningful connections with like-minded individuals. I am discerning in my associations, seeking allies who align with my vision and can support its realization.

When analyzed through Numerology, my purpose is a humanitarian calling driven by a deep concern for the world's well-being. I am characterized as an idealist, a dreamer, and a healer endowed with boundless compassion. My journey has granted me insight into the interconnectedness of all existence.

My healing abilities manifest through various forms, including writing, composing, and teaching. As an educator, I am dedicated to serving others and seeking innovative solutions rooted in inspiration, intuition, and creativity. A fundamental lesson of my path is to give selflessly, without expectation of reciprocity—a challenging yet invaluable principle to embody.

Balancing the needs and aspirations of others with my innate desire to contribute to those in need has been a central focus of my journey. Despite the complexities, I remain committed to fostering harmony and positively impacting the world.

I've often pondered what the future holds for me as I embark on a period of profound transformation. The opportunities ahead are too promising to overlook, compelling me to take action and seize them with both hands. With numerous significant changes on the horizon over the next year, I am vigilant for one particular opportunity: the chance for true love.

My journey hasn't always been smooth, especially concerning heart matters. However, amidst my personal growth and rediscovery of my true purpose, I've realized that the years ahead hold several auspicious moments for love and romance. During this time, my allure has been amplified, making it easier to forge deep and meaningful connections with others.

After being single for an extended period, fate intervened, leading me to encounter someone special. Now, in a relationship, I recognize the importance of transparency and honesty in fostering a healthy and fulfilling bond. It's a time for open communication and healing any lingering doubts or insecurities between us.

I've often felt overlooked and underappreciated, yearning for the recognition I believe I deserve. It's disheartening to feel unseen, especially when acknowledging my unique gifts and talents. However, there was a specific period in my journey where everything changed, thanks to a significant influence on my rising star—the aspect of my destiny that shaped my first impression of the world.

During this transformative time, I noticed a remarkable shift in how others perceived me. Friends and acquaintances couldn't help but wonder what had sparked this newfound magnetism within me. Under the influence of this cosmic alignment, I exuded charm and charisma, effortlessly leaving a lasting impression on those I encountered. I also stepped into leadership roles with confidence and grace during this period.

Determined not to squander this surge of energy and opportunity, I consciously committed to focus on my personal growth and development. Every self-improvement endeavor I undertook during this influential phase played a crucial role in shaping my path to success.

At work, a significant shift unfolded as I embarked on a transition period marked by the influence of my Mid-heaven—the cornerstone of my professional aspirations. This transformative phase brought forth opportunities for advancement, entrepreneurship, and even the possibility of relocating for a fresh start.

After dedicating countless hours to my career, I felt a sense of deservingness for greater recognition and fulfillment. This year, in particular, has been a time of abundant rewards, where the seeds of my hard work have finally begun to bear fruit. As I navigated through this period of change, I learned to recognize the subtle signs pointing me toward new horizons, allowing me to ride the waves of opportunity with confidence and grace.

While some ventures, like my entrepreneurial endeavors, may have faced challenges and remained in their infancy stage, I remain hopeful for their revival in the future. Despite setbacks, I continue to align myself with the energy of growth and possibility, trusting that my efforts will eventually lead to success.

My vibrant personality shines through in my communication skills, creativity, and ability to forge connections with others. Unsurprisingly, I attract numerous opportunities through my extensive social network and relationships. My infectious enthusiasm and charm have garnered many friends throughout my life, and my gift of gab ensures that people genuinely enjoy my company. My good sense of humor and outgoing nature have proven invaluable in navigating various social situations.

However, I've realized the importance of caution. I tend to spread my energies too thinly in my quest for acceptance from others—a phenomenon akin to the Shiny Object Syndrome. My propensity to chase after new ideas, trends, or goals rather than maintaining focus poses a significant challenge for me. Consistency, follow-through, and cultivating a sense of self-acceptance are areas where I strive to improve.

With my vast array of interests and passions, committing to any pursuit is often challenging, making me overly critical of myself. Yet, I understand that embracing my flaws and acknowledging my innate gifts are essential to attracting the ideal circumstances for my success.

Yearning for a glimpse of prosperity and abundance, I must admit that fortune has smiled upon me, and I am more than ready to embrace it. Thanks to Jupiter—the celestial harbinger of Fortune and Wisdom—a harmonious alignment with my destiny has unveiled a concealed window of opportunity, infusing my life with a sense of abundance akin to the Midas touch. The path to triumph lies clear before me.

However, I am not content to wait for miracles to unfold. Instead, I have taken proactive steps by creating a vision board, a tangible symbol of the clarity and prosperity I now feel. Moreover, I am rekindling connections within my social circle, recognizing the potential for their support in my upcoming endeavors. A series of synchronicities hint that I am on the brink of something extraordinary, within reach of a spectacular opportunity.

Under this fortuitous influence, I trust in the wisdom of my heart and intuition, remaining vigilant for signs and signals that guide me along the right path. With the proper guidance, I position myself at the nexus of opportunity, ready to seize the moment when it presents itself. By understanding the timing of these cosmic influences, I empower myself to make decisions that align with my highest good, confident that the universe is conspiring in my favor.his juncture in my life holds profound significance. Over the past few years, I have realized that what I once believed to be my purpose was merely a shadow of the truth. Within the tapestry of my destiny lie two pivotal days, each bearing profound karmic implications that illuminate the path toward my authentic purpose.

The first of these days offers a tantalizing glimpse into the potential of a life lived in alignment with my true self. On this day, I encountered someone whose presence opened the door to a realm of possibilities—a world intricately attuned to the essence of my soul.

Conversely, the second day serves as a beacon, illuminating the obstacles and hindrances that stand in the way of embracing my newfound purpose. It is a stark reminder of the beliefs, patterns, and attachments that no longer serve me, hindering my progress toward love and abundance.

Both days are equally significant, offering invaluable insights into the trajectory of my life's purpose. I understand the individuals, circumstances, and energies shaping my path forward by paying heed to the lessons embedded within these moments.

Of course, it would be remiss of me not to acknowledge the obstacles that lie ahead. As I navigate this journey of self-discovery, I recognize that personal challenges will inevitably arise. Yet, I am steadfast in my commitment to overcome them and forge ahead toward my true purpose.

My faith encourages me to contemplate the divine, whose ultimate wish is to pursue my life goals with determination and purpose. It is a goal that encompasses realizing the future I have long envisioned, the dream that resides deeply within my heart and for which I have been uniquely equipped. Through special skills, gifts, and abilities bestowed upon me—attributes that are exclusively mine—I am empowered to journey towards fulfilling that dream. The divine desires me to taste the sweet fruit of success and experience the joy of its attainment.

Visualization is a powerful tool in harmonizing my nervous system with the entirety of my being. It acts as a bridge connecting my past, present, and future experiences with equal significance. I absorb environmental cues through the five senses, relayed to the central nervous system. Understanding the importance of the questions I pose to myself is paramount, as they shape the trajectory of my life. It's not solely about my present identity but the sacrifices I will make to realize my future self.

As we traverse life's journey, we often become entangled in externally imposed norms, gradually losing sight of our true essence and purpose. We find ourselves confined by self-imposed limitations, held back by false beliefs such as unworthiness or fear of failure. These beliefs act as shackles, hindering our progress and clouding our vision. Yet, the truth remains that we possess all the necessary resources within us—the time, the money, the knowledge—they merely await our recognition and utilization.

In reality, these resources are scattered, much like the fragments of our soul, waiting to be pieced together. It's a daunting task that promises a life of fulfillment and abundance. If we sense a calling towards a more rewarding existence, it is within our power to seize control of our destiny.

I am intricately woven into the fabric of my environment, shaped by its influences and molded by its norms. It's a reciprocal relationship where I absorb the values, beliefs, and behaviors that surround me and, in turn, contribute to shaping the environment itself. Together with others in my community, we form a collective culture, a tapestry woven from the threads of our shared experiences and beliefs.

At the heart of this cultural identity lies our faith, our belief system, which guides our interactions and perceptions. Through this sacred dance between religion and culture, we find our place as participants, each embodying the essence of our shared beliefs and values. In this dance, we are not mere spectators but active participants, shaping and being shaped by the dynamic interplay of our collective identity.

Our faith mirrors the essence of our culture just as our culture reflects the nature of our faith. Embedded within our culture lies a profound yearning, an innate longing for that which holds the center of our individual and communal identities. This central force, though ineffable and indescribable, exerts a profound influence, compelling us ever forward.

Throughout our exploration, community members undertake various rites of passage, each marking a step closer to the elusive center. It's a pilgrimage of hope, a steadfast belief in the unseen, guiding us toward the heart of our collective existence. This faith, this unwavering assurance in the unseen, propels us forward, anchoring our journey in the conviction that we are moving closer to our shared center.

The rich melting pot of culture and faith within our community finds its continuity and progression through the sacred practice of tradition. These rites of passage, deeply ingrained in our collective identity, serve as the conduit through which our cultural and spiritual heritage is transmitted from one generation to the next.

Revered and cherished tradition balances preserving our unique identity and remaining open to the world beyond our community. It acts as a bridge, allowing us to honor our roots while engaging with the broader society.

Embracing the rhythm of life's seasons has been a passage of profound revelation and self-discovery for me. In my 40s, as the pace of life slowed, I found myself drawn to introspection and reflection, seeking to unravel the essence of my being and discern what truly matters in life. Amidst the whirlwind of earlier years, I realized that the answers I sought were not to be found in the speed of the chase but in the stillness of self-awareness.

On the brink of Chapter 50 of my life, I carry the wisdom gleaned from seasons past. It is a fabric woven with the threads of youthful exuberance, the quest for identity, and the recognition that life's most significant revelations often come when we surrender to the ebb and flow of existence. Each phase of my journey, from the frenetic pace of my twenties to the adventurous spirit of my thirties and the contemplative introspection of my forties, has played a vital role in shaping the person I am today.

In this poignant moment of introspection, I find myself on the cusp of a new chapter in my life, brimming with anticipation and a sense of purpose. With each passing year, I've realized that life is an ever-evolving journey of self-discovery, rich with lessons waiting to be learned and experiences waiting to be embraced. As I reflect on the chapters of my past, I am reminded of the invaluable wisdom they have bestowed upon me, guiding my steps and shaping my perspective.

Armed with this profound understanding, I stand at the verge of the following fifty chapters with renewed purpose and determination. I approach the unknown with gratitude for the lessons of the past, resilience in the face of challenges, and an open heart ready to embrace the countless possibilities that lie ahead. With each step forward, I am propelled by the belief that the journey is not merely about reaching a destination but about savoring the beauty of the path itself.

I am also struck by the realization that every passing year adds another layer to the intricate collage of my existence. Gone are the hurried steps of youth, replaced by the measured strides of experience, each footfall a testament to the lessons learned, and the roads traveled. The echoes of past adventures reverberate softly in the background, a reminder of the richness and depth of my narrative.

In this moment of reflection, I am filled with deep gratitude for the wisdom that comes with age – wisdom born not just from years lived but from the willingness to embrace life's myriad experiences with an open heart and a curious mind. With each passing season, I have come to appreciate the beauty of the journey, recognizing that every twist and turn has played a vital role in shaping the person I am today.

My life's story is a mosaic of experiences – from the exhilarating highs of exploration to the profound depths of introspection. Along the way, I have navigated the complexities of relationships, weathered the storms of adversity, and discovered the transformative power of moments of stillness. Each chapter has brought its challenges and triumphs, yet through it all, I have emerged stronger, wiser, and more resilient than before.

As I stand at the precipice of the future, I am filled with excitement and trepidation, for I know that the uncharted territory of the unknown lies beyond this horizon. Yet, precisely, this uncertainty infuses my spirit with anticipation, for I understand that the most profound growth occurs within the realm of the unfamiliar.

Each chapter of my life thus far has been a stepping-stone, guiding me toward self-discovery and personal evolution. From the innocence of youth to the wisdom of experience, each phase has left its indelible mark, shaping the person I am today and laying the foundation for the person I am yet to become.

With a heart open to new possibilities and a mind eager to explore, I embark on the next leg of this odyssey. I am acutely aware that the journey ahead will be fraught with twists and turns, challenges and triumphs, but I embrace these uncertainties with a steadfast resolve and a sense of adventure.

For in the ebb and flow of life's seasons, I find solace in the knowledge that each moment, each experience, is an opportunity for growth and discovery. And so, with courage in my heart and faith in the journey, I set forth into the great unknown, ready to write the next chapter of my life's story.

In the grand plan of my life, the threads of resilience and growth are intricately woven, creating a mosaic of experiences that define who I am. I am filled with profound gratitude for the journey that has brought me to this moment. It is not merely a milestone but a vantage point from which I can reflect on the landscapes of my past and gaze upon the vast horizons of the future.

The pursuit of self-discovery has been a lifelong expedition marked by twists and turns, triumphs and tribulations. With each step forward, I carry with me the wisdom gleaned from the journey thus far, etched into the lines of time that adorn my face. Every laugh line and every furrowed brow bears witness to the richness of my experiences and the depth of my resilience.

I have come to understand that the true beauty of life lies not just in the destination but in the intricate brushstrokes of the journey itself. In the moments of joy and sorrow, triumph and defeat, we discover the true essence of our being. And so, as I embark on the next chapter of my life's adventure, I do so with a heart full of gratitude and a spirit buoyed by the knowledge that each new day brings with it the promise of growth, discovery, and transformation.

I am filled with anticipation and reflection, much like a seasoned protagonist in an epic tale. The sun sets on previous chapters, casting long shadows of memories and experiences, while the promise of new beginnings looms. With each passing day, I am reminded that my life is a symphony of moments, each contributing to the melody that is uniquely mine.

In the rhythm of life's moments, I discover significance and significance by intertwining joy, sorrow, love, and loss into the intricate and often stunning fabric of my being. During moments of silence, between heartbeats, I uncover deep truths that influence my story and determine my identity.

Chapter 50 signifies a transition rather than a conclusion, symbolizing the start of something new. With thanks for the past and an open heart towards the future, I move into the unfamiliar, prepared to welcome whatever comes my way. With bravery, inquisitiveness, and a resilient attitude, I am ready to begin crafting the following section of my life's monumental story, one step at a time.

Chapter 50 is a juncture marked by reflection and anticipation. The journey ahead unfolds like a sprawling epic, with familiar landmarks dotting the landscape of my memories and uncharted territories waiting to be explored.

In embracing this milestone, I am reminded of the great variety of experiences that have shaped me—a mosaic woven from threads of triumphs, setbacks, laughter, and tears. Each chapter has added depth and complexity to the narrative of my life, contributing to the vibrant tableau of my existence.

Standing on the cusp of the unknown, I am guided by the wisdom gleaned from past adventures and the resilience forged in the crucible of challenges. With their ever-changing rhythms, the seasons are my compass, guiding me through the ebb and flow of life's tides.

With each step forward, I am propelled by a sense of purpose and curiosity, eager to fill the blank pages ahead with stories of growth, discovery, and transformation. The symphony of joy and the cadence of challenges will accompany me on this journey, reminding me of the beauty and complexity inherent in the human experience.

The collection of memories of my life is woven with threads of countless experiences, each imbued with its unique hue and texture. From the bold strokes of adventure to the delicate intricacies of everyday moments, every memory adds depth and richness to the canvas of my existence.

In the quiet moments of reflection, I find solace in the realization that life's true beauty lies not in the grand spectacles but in the simple joys surrounding us. In the warmth of a shared smile, the comfort of a familiar embrace, and the serenity of a tranquil dawn, I discover the magic woven into the fabric of everyday life.

Standing at the crossroads of past and future, I am reminded of the boundless potential that each chapter holds. With each turn of the page, there is an opportunity for growth, discovery, and connection. As I embark on the next leg of my journey, I do so with an open heart and a spirit eager to embrace the unknown.

Age is but a number, and I refuse to be defined by the limitations it imposes. Instead, I greet each new chapter with a sense of wonder and possibility, ready to explore the depths of my potential and savor the richness of each moment life offers.

I've been yearning for change in my life, believing wholeheartedly that when I set my intentions, the universe conspires to bring them to fruition. Yet, this isn't just any change—it's a profound shift beyond surface transformations. I stand at a pivotal juncture where every decision I make carries weight and significance.

It's as if I'm transitioning from a phase of seeking to one of exploration, shedding the cloak of doubt and confusion that once clouded my vision. Like the lifting fog at dawn, the veil of illusion and uncertainty dissipates, revealing clarity and purpose with each passing moment.

Continuing my journey, I am drawn toward practical application, spirituality, and a deeper understanding of myself. This calling has likely been brewing within me for quite some time, but now it feels more tangible and urgent than ever before. What makes this divine soul mission particularly profound is the realization that I am uniquely positioned to assist others in their transitions.

I've come to recognize that my strengths and experiences align perfectly with the challenges and needs of those around me. Through my career as a chaplain and mental health therapist, I've honed the skills necessary to navigate conflicts and provide support during times of uncertainty. These abilities can be leveraged to address immediate concerns and facilitate more profound personal growth and transformation.

So, I've taken the foundation of my strength in conflict resolution and expanded it to develop parallel skills in mediation and negotiation within my career. This realization is just one of the many insights my spirit guides have revealed during this exploration period. As I delve deeper into my journey, I discover endless possibilities.

This journey involves honing my emotional intelligence and effectively leveraging my strengths. It's not about boasting or overstating my gifts but rather about recognizing and honoring the unique abilities that I bring to the table. By doing so, I can unlock new possibilities and navigate the twists and turns of my path with confidence and grace.

The Mindset of a Problem Solver

In the journey toward discovering my true purpose, I've learned that life presents problems not as obstacles but as stepping-stones toward growth. Every challenge becomes an opportunity for deeper self-awareness, and with the mindset of a problem solver, I embrace each one with resilience and curiosity.

Instead of being deterred by difficulties, I approach them with a sense of curiosity, knowing that each problem contains the seed of its solution. I have developed the ability to break down complexities, understanding that the unveiling of my purpose isn't a single, dramatic moment but an evolving process shaped by my willingness to engage with life's uncertainties.

In solving problems, I sharpen my skills, fortify my mind, and enrich my spirit. Every solution brings me closer to the essence of who I am and what I am meant to contribute to the world. It is through facing the unknown, seeking creative answers, and persisting when the path seems unclear that I carve out my purpose with clarity and conviction.

My purpose isn't a distant dream or an abstract concept. It reveals itself in my daily choices, how I engage with the world's challenges, and the mindset I cultivate as I turn problems into opportunities for growth and transformation.

As a problem solver, I embrace this process, confident that each step brings me closer to unveiling my true purpose.

13

Conclusion

My journey unfolds as a poignant exploration of personal growth and self-awareness, marked by a profound evolution in perspective. Initially, I grappled with the shadows of my past, hiding behind a façade of strength and avoiding vulnerability at all costs. However, as my narrative unfolds, I embark on a transformative journey of self-discovery, confronting my inner shadows with courage and introspection.

Through this process, I learned to embrace the inherent complexities of the human experience, recognizing that shadows are a collection of memories, experiences, and emotions that shape our identity and define who we are. Rather than shying away from discomfort or pain, I learned to lean into these shadows, understanding that they hold valuable lessons and opportunities for growth.

The overarching theme of "embracing shadows in the rain" is a metaphor for me to embrace life's darker, more challenging aspects with courage and resilience. I find liberation and empowerment by acknowledging and accepting these shadows, paving the way for profound personal transformation.

Examples of my evolution can be seen in my journey of self-reflection, my willingness to confront past traumas, and my commitment to embracing vulnerability in relationships. Through these experiences, I learn to navigate the complexities of my emotions with grace and authenticity, ultimately finding strength and wisdom amid life's storms.

My journey of self-discovery unfolds as I struggle with the complexities of my emotions and experiences. Initially, I shield myself behind a façade of strength, reluctant to confront my vulnerabilities. However, through introspection and growth, I gradually realize the significance of embracing my shadows and imperfections.

This transformation is exemplified by moments of reflection and personal insight, where I confront my fears and insecurities head-on. The overarching theme of "embracing shadows in the rain" symbolizes accepting the darker aspects of my identity as integral to the human experience. This process taught me that genuine authenticity and meaning emerge from acknowledging and embracing these shadows.

Cultivating a deeper understanding of myself, I find healing, clarity, and genuine connection with others who share similar struggles. Examples of this evolution may include instances where I confront past traumas, engage in therapy or self-reflection, and ultimately learn to embrace vulnerability as a source of strength and authenticity.

In my journey, I navigate through moments of struggle and growth, gradually shedding the layers of pretense and embracing my true self. This evolution is evident in my interactions with others, where I learned to communicate openly and authentically without fear of judgment or rejection. Additionally, my newfound acceptance of vulnerability allows me to form deeper connections with those around me, fostering meaningful relationships built on mutual understanding and empathy.

Moreover, the theme of embracing shadows in the rain serves as a powerful metaphor for confronting the challenges and uncertainties of life with courage and resilience. Just as rain brings nourishment and growth to the earth, embracing one's shadows can lead to personal growth and transformation. In my journey, I learn to find beauty and strength amid adversity, embracing both the light and the dark aspects of my existence. By facing my shadows head-on, I discover newfound resilience and courage, allowing me to navigate life's storms with grace and determination. Through this process, I cultivate a deeper self-awareness and acceptance, ultimately finding liberation and empowerment in embracing the full spectrum of my experiences.

Ultimately, my evolution reflects a profound shift in perspective, from hiding behind a façade of strength to embracing vulnerability as a source of authenticity and empowerment. By confronting my shadows and embracing the complexities of my emotions, I embark on a transformative journey of self-discovery and healing, finding greater meaning and connection in the process. This evolution is marked by moments of introspection and self-reflection, where I confront my fears and insecurities with courage and resilience. Through this journey, I learn to embrace the full spectrum of my experiences, finding beauty and strength in both the light and the dark. As I cultivate a more profound sense of self-awareness and acceptance, I discover a newfound sense of purpose and fulfillment, allowing me to live authentically and fully embrace life's challenges and joys.